PLAIN SPEAKING

A Sudra's Story

PLAIN SPEAKING

A Sudra's Story

A.N. Sattanathan

edited, with an introduction and notes
by

Uttara Natarajan

permanent black

Published by
PERMANENT BLACK
'Himalayana', Mall Road, Ranikhet Cantt,
Ranikhet 263645
Email: perblack@gmail.com

Distributed by
ORIENT BLACKSWAN PRIVATE LIMITED
Bangalore Bhopal Bhubaneshwar Chandigarh Chennai
Ernakulam Guwahati Hyderabad Jaipur Kolkata
Lucknow Mumbai New Delhi Patna
www.orientblackswan.com

First published in 2007

First paperback printing 2020

ISBN 978-81-7824-554-6

Typeset in Agaramond
by Guru Typograph Technology, Crossing Republik, Ghaziabad
Printed and bound by Sapra Brothers, Noida, U.P.

For the New Generation

Lars and Jules Sattanathan; Malaika, Neel, and Amar Ramachandran; Abhimanyu and Samyukta Natarajan; Sahir and Surabhi D'Souza

செடி கொடி வளர

Contents

Acknowledgements

That this book has been published is owing first of all to Rajeswari Sunder Rajan, who generously agreed to read the typescript, and, when she had done so, put me in touch with Rukun Advani at Permanent Black. In the warmth and enthusiasm of both Raji's responses and Rukun's, I found much-needed confirmation of my own view of my grandfather's writing. The idea of putting the memoirs and lectures together was Raji's. Rukun's interest in the project has stimulated my own, and, as we argued about titles, I found I had made a friend. Also the *sine qua non* of this publication is my mother, Ramani Natarajan, who, without stinting, has answered queries, gathered information, and acted as sounding-board; indeed her contribution has been so fundamental and so wide-ranging that I can hardly describe it fully.

In my work on the annotations, I have had, besides, invaluable assistance from my father, N. Natarajan, and my aunt, Aruna Pillai. I should also like to thank the Alumni Office and Registry of the London School of Economics, Judith Curthoys at Christ Church, Oxford, Gayatri Krishnaswamy and K. Krishnaswamy; Laura Ley at Trinity Hall, Cambridge; Mammen Matthew of the *Malayala Manorama*; Giti and Tom Paulin; B. Periasamy, N. Ram of *The Hindu*, Kalpagam Raman, Vasanta Ramakrishna, K. Ramamurthy, G. Ravikumar, R. Shanmugasundaram, M. Subramanian, and S. Suresh. For background information and general knowledge, I have trawled very many written sources, not all of which have been cited individually: I should like gratefully to acknowledge my extensive dues to existing scholarship, especially on South Indian culture and politics.

The staff of the Indian Institute Library at Oxford have been exemplary in their helpfulness and courtesy. I am grateful to the University of Madras for permission to republish the lectures. Tahmina Sorabji and Graeme Stones have been sympathetic participants in my day-to-day progress, and every kind of support and encouragement has come, as always, from Meena D'Souza, Latha Dulipsingh, and Kartik Natarajan.

For what I owe to Ravi Vaidyanathan, for daily succour and cheer, no words are adequate.

Introduction

The memoirs of the late A.N. Sattanathan, Chairman of the first Tamil Nadu Backward Classes Commission, were written in 1958, in his close, cramped hand, from the first to the last page of a ruled notebook of the kind that children use in schools. In the present book these memoirs comprise the first part, entitled 'An Exercise in Biography (1958)'. They cover the period of his life from his birth in 1905 till his second job in 1928. There, where the notebook ends, they break off abruptly. Sattanathan had at one time intended a fuller account, but never resumed his narrative. Instead, some years later, he began to think about publication, at which time he gave the memoirs their title, possibly partly suggested by, or humorously alluding to, the 'exercise' book in which they were written. Nothing came of those publication plans in his lifetime. The one or two people Sattanathan spoke to were not encouraging, and he himself took a rather deprecatory view of the memoirs: their style, he is known to have said, was like that of his Civil Service reports.

In 2001, I came across the notebook and began to type up its contents, and so also began the process that led to this book.

The second part of the book comprises three lectures delivered by Sattanathan, in 1981, on the Dravidian Movement in Tamil Nadu.

The overarching title, *Plain Speaking: A Sudra's Story*, was an editorial decision, agreed with the book's publisher.

A.N. Sattanathan was born on the 6th of May 1905, in the town of Shencottah in what is now southern Tamil Nadu, the second child and first son of Armuga Nayakar and Ayanammal, of the Padayachi caste. Growing up in abject poverty—his very name, as he tells it in chapter 6 of the memoirs, was acquired as a means of currying patronage—Sattanathan managed to obtain, step by step, first a school, then a college education, financed largely by a wealthy family of the town with whom he could claim a connection. In 1926 he qualified with a first-class Honours degree in History from the Maharaja's College, Trivandrum. After a few years' employment as a college lecturer in Trichy and Madurai, in 1929, fulfilling a long-cherished ambition, he qualified for the Superior Civil Service. He was allocated to Customs and Central Excise, his first posting, as Assistant Collector, being to Chittagong in present-day Bangladesh (then East Bengal). Six months later he married Meenakshi, of the village of Sundarapandyapuram, in his home region. They had four children, a son followed by three daughters. Sattanathan's middle daughter—his third child—is my mother.

Sattanathan had a distinguished career in the Services. He is credited with formulating excise procedures, during his posting to the Collectorate of Salt Revenue and Central Excise in Madras in 1942–4, that were subsequently adopted for the rest of the country. In 1945–8, posted to Simla at the time of Partition, he was in charge of laying down the customs and excise frontiers between the newly divided nations. In 1947 he was a member of the Indian delegation to the United Nations Narcotics Commission in New York, and in 1950 and 1951 he was Chairman, respectively, of the fifth and sixth sessions of the Commission. In 1956 he took early retirement on health grounds, his last posting being as Collector of Customs and Central Excise, Calcutta.

Retirement was another kind of intellectual beginning for Sattanathan. Settled in Madras, he took up the study of Sanskrit and began to read classical Tamil. He was able to indulge to the full his lifelong love of the theatre. Most importantly, he started to write prolifically, contributing articles on politics, economics, and current affairs to newspapers and journals all over India. The memoirs were written early in his retirement. He also wrote two books for children,

The Jester, the Judge and the Minister, and *Folk Tales from the South*, both, sadly, now out of print. It was not until the late 1980s that declining health brought with it an intellectual decline. He died in Madras on the 19th of June 1990.

Perhaps Sattanathan's greatest contribution to national life was his Report, submitted in November 1970, of the findings and recommendations of the first Tamil Nadu Backward Classes Commission. The Commission was appointed by the DMK Government under M. Karunanidhi in 1969, with Sattanathan as Chairman. If Tamil Nadu has been a pioneering example in the history of reservation in India, then Sattanathan has played a leading role in that history. Among other recommendations, his Report prescribes an income limit for reservation: the implementation of this recommendation and, on its heels, the *volte face* in which the economic criterion was withdrawn, has had a significant impact on the shape of Tamil Nadu politics. Sattanathan's phraseology in arguing for the removal of the 'upper layer' or 'upper crust' of the backward classes[1]—the phrase is repeated in the lectures published in the present volume—anticipates the current catchphrase, 'creamy layer', which has come into use since the Supreme Court's ruling of 1992 on means testing for reservation.

In the light of Sattanathan's memoirs, we can read, in every line of his Backward Classes Commission Report, his intimate knowledge and firsthand experience of social disadvantage and marginalization. He worked indefatigably to compile the Report and refused to accept an honorarium. At the beginning of the Report, closing his prefatory letter to the Chief Minister, he writes, with all the sincerity of his plain, strong prose: 'It has been to me a labour of love, working on this Commission, and it is my earnest hope that the Report will be of some use to your Government which has evinced so much interest in the welfare of the weaker sections of society.'

[1] *Report of the Backward Classes Commission, Tamil Nadu* (Madras: Government of Tamil Nadu, 1974), I, 100–1.

The timing of this book has been opportune. The interest in Indian life-writing has burgeoned recently, not so much for the general reader, for whom biography and autobiography have always held an appeal, but for the academic specialist. Life stories—and Indian life stories in particular—have been found to compass the dialectic of self and society, of individual consciousness and collective identity (of a class, or a caste, or a culture), distinctively, in an engaging and personalized form. In particular, the life-narratives of the marginalized, emerging into a wider awareness, are being recognized and celebrated as sites of resistance.[2]

To the growing body of such narratives, Sattanathan's autobiographical fragment makes a quite unique contribution. First of all, in respect of content: although narratives of Dalit lives are reaching the public domain in increasing numbers, the same cannot be said of those communities which, as one recent commentator put it, are '(just) above the traditional pollution line'.[3] These are the lowest of the 'touchable' Sudra castes, or by the present-day classification of the Government of Tamil Nadu, the 'Most Backward Classes'. In Tamil Nadu the largest of such communities, the Vanniyar or Padayachi community to which Sattanathan belonged, has had some political impact. But to the English-educated reader, especially, the community has remained largely invisible. Upper-caste readers, indeed, are barely aware of the huge variations in social status across the Sudra castes of Tamil Nadu, or of the possibility of distinction between 'Sudra' and 'Dalit'. By bringing into view a disadvantaged section of society not locatable in the binary domain of 'upper caste' and 'Dalit',

[2] For a recent and cogent survey of the characteristics and appeal of Indian life-writing, see David Arnold and Stuart Blackburn, 'Introduction: Life Histories in India', in *Telling Lives in India: Biography, Autobiography, and Life History*, ed. David Arnold and Stuart Blackburn (New Delhi: Permanent Black, 2004), 1–28.

[3] P. Radhakrishnan, 'Backward Class Movements in Tamil Nadu', in *Caste: Its Twentieth Century Avatar*, edited and introduced by M.N. Srinivas (New Delhi: Penguin, 1996), 110–34: 127.

Sattanathan provides an exceptional insight into the spectrum of caste prejudice and its objects. This is not in any sense to claim a parity between Sattanathan's and Dalit experiences: no such claim could be tenable. Nonetheless, a grasp of the plurality of the identity and experience of the lower castes must in some degree loosen the totalizing tendencies of the uninformed reader. The emphasis on particularity must vitally enhance the raising of awareness.

Another notable aspect of Sattanathan's memoirs is that they are written in English. I have no wish to enter here into a debate about the 'nativity' of English as a medium of expression for Indian writers; in Tamil Nadu, with its decades-long history of anti-Hindi agitations, and its two-language formula, the position of English is especially complex. Sattanathan himself has some illuminating observations to make, in chapter 5 of the memoirs, on the teaching of Tamil in the schools of his time. But it is certainly the case that his memoirs belie many of the generalizations that have been made in the past about English-language autobiographies by Indians, for instance, by Judith Walsh:

> . . . one of the characteristics of Indian autobiography is the tendency of authors to obscure, rather than to emphasize, the regional and cultural backgrounds from which they came. As a rule, the autobiographers . . . chose to obscure items of indigenous culture and tradition . . .
>
> English language autobiographies remind us of the degree to which Indians from different regions, cultural traditions and even historical periods could be members of one group—the Westernized, English-educated elite.[4]

Sattanathan's memoirs expose the inadequacy of this kind of homogenizing paradigm. And more: whatever might be said of its other problematics, his use of English has at least this in its favour, that it

[4] Judith C. Walsh, *Growing Up in British India: Indian Autobiographers on Childhood and Education under the Raj* (New York and London: Holmes & Meier, 1983), x.

makes him more completely the author of his own story than the translated author of an Indian-language text. When he speaks in his own voice, we grasp, more fully than otherwise, the humanity of the speaker, his individuality, his agency in his own story.[5]

Indeed, it is one of the peculiar strengths of Sattanathan's narrative that it repudiates categorization. Partly, this is due to its anachronistic character. Its time-span is the early decades of the last century; its date of composition the mid-twentieth century—at the beginning of the second decade of Indian Independence; and its publication in the early twenty-first century. In its content and stance it stands apart both from the elitist English-language narratives of the first half of the twentieth century (to which Walsh refers), and from the more deliberately oppositional narratives of the marginalized peoples of India that began to appear from the 1980s onwards. Although oppositional relations of various kinds are certainly inscribed here, and in more than one pairing—Brahmin and Non-Brahmin, rich and poor, and perhaps also, and more subtly, North and South—the memoirs themselves cannot be described as either oppositional or collusive. Instead, Sattanathan manages to inhabit, without apology or defence, a range of polarities: a love of Hindu mythology, for instance, as well as a hatred of the caste system; or, equally, a sympathy with the Non-Brahmin movement as well as a fervent nationalism. In so doing he manifests neither irresolution nor complicity, but a generous and ample humanity.

The form of the memoirs is also unusual. They are incomplete, not in the sense that all autobiographies, insofar as they do not and

[5] I am here adapting some of the terms of Alok Mukherjee in his essay, 'Reading Sharankumar Limbale's *Towards an Aesthetic of Dalit Literature*: From Erasure to Assertion', in Sharankumar Limbale, *Towards an Aesthetic of Dalit Literature: History, Controversies and Considerations*, translated from the Marathi by Alok Mukherjee (New Delhi: Orient Longman, 2004), 1–18. Mukherjee declares that an important 'facet of the revolutionary project of Dalit literature . . . is the establishment of the full humanity of the Dalit. This literature asserts the Dalits' selfhood, history and agency' (ibid., 15).

cannot represent a whole life, must be incomplete, but more overtly, in that they are in the form of a fragment, a form which, like autobiography itself, has been identified as a characteristically Romantic form. Much has been written about the Romantic fragment: it has been argued, on the one hand, that what is incomplete can the more effectively capture the entirety that it does not attempt to embody, and, on the other, that the eliciting of totality from what is incomplete is an act of bad faith, entailing the smoothing of fissures and tensions into an ideal (and ideologically suspect) whole.[6] In either case, and whether we celebrate or indict it for the comparison, Sattanathan's prose fragment is like its Romantic forebear in that what is fragmentary here is also, paradoxically, capacious. The full humanity of the author, the polarities and contradictions that he occupies, are appropriately accommodated in a form that eschews finality or closure.

At the same time, a wholeness of another kind has been constituted by the publishing of the memoirs in conjunction with Sattanathan's lectures on the Dravidian movement, delivered in 1981 as the E.V. Ramaswamy Endowment Lectures at the University of Madras. Some of the statements in the lectures might well be contested, but as a whole the lectures offer a lucid and non-partisan view, and in so doing, stand as a useful introduction to the topic that they treat. As a composite text as well as singly, and in ways that are complementary to each other, the memoirs and lectures exemplify the dialectic to which I have referred, of personal and social history. If the memoirs can be read as social history written as a life, the lectures, no less, contain a personal history between the lines that describe a social movement. Here I should clarify that the word 'Sudra', in my subtitle for the composite text, reflects Sattanathan's own usage in the lectures;

[6] For an example of the first view, see, for instance, Edward Kessler's defence of Coleridge's late poetry, *Coleridge's Metaphors of Being* (Princeton, N.J.: Princeton University Press, 1979); for a classic exposition of the second, see Marjorie Levinson, *The Romantic Fragment Poem: A Critique of a Form* (Chapel Hill and London: University of North Carolina Press, 1986).

it pre-dates recent political usage, such as that of Kancha Ilaiah, for instance, to which it is not quite congruent, except—and importantly—as an assertion of low-caste identity, an affirmation.[7]

I prepared the text of the memoirs from the notebook in which they were dashed off—without prior planning or preparation, and with only a very few afterthoughts or revision—by the author. A certain (minimal) amount of editorial intervention I judged to be not only permissible but necessary. Such intervention has been mainly to do with the arrangement, not the wording, of the narrative. There is a greater degree of paragraphing and punctuation in the present text than in the notebook, and in one or two instances I have transposed sentences or sections of paragraphs. The first two chapters are one in the notebook. I split the second chapter as it now stands off from the first and gave it its title. All other chapter divisions and titles are the author's, although the title of the volume as a whole, for the reasons given earlier, is mine. I have left untouched the distinctive constructions and cadences of Sattanathan's writing, but have had to rectify the odd grammatical error of tense. The author's recollected experience was so immediately present to him that he occasionally sacrificed grammatical consistency to drop unconsciously from past tense into present, sometimes within the same sentence. On the other hand, I have retained spellings now no longer in use, and the author's variant spellings of the same word in different parts of his text; also some of his (sometimes inconsistent) capitalization of words (Sattanathan's varying use of upper and lower case for the word 'brahman' is especially indicative.) The italicization in the text is mine: I have italicized, and glossed in my notes, transliterated words and phrases, but not those words of Indian origin that can be found in the *OED*. The

[7] See Kancha Ilaiah, *Why I am Not a Hindu: A Sudra Critique of Hindutva Philosophy, Culture and Political Economy* (Calcutta: Samya, 1996).

same policy of italicization has been adopted in the lectures. Otherwise, except in one instance signalled in my annotations, the text of the lectures, being prepared from a previous publication rather than from manuscript, has required little more than the amending of typographical errors, and the occasional substitution, in the interests of clarity, of a noun for its pronoun.

So as not to intrude upon the narrative in any way, my notes to the text are nowhere signalled in the text itself, but are given at the end, each attached to a phrase tag, and with a page reference. These annotations have turned into a parallel text, a patchwork of local customs and traditions, religion, literature, mythology, figures of personal, local, or national importance, regional and national contexts. Starting with a vague notion of providing information for a 'general reader', as I progressed my picture of that reader became more and more eclectic, and with it the nature of the information I was supplying. By the time I finished, the descriptors of 'general' or 'useful' information also disappeared; in very many instances I sought information merely—as an end in itself. Not that I have succeeded, or not at least as fully as I had hoped. But if I have succeeded at all, the annotations should pick out, for anyone who might be interested, some of the constituent threads and colours of the fabric of Sattanathan's text. My searching has taken me far beyond my usual fields of scholarship, and also far back, into my own personal and political history, and into lost or forgotten knowledge of which I was already in possession: what might have been new has turned out to be after all intensely familiar. I have tried to keep to a minimum the expression of my personal involvement in this work. Yet I cannot leave unwritten here my immeasurable debt to a dearly beloved grandfather, who, having lit up my childhood and young adulthood from the great stores of his knowledge, has thus still been the means, so much later in my life and so long after he is gone, of my ongoing education.

PART ONE

AN EXERCISE IN BIOGRAPHY (1958)

1

A House of Women

15 May 1958. Today is my official birthday. It struck me only when I noted the date on the calendar. Not that it has any significance; but it is interesting that I should start writing these notes on the day that I am 54 (completed 53) according to the date entered in my school and official records. The actual date of my birth is really 6th May—which I have often remembered celebrating, but not regularly.

Celebrating birthdays is the custom of the rich and the religious. I don't remember my even thinking of my birthday as anything special till I was 25 or 26 years old. Among my friends and acquaintances during that period it was fashionable to celebrate birthdays, and my family also thought of flattering me by copying this custom. I never felt particularly cheered by this. I always thought it was vain. Having been born in poverty, I always had the plebeian dislike of all plutocratic habits.

Most people feel a certain sense of pride about the place of their birth. It is rather difficult for me to analyse my feelings about Shencottah. That I was born there is a matter of pride to some people. To me, it was more in the line of an accident.

My recollection of the house of my earlier days is that of a crowd of ill-assorted old women. It has always remained to me a house of women. There was my mother, my grandmother (mother's mother), her mother, an aunt of my mother's (widowed), and another woman relation who was perpetually drinking water and lying ill. The women were dominated by my grandmother, a domineering personality.

She was very fair, by our standard at least, almost yellowish in complexion, very thin, and very tall. She was pretty well advanced in age at the time of my earliest remembrance of her. She apparently was suffering from a chronic ailment. I did not know then what it was. All that I can remember is that she was constantly coughing. A spittoon was her companion. I cannot remember her going out of the house very often. She was a wiry, almost thin woman, and when not bedridden, was very active, doing all the chores of a big household. I often thought even then that she must have been a beautiful woman in her younger days. But when I remember her it is as a woman with deep and secret sorrows and disappointments. She had a temper. I have heard her swear and scold her household of women, as I have never heard since. Many older men and women used to visit her to unburden to her their sorrows and to seek her counsel. She did not spare them either. No one seemed to resent her vitriolic tongue. They took their doses of her medicine with philosophic resignation. None got the better of her in an argument. Beaten, they used to retreat sadder, but not angrier.

For her female relations she laid down the law and expected and obtained implicit obedience. Nevertheless I cannot remember her ever getting angry with me. I do not know whether I was treated as the apple of her eye. She was not one for demonstrative affection. In that household of grim, sad, hard-working women, in that atmosphere of poverty, there was no place for demonstrative affection. But I was always drawn to my grandmother. I felt I was under her special protection, though I do not recollect receiving any special expression of her grace, love, or bounty. That she was very fond of me was certain. I always looked up to her, and imagined that she must have had a stormy life, with her undoubted beauty, and fierce temper.

Her mother, that is, my great-grandmother, was a contrast to her daughter in many ways. She was sweet and soft-spoken. She was darker and very much shorter—a little dumpling. She was quiet and mild, and went about her work unobtrusively. Her gentleness pervaded wherever she went. She was demonstratively fond of me, and I still remember her using the fondest and most endearing epithets in caressing me. She had, as long as I can remember, two white coarse cotton sarees, the type poor old widows wear. How she kept them spotlessly clean all the time used to mystify me even then. Soap was not in such common use in those days. Some kind of earth village washermen used to excavate from near river beds and tank bunds served instead. The old lady probably knew this recipe—her clothes were always clean and washed.

The combined influence of these two old ladies must have been comforting to the meek little child—the hope of a family dominated by several women of three generations.

This gentle old lady was called the golden mother (*thanga thaai*) by all of us children. There is a story behind this. When one of the younger children of the family was brought away from the parents during a quarrel, the little child asked for the mother when she woke up. The gentle old lady fondly caressed the child and said that *she* was her mother. The child lisped back, 'my golden mother', and the same name stuck. She was such an affectionate and self-effacing old woman. She remained our golden mother till she died.

When I was about 13 years old I suffered from a bad spell of an unnamed fever—might have been influenza, which was a dread scourge in the years following the First World War. I was scorched with the fever for nearly three weeks, and the old lady said, squatting beside my pillow, 'Why should this child suffer, I would willingly die happily if this child could recover.' I got better and within a month thereafter the old lady passed out of life as gently as she had lived through it. Talk of Humayun's legendary story!

There was yet another woman, only a little older than my mother, who was foster mother to us children. In fact we used to call her 'mother' (*aathal*). In Tamil, *aathal* is the proper word for 'mother', and the term *amma* is used only by the more sophisticated and Sanskritized middle classes. She was the widow of my grandmother's brother who died perhaps a few years after her marriage. She made her home with the domineering sister-in-law of hers, and did all the drudgery of the house ungrudgingly. In that household of intelligent and competent women, she suffered from an inferiority complex. She never tried to assert herself, but was contented to be the foster mother of two generations of children.

I often wondered how this family of women came to be there, and where they came from. Family records have no place among the poor. Even remembrance does not go beyond two or three generations. My grandmother's father built the house on the plot where it now stands, though very much changed now due to successive alterations and rebuilding. For a long time, our house was the only one with a tiled roof in that street of thatched huts. The old man must have had some pretensions to gentility and must have been of a class slightly superior to the neighbourhood. He had a brother and sons. All seem to have withered away, leaving the legacy to the tall fair wench who even as a girl appeared to have dominated her father's family, as she dominated her daughter's in later years.

It was fairly obvious to me even as a child that there was something out of the ordinary about this matriarchal lady and that she had had a colourful past. The absence of a grandfather around the house and veiled references to a shadowy one would not escape curiosity. The story that I gleaned was not very pleasing to one's sense of pride in family history. But there it was, for good or bad, and it had influenced the lives of my parents, and mine, to some extent.

The young girl, because of her beauty and daring, must have had admirers amongst the young men—friends and acquaintances of her father. Apparently she enjoyed more freedom in her household than most young girls in villages. One young man (whom I shall refer to as 'K') was attracted to the girl. He was a remarkable man in many ways. Though unlettered (he could barely sign his name in Tamil, and with difficulty write a few lines), he was ambitious, far-seeing, and hard working. Starting life as a servant boy and cook, he was already building a fortune by successfully handling small contracts for the supply of provisions and labour to the coffee estates prospering in the nearby forests. The girl's father was associated with the young man in some business of theirs, jointly, and he was a welcome visitor to their house. He found the girl not only attractive, but of kindred spirit. Their intimacy could not have remained a secret for long. Marriage was out of the question, as they belonged to two different communities. They had to be separated in their own interests.

The girl was given away in marriage to a meek and incompetent man, of poor means, in a village about twenty-five miles away. Those were the days when the South Indian Railway had not ventured south of Thirunelveli. Village folk married away near relations in the village, or in nearby villages within easy walking distance. Only very well-to-do people, who could afford transport by their own bullock-carts or palanquins or horse-drawn vehicles, ventured to go beyond this small radius in search of marriage alliances. In these conditions, this marriage was somewhat unusual and perhaps the girl's father sought to place his rebellious young girl out of harm's way, or K's way. He did not appear to have succeeded in this. Temperamentally the girl and her husband were ill-matched. She seemed to have developed neither love nor respect for the man to whom she was wedded by force. I do not know how long she lived there. She must have taken any convenient pretext to come back to her father's house for short or long spells, as her whims dictated. I have also heard that K used to visit her husband's village now and then. How they carried on the surreptitious love affair beats me, as facilities for such meetings must have been few and hard to arrange in those days. Her husband appears to have been a patient and long-suffering person, very fond of his good-looking but intractable young wife, and prepared to endure her tantrums and vagaries if only she would abide with him.

It was not to be. After a few years, K literally stormed her feeble fortress and carried her away, defying decorum and prejudices. She came back to live with her father. The old man eventually got reconciled to his daughter's waywardness. She dominated him and became the mistress of the house, sending her gentle little mother to the background.

The liaison between the rebellious and impetuous girl and the ambitious K did not appear to have lasted very long. He was already rapidly amassing wealth and building up local influence. He was soon recognized as the richest man of the town and the most influential person in the locality. A marriage, even in our polygamous society, outside his caste, was inconceivable in those days—the eighties of the nineteenth century. He had his wife and many children already. He was far too deeply engrossed in the business of amassing wealth and building up respectability. He was also passing the prime of life. He slowly drifted apart. The liaison produced one child—my mother.

The clever old adventurer apparently had a soft corner for this love child of his in his heart. Though he ceased his regular patronage of the house after this child was three or four, she used to be taken to see him frequently. His own sons and daughters knew of the relationship and somehow treated the little girl with consideration and sympathy, mixed with a little disdain, inevitably.

I have a faint recollection of the celebrity visiting the house when I was a very young child. He was making a spot investigation in the neighbourhood in connection with some matter he was interested in. My grandmother was fairly bedridden at the time, and word was sent to him that she would appreciate his coming over for a minute. He did, followed by his retinue. He seldom went out without at least a dozen courtiers, hangers-on, and relations following him. He was affectionately and respectfully greeted by his daughter, but the old lady, after a brief moment of crying—she did not actually speak to the old man—began hurling curses and abuses. He stood in the front yard listening for a while very intently, and then walked out without a trace of anger or bitterness. He must have been seriously affected by the outburst—for the house soon had evidence of his benefaction. He was a grand man, very large-hearted, and intensely human.

I used to be taken to him occasionally—perhaps once a year, or in connection with some social event. He always made very kindly enquiries, encouraged me to study, perhaps gave me a rupee or two, or sometimes he arranged for a new piece of cloth to be given to me. He was aware of the poverty in which his daughter's family was living. He would have liked to do something for them. But like all self-made men, he was loath to part with the wealth he had accumulated so carefully and painstakingly. He must also have been postponing things, as most old people in such circumstances tend to do. Once or twice, he asked my mother what she would like to have. She had neither the imagination nor the courage to ask for anything substantial. She only asked for a piece of rice-growing land on his estate, hardly worth Rs 1000, which was within a furlong or two of our house. It was this bit of land that she got as a gift just a few days before he died. He might have given more if he was asked. In poverty one does not even know how and what to ask.

I have one very clear picture deeply ingrained in my memory about this old gentleman. There was a big crowd in front of his house soon after he died. I also made my way into the crowd and came quite close to see what was going on in the centre of the courtyard. The venerable gentleman's dead body had been bathed, and the last rites in which the women of the household participate prior to the last journey were being performed. A large number of women mourners with their wet sarees, dishevelled hair, and loud lamentations were going round the decorated wooden platform on which the body was laid. In that crowd I saw my mother also, taking the second place among the mourners, the first being taken by the old patriarch's legitimate daughter, who resembled my mother remarkably, except for the changes affluence effects in a person. No-one seemed to resent or comment on my mother's taking part in these last rites. It was natural, and in sadness and bereavement, blood was thicker than economic or legal differences, or differences in caste and status.

There is yet another unforgettable episode connected with this funeral. After the body was laid in the family palanquin, it was taken in procession to their private garden beyond the little stream, where all their dead were cremated. It was forbidden for women to accompany this procession. There was one girl—a granddaughter—who clung to the palanquin, and followed it. She was about 11 or 12 about that time, and her heroic performance impressed me a great deal. From that day onwards I always had an admiration for this courageous girl. She married a cousin and has been living an undistinguished life—a failure, I am sure, by her own standards.

Brought up in the shadow of a domineering mother and several other women, my mother always appeared sad to me. She must have had her problems living in this household of women, bereft of the beneficial influence of a father and the guidance of a strong male head of family. In her childhood days, I don't think she suffered from want. As the only child, she was affectionately brought up. There could, however, have been no pampering. Her mother was incapable of pampering or spoiling a child by kindness or too much laxity.

Though there was a certain amount of caste ostracism, it appears to have worn off gradually. My grandmother made staunch friends. Those whom she did not like she cut out of her life, sharply. Even they did not bear any rancour against her. She did not therefore have very many enemies as another woman in her position would have done, especially with her temper and outlook. The family had good friends among people of other castes and faraway relations. Therefore she did not have much difficulty in getting her daughter married off.

From bits of conversation I have heard over the years, I gather there were apparently several suitors for my mother's hand. Most eligible young men in the community in neighbouring villages were eager for the match. In spite of a somewhat lurid background, the young girl had made a reputation for herself as a gentle, home-loving, and well-behaved person. The family had pretensions to gentility always. Though they always lived at near-starvation level, their means being limited, they were always regarded as respectable middle class. Their standard of cleanliness, observation of social and religious rites, and external appearances were distinctly superior to those of their immediate neighbourhood, and of the people of the caste. When they entertained an occasional relation or guest, he was impressed, and the people of the caste generally observed that the food in the house was such as is not ordinarily cooked in other houses. This reputation for affluence and a standard above the reality of the situation had always clung to the family for generations. In those days when my mother was of marriageable age, many suitors also perhaps thought there was some wealth hidden away somewhere. The marriage was, I have heard, celebrated with some amount of pomp, and the bridegroom's people were impressed.

2

My Father

My father came from a village, Pavoor, some ten miles to the east of our home town. He was the second of five brothers and two sisters. I have distinct recollections of my father's mother, a large, square-built lady of unusual cheerfulness and grace. She was of a complexion which for that part of the country could be called very fair. She was of an extreme religious disposition and was devoted to the family deity for whom there was a temple at the rear of their home. The grandfather was a sturdy, rough, peasant type of person. The thing that impressed me forcibly in my childhood days was the abundant good health of all the people on my father's side. My father's brothers were very sturdy and big-built and so were their womenfolk. All these men and women worked on their fields—they owned small plots of paddy land and dry land where maize and coarse grains were cultivated. The women did more work in the fields than the men and often they worked for daily wages for others, when they had no work on their own land. The men took to other avocations also—the most popular at that time among those who had the talent for such work was playing musical instruments.

My mother did not live in father's village for more than three or four years. The gentle girl did adjust herself to the life of the big joint family and learnt to do the rough and strenuous work that womenfolk were accustomed to do then. She won the affection and respect of all her in-laws. Her mother-in-law was genuinely fond of her. Whatever mother brought from her mother's house was shared by the in-laws.

Gradually father fell out with his brothers. One younger brother was a hot-tempered young man, ready to pick a quarrel on the least pretext. The brothers had their quarrels—but they just as easily made up. Then father had a bad attack of chicken-pox. It left his face and body badly scarred. There was an unhealed scar near the eye. When he was still recovering from the ravages of the pox, there was a family quarrel. The brothers exchanged blows, and father was hurt in his already injured eye.

Grandmother heard about this and felt it was time she interfered. She decided it was time her daughter and son-in-law came to live with her. The house in Shencottah badly needed a man. Father and mother packed up whatever few possessions they had and followed the old matriarch home. At the time of leaving, the brothers wanted that he should relinquish whatever right he had to a share in their meagre family property. The old lady, my grandmother who had made and squandered money in her own ways, advised father that he did not need any share of his family's petty possessions. So father literally washed his hands off. The Hindu religious ceremony of renouncing rights consists in washing your hands off with water over whatever you are renouncing.

Life for father and mother in their earlier days in grandmother's house was neither peaceful nor prosperous. Day-to-day existence and keeping up pretensions of middle-class respectability were an effort. The family's income from land was utterly inadequate to feed its several members. Then there were the children—additional mouths to be fed. In addition to cultivating the little bit of land they possessed, the family had recourse to several other petty avocations. The women of the household bore their full share in this.

Father carried on his services as a musician. The musician has to have his troupe, a minimum of four: the piper, the drummer, the *taalam* or time keeper, and the background piper. If it was a heavy engagement, like attending to a Temple festival or an important marriage celebration, there was always a second piper, and a second drummer sometimes. Father had the co-operation of his brothers and near relations in this matter. The marriage season and the Temple festival season fall as always during the months of April, May, and June. There were two or three dull months in the year. In certain areas in the district and neighbouring districts, marriages are celebrated in January–February. To get the engagements for performing music in the houses of leading landlords in important villages, a considerable amount of advance solicitation is essential. Temples do not pay as well as marriage houses. For a few weeks before the marriage season, father and one of his associates used to be away making a round of calls and getting the bookings for engagements a month or two ahead.

A Brahmin wedding used to last five days. Formal music had to be played in the *pandal*, morning and evening. This was supposed to be auspicious. The original object must have been publicity—to make known to the neighbourhood that a wedding was on, and that people were welcome. In addition to the formal performance of music in the mornings and evenings, music was expected to be played when the various religious and social ceremonies and rites were being performed. The wedding ceremony proper lasted two hours. Music must be continuously played for the duration and for an hour before and after. In rich weddings, two sets of pipe musicians used to be engaged, and both must play simultaneously, from two different sections of the *pandal*. One can imagine the din.

The biggest occasion for the musicians to show their talent was the procession of the bride and groom. Sometimes there were two of these processions. But the main procession was the day after the wedding ritual. The boy and the girl (those were the days of child marriages, and a brahman bride was seldom more than thirteen, and usually about ten or eleven) decked in silk and jewels, covered with flowers and garlanded, were seated in a palanquin and taken in solemn and slow procession round the main streets of the village or town. This procession, in a rich wedding, lasted four to six hours, beginning from eight or nine, after dinner. The palanquin was preceded by all the relations, guests, and the leading gentry of the locality (sometimes invited and sometimes uninvited), and followed by the rabble, street urchins, and sightseers. The musicians were generally a few yards ahead of the palanquin. They were expected to face the palanquin and not show their backs to it. In slow motion, the procession would march for a few yards and then stop for fifteen minutes or half an hour. This was the occasion for the musicians to elaborate their musical theme. The crowd in a South Indian village, especially Brahmans, was always appreciative of good music, and heads would nod and hands clap in rhythm, with occasional exclamations of '*Balai*!', '*Sabaash*!' Sandal paste mixed in rose water was passed round to the musicians and the main guests to refresh themselves. The bridegroom often used snuff to keep himself awake and the bride was gently nudged by an attendant relation to keep awake. A procession was an exacting experience for the bridal couple, and for those whose business it was to look after the arrangements. The musicians used this as an opportunity to advertise their prowess and to win general applause. A musician who failed to rise up to the expectations of the critics of the village in an important procession would get no more engagements in that locality and his market value would crash.

As a child of five or six, I have followed my father when he was performing with these processions. I have returned home exhausted after following processions, on many occasions after midnight. I remember to have kept time (*taalam*) for the party occasionally. Mostly I was a hanger-on, and was handy in case my services in such a capacity were needed. My particular aesthetic delight was limited, for I did not have a scientific appreciation of music—but the palanquin, the crowd, the noise, and the fireworks display in front of the procession could not but provide welcome entertainment for a child. However, I later developed a loathing for the procession as a part of the marriage celebration—especially the display of a sleeping child bride in a palanquin or a decorated chariot.

The participation of father's music troupe in a big marriage celebration was a welcome interlude in the humdrum life of the house. During those few days, there was plenty of everything. If it was a Brahmin or a Pillay wedding, big basket-loads of cooked rice, vegetables, and sweets used to be brought from the marriage feast for the troupe. Otherwise, uncooked rice, vegetables, pulses, coconut and jaggery, oil and ghee used to be sent. Everyone in the house ate well for those few days. The musicians received other gifts also, if their performance was pleasing and their services otherwise satisfactory. These gifts normally took the form of dhotees and occasionally, gold trinkets were also presented. After a big wedding service was over, the house had plenty of provisions left over for use for a few days.

Another socio-religious custom that gave opportunities for musicians in our villages in those days was the *kaavadi*. There were a few temples nearby dedicated to Subramania, the deity of the ancient Tamils. There was one very near our village, situated on the top of a small hill. This was very popular with all classes of people, and on Fridays, large crowds from nearby villages went up the hilltop to offer prayers to the Hill God. If anyone was seriously ill, the family elders used to make a vow that the patient on recovery would make a pilgrimage to the temple with a *kaavadi*. The *kaavadi* was originally a mendicant's equipage. It was in the shape of a short bow in reverse, the beam connecting the two ends of the bowed frame, made of stout bamboo, resting on the man's left shoulder. Tied to the beam, hanging on either side of the shoulder, were cloth bags, in which the mendicant collected alms of rice and other grains. Religious mendicants travelled the country with this equipage, begging from village to village, and visiting temples en route. The really religious offered at least part of the alms they collected to the needy people, or fed the poor and the mendicants who generally throng our temples. Others took to this way of life just for an easy living.

The custom of a young man from a good home making a pilgrimage to the Temple of Muruga or Subramania as a mendicant with the *kaavadi* was an ancient one. It taught humility to the man, respect for religion, and was a deep personal religious experience. In some families, young men performed the pilgrimage as a ritual before their wedding. There were variations in the ritual. Some had this for three days; others were satisfied with a single day's pilgrimage. The *kaavadi* for such purposes was a highly ornamental and artistic piece of work. The bowed portion was in a frame of silk fringed with tassels, and on either side were clusters of peacock feathers. The mendicants' pouches were of saffron cloth. The whole contraption was covered with white flowers. The devotee was expected to abstain from meat and other kinds of objectionable food, eat only one meal, of milk and fruits, and generally lead a life of prayer and meditation for a week prior to the auspicious occasion. On the appointed day, early in the morning, after elaborate prayer and invocations, he was initiated by the priest and asked to shoulder the *kaavadi* to the accompaniment of pipes and drums and the chanting of hymns. The common belief was that the spirit of the deity possessed him and the initiate would go into a state of trance. The really religious (or superstitious, as one might like to call him) hypnotises himself, and for the next day or two, till the pilgrimage is over, he is in a state of semi-trance for most of the time. In this dazed state, he is taken in procession to the nearest temple and from there to the houses of friends and relatives where 'alms' are given to him in the pouches carried on the *kaavadi*. The devotee from a well-to-do family begs alms only from five houses of his nearest relations or close friends. The ordinary devotee from a poor family receives alms from any house that invites the *kaavadi* party. On the appointed day, which is generally a Friday, considered sacred to Muruga, the devotee walks up to the Hill temple, offers prayers, and then the poor are fed.

For the *kaavadi* pilgrimage, high-class musicians do not play. Only devotional songs and light music are permitted, and some musicians specialize in this. Musicians from among some of father's relations used to visit on plea of these functions and stay in our house. Almost every season there were half a dozen *kaavadi* offerings from men of our neighbourhood. I was always impressed by the simple faith of the poor and the devotion to their Gods even of the rich. Much of it was sheer superstition, but the origin of this custom, founded on religious humility and self-denial, impressed me always. Nevertheless, when my family suggested later that I should do a *kaavadi*, I stoutly refused, describing it as rank superstition.

Another part-time endeavour in which my energetic grandmother was engaged, as a means of making some money for the family, was the supplying of provisions to small labour gangs employed in the coffee and rubber plantations which flourished in those days, the early decades of this century, in the nearby forests. The leader of the gang was known as a *kangaani*. His business it was to recruit workers, men and women from the villages, and supervise their work and conduct during the brief periods when they were working in the factories or estates. The *kangaani* arranged with a contractor for regular supplies of rice, spices, and pulses for the use of the labour working under him. Grandmother had one or two of such small contracts and the stuff was sent up by head loads or bullock-cart once or twice a month. The profits in this business were meagre, as the commodities were local produce on which a high margin of profit could not be charged. There were also certain intermediaries and agents who had to be given a share of the profits.

I remember one of these agents who was an old friend of the family. He was a Muslim. Among certain sects of Muslims, during Id, there was the custom of 'playing the Tiger'. The person who has taken the particular vow paints himself in the colours and stripes of the tiger, and prances like one, within a wooden cage mounted on a gaily decorated bullock-cart. With music and shouting, the cart is taken through the streets where the tiger's friends live and the tiger used to clamber down the cart to call on his friends. One such visit to our house by the friendly tiger I distinctly remember. He was very sporting and made his visit memorable. I must have been not more than five years old at this time. I remember seeing this tiger in his normal human form later on several occasions in our house. He was a particular friend of father's, and took a lot of interest in me.

3

Experiments with Schools

My education started in the old-fashioned primitive single-teacher school run by a professional teacher in a shed at the end of our street. I was initiated at the age of five. The 'initiation' ceremony was a relic of the old *gurukulum* system which was popular in ages gone by.

I was given a ceremonial bath and new clothes on the auspicious day, the day following Saraswathi *pooja*, *Vijaya Dasami* day. This was always considered by good Hindus as the most appropriate day for starting to learn any art or craft. The village goldsmith, who generally attended to the requirements of the family, was invited to pierce the ears of the boy and stick a tiny gold ring in each. No child was considered fit to receive learning without this preliminary ear-boring. After this the teacher selected by the family elders took the child over and asked him to utter the sacred names of the Gods: *Om Shiva* etc. Thereafter fine river sand was spread on the ground and the child's fingers were guided by the teacher to trace the sacred symbols and then the first letter of the Tamil alphabet on the sand. The ceremony was followed by distribution of sweets, and feasting. In the houses of the wealthy, the child was taken in procession in a palanquin to the temple and round the main streets. I was spared this ordeal.

I went to the one-teacher school for nearly a year. After the first few days, I had a slate and a pencil. After a month or so, I was taught to write with a steel style on palmyra leaf. I left the school after a year, much to the teacher's regret, to join the Government-run elementary school.

My first schoolmaster in this primitive type of school belonged, as I said, to a family of hereditary teachers. He was a kindly old man, with considerable proficiency in the religious lore of the Tamil land, and he had an abhorrence for English and modern schools and methods. He attended my initiation ceremony, having left the school to be managed by his nephew who was hardly dissimilar to the village roughs.

The teacher sat on a raised stool while all the pupils sat on the floor with sand spread before them. Each child was given from time to time, according to the state of his progress, a piece of palmyra leaf with the Tamil alphabet written in stages. In the course of a month or two, the child had the entire set of alphabets in a bunch of palmyra leaf cards neatly punched in the centre and held together by a cord running through the centrally punched hole. The child was taught to write on the sand with the forefinger, and after some time, to write on the slate and also to write with the steel pointer on the palmyra leaf itself. Proficiency in writing on the palmyra leaf was the high-water mark of learning. After the alphabet was mastered, the combination of letters to form simple words was taught. Numbers and simple arithmetic tables were also taught in this manner. Memorizing was an important aspect of training in this school. The children were made to repeat the alphabet and numerals, and later the word spellings and simple tables of arithmetic, in chorus and also individually. Printed books were not used at all in those days in my school. The teacher himself wrote out all the days' lessons on the palmyra leaf book for all the pupils. When proficiency was reached in the alphabets, arithmetic, and writing, simple songs and poems from the ancient Tamil poets and minstrels were taught. These songs were memorized and repeated to the teacher.

The teacher was a hard taskmaster and did not spare his pupils if they did not do their lessons properly. He had his own code of punishments. If the child would not write on the sand properly after the initial demonstration or was careless of his guidance, he would catch hold of the child's forefinger and rub it on the sand, tracing the letters firmly and hard. If the finger did not bleed or if the child did not improve, he would be wild. If the child could not write with the steel style on the leaf legibly, the style would be used as a hammer on the knuckles. The teacher resorted to caning frequently only with the advanced pupils. Discipline was perfect. The children had a wholesome respect for the teacher. Disobedience of any sort was unthinkable.

I paid a fee of four annas a month. The school had a strength of about thirty pupils. I don't think the senior pupils paid more. The teacher had some other income besides the fees. During harvest time most of the pupils brought him small quantities of rice or paddy, pulses, and other grains. Those who had coconut groves brought him a few coconuts. Whenever there was a religious or social function in the house of a pupil, the teacher was an honoured guest and had some customary perquisites. When a pupil was first admitted to the school or initiated ceremonially, the teacher received a rupee or two, and sometimes the gift of new clothes. On the whole, he made a decent living out of his school. It was not a school recognised or inspected by Government. He did not therefore receive a grant from the authorities. The section of the village where the school was situated, however, saw to it that the teacher kept the school, so that the children were saved the trouble of going to a Government school at a distance. It was an institution bound to the old village economy, which believed in co-operative self-sufficiency.

My progress in the school was quite rapid. I was a quiet child, had no other distractions, and was very much liked by the teacher. He would have liked to keep me there and in course of time, I might have become enough of a scholar to become his assistant. But my father, who was receptive to progressive ideas and was keen on giving me a modern education, removed me from that school and got me admitted to the Government elementary school, which was popularly known as the Malayalam school. It was housed in a substantial building, about half a mile away from our house, near the Brahman quarter and the big Bazaar. It was known as the Malayalam school because Malayalam was taught as a compulsory second language besides Tamil.

My home town was the Headquarters of what was the frontier taluq of the Princely State of Travancore. Malayalam was the official language of the state. In the Tamil areas like mine, Tamil and Malayalam were taught up to a certain stage. The population was Tamil and the social customs and practices were of the Tamilians. But the upper and middle classes learnt Malayalam and most of the Government servants, including even such lowly personnel as police constables and peons in offices, were Malayalees. The school teachers, both in the Malayalam school and in the other bigger school (known as the English school), were mostly Tamil Brahmans, whose proficiency in Malayalam was as good as that of the Malayalees of Travancore.

I had no difficulty in picking up Malayalam. In fact, I showed a remarkable predilection for it and could soon speak the language without noticeable traces of Tamil influence. The teachers in the school treated me with affection mixed with a certain condescension. There was a general feeling in the country even then that Brahman teachers treated children of other castes with contempt. Whatever the truth may be, I did not feel that I was being treated unfairly. Perhaps the teachers, being themselves very poor, may have felt some sympathy for a poor child like me evincing earnestness in my studies.

About this time, my father was engaged in another lucrative part-time occupation. He was taking two or three pupils at a time, for teaching music. Some were Malayalees—perhaps the more earnest amongst his pupils who stayed with him for any length of time were Malayalees. Some stayed for a few months—a few stayed for two or three years. The teaching of music was done in the *gurukulam* tradition. The pupils stayed with us in the house and had food with us. They were treated as part of the family and were asked to do all the little jobs arising in the house, even to attending to the cultivation of our small piece of land. They accompanied my father when he had a music engagement to fulfil, and the wages for their share were surrendered to the master. They were expected to get up at four or five o'clock in the morning for their practice. They received instructions from father who also accompanied them on their instruments for a few minutes as need be.

Quite a number of our relatives and friends expected father to initiate me in music. His proficiency as a music instructor was greater than his reputation as a performing musician. But at no time did he show any inclination to make a musician of me. All craftsmen and artists in India in those early decades of the century had an abhorrence for making their profession hereditary, strange as it may seem. Every father, however eminent he may have been in his particular craft or art—be he a good goldsmith, mason, locksmith, or musician—wanted his son to get a smattering of an English education and to become a holder of a Government job. The attraction of a Government job in Travancore in those days was irresistible. Even a peon or a police constable was regarded as highly respectable. It was the beginning of the breakdown of the occupational basis of the caste system. The social taboos and stratification according to birth showed no signs of decline, but there was a flight from hereditary avocations. To become a clerk or a sub-inspector of police was the height of ambition. Many fathers spent their hard-earned savings to educate their sons, so that they might become clerks in Government offices. They might be indifferent clerks, making far less money than their fathers did as masons or carpenters, but the fathers wanted to see their sons dressed in shirt and coat and sitting in an office chair.

My father, experiencing as he had poverty in all its manifestations and the taboos of caste and caste professions, wanted to see that I became a Matriculate and a Government servant. He was not a very devoutly religious person, but he always had a deep faith that God was going to look after me in some special way. He was not demonstrative either in his affections or in his faith, but he was silently stubborn in his resolve that I should study. Any kind of play on my part met with his stern disapproval. He thought any play was a waste of time and effort and would distract me from my studies. He would not let me take part in the small games with pebbles and sticks children indulge in on streets in villages. I grew up without playing any games at all. True to his resolve, he was always thinking of short-circuiting the tedious course of education through different levels. He removed me from the village schoolmaster when he thought I could profitably study in the Malayalam school in a class slightly more advanced than would be justified for my age-group. After a year and a half in the Malayalam school, he thought it was high time I began learning English. In the Malayalam school, English was not taught. I had to pass the fourth standard, and then go on to the English school (secondary school) to join the Preparatory class where the English alphabet was taught. That was the system followed in Travancore. To my father, whose most remarkable quality was impatience, this was too slow and wasteful. He was thinking of some method of introducing me to English education quickly, so that I could join the English school in Form I (Form VI being the Matriculation standard) ahead of my contemporaries.

I was about seven years old at this time. An event took place in the family which enabled father to take his decision about the next stage of my education. That was the marriage of my elder sister. She was about four years older than me. Like all girls in poor families of our caste, she was unlettered. In fact, few girls even of richer families were given an education. In some houses, they were taught the alphabet and the numerals at home by an elder. In the socially and culturally advanced homes, girls were sent to the separate school for girls run by the state, for a few years. They were generally withdrawn by the time they were eleven or twelve. This luxury poorer families could not afford. The girls worked in the house and in the fields from the age of five. Except among Brahmans, it was not the custom, however, to get the girls married off before they were fourteen. The average age of attaining puberty was thirteen. Among the working classes and those who did physical work in the fields and at home, my recollection is that the age of puberty was even higher. It was considered proper to get girls married off within a year or two after they attained puberty. This was called the marriageable age. Among the lower middle-class non-Brahmans in those days, sixteen was regarded as the respectable age for marriage. Anything later was treated with suspicion. A girl remaining unmarried long after seventeen was considered deficient in some qualities and therefore not desirable. By the same reasoning, the more desirable girls were married off soon after attaining the marriageable state or in anticipation of it. Only very desirable girls were taken in marriage at an earlier age.

My sister was married off at the age of eleven. The custom amongst our people was for the bridegroom's people to come and seek the bride. This was the reverse of the Brahman custom. I cannot even now understand why an offer of marriage came so soon to my sister. We were not rich. There was no big dowry in the offing. The girl was comely—but was not 'fair'. Fair colour was always a desirable asset for a bride even among the poor! The bridegroom was not a close relation who had, by caste convention, a right to demand the girl's hand in marriage. Certain cousinly relations alone have that right, and in some cases, to prevent the girl slipping from their hands, early marriages were arranged. There were two sisters of my father married in that village. At least one of them had a son who had the traditional claim to the bride from our house. The sisters of father did not press their own legitimate claim, but wanted this child-bride for a relation. The bridegroom was an eligible young man by our standards, following the usual professions of the caste. He was a cousin of my father's sister's husband. The whole affair was unconvincing—but events in life do not always follow a logical sequence.

Marriages in our society were always arranged. But in the arrangement there were always certain reasons and aims. This marriage had neither. We say marriages are made in heaven. This particular marriage was made in hell. But that is anticipating events by several years.

My sister's wedded home, as we call it, was in a village about 12 miles away from ours. It had a big Christian population and a mission school where English was taught from the earlier standards. Father thought I should go to this school and be looked after by my sister and her husband. So before I was eight, during the middle of the school year, I was transplanted to this Christian mission school in Surandai.

Surandai was a twin-village. The Christian converts had moved out from the main village during the course of years, and with the help of the mission, built another village about a mile to the east. Most of the houses were tile-roofed, as distinct from the thatched huts in the original village. The missionaries—Indian and European—had small Bungalows. There was a school and an impressive church. The new village came to be called 'Bungalow Surandai' and was the pride of the Christian community for miles around.

In those days, the members of a particular caste—toddy-tapping being their hereditary profession—were converted to Christianity in large numbers. They got free education and the educated young men and women had no difficulty in getting suitable employment in Government Departments and in educational institutions. The women trained in nursing were rapidly filling up the hospitals. Indian Christian women were the first to take up nursing as a career. A community which was regarded as backward was soon in the forefront of advancement as soon as they changed the religion. It was due to the interest taken by European missionaries and the active support they received from the Government and the European civil servants who were all-powerful in those days. Soon, from the Christian villages in the District of Tinnevelly, there went out all over the state, doctors, lawyers, teachers, and nurses. Their new-won prosperity was reflected in their parent villages where the older people lived while men and women of the younger generation were out in Madras and in distant towns, earning comfortable livings owing to the benefits of missionary education.

The village of Bungalow Surandai could boast even then of several graduates and doctors and teachers. It had a clean, healthy, prosperous appearance and the school was the central show-piece. It had extensive playgrounds and shady avenues of trees, and the atmosphere was conducive to education. The teachers were Christian converts, and some of them were really gifted men indeed.

To this school came pupils from many neighbouring villages. The school was partly residential, but the facilities for boarding and lodging it provided were not taken advantage of by the non-Christian students, though there was no restriction against them. Some boys walked four and five miles from their villages, morning and evening, carrying a little packet of cooked rice with them for the midday repast. Brahman boys also attended the school, though orthodoxy in the villages in those days was very severe. But orthodox or otherwise, they were quick to take advantage of educational facilities wherever they were available. Brahman boys on returning from school used to remove their school clothes and keep them apart in an outside apartment, and enter the house only after a purifying bath. Boys who came from distant villages outside the range of walking distance boarded with the families of friends and relations, and some well-to-do boys kept their own establishments in the village—either the new or the old one.

When I was taken to Surandai, I first stayed in my sister's house. Afterwards I stayed for some time in the house of one of my aunts. For brief intervals, my grandmother or great-grandmother and I stayed in a rented room in the vicinity of the school in the Christian village, and the old lady cooked for me. It was no great trouble, nor was it frightfully expensive, living that way. We brought the rice and pulses and condiments from our home once in two or three months, and little sundries we bought in the village bazaar, and the vegetables in the weekly market. Rice was cooked once a day either at noon or at night and the leftover was preserved to serve for the other meals.

This little personal establishment to look after me was found to be necessary as I used to fall ill when I stayed in the old village with my relations for more than a month. I had to leave the house before 9 a.m. after a breakfast of fermented rice and curry left over from the previous night, and walk nearly two miles in the hot sun. I used to carry some rice in a leaf packet or in a small utensil, to be eaten during the noon interval. Often I threw away the rice and preferred to starve. In the evening, again I walked back two miles. The night meal—the only satisfactory meal of the day—was at seven p.m. Even this meal was much worse than what I used to get in our house where, in spite of our poverty, the food was clean and tasty, and we had at least one satisfying meal a day.

I was a very delicate child and my pigeon-chest was my mother's and grandmother's constant worry. My chest was rubbed constantly with an awful-smelling oil—some kind of crude fish oil—and I was asked to stand in the early sun. No wonder therefore that spells of boarding with my relations—who were constantly living at starvation level—reduced my health, and I used to trudge home for long weekends with my pigeon-chest more pronounced than before. This would provoke my grandmother to fury and she would order one of her aged relations to escort me back when I returned to school, and to keep house for me, however expensive this proved to the family, with its scanty resources.

This sojourn of a year and a half in Surandai brought me in touch with the life of the poor outside my own family circle. Men, women, children, and the aged worked incessantly at any kind of occupation that was within reach in the village, to earn a few annas or half a measure of rice. Women shared the burden with the men. When there was no work to be had, idleness was forced on them. Nevertheless they married young, and before a girl was twenty-five, she would have several children, some still births, some abortions, and the toll nature and poverty had taken on her would be evident, for she would already look like an old woman. Quarrels in the family, between husband and wife, between mother-in-law and daughter-in-law, between father and sons, between brothers, between neighbours and relations, were an everyday occurrence. Living in the village amongst our relations, I witnessed their quarrels almost every day. It was not unusual to see a young husband beat his wife mercilessly with anything he could lay his hands on, for the simple offence that she did not keep hot water ready for his bath when he returned home in the evening. Children were also mercilessly beaten. The daughter-in-law of the house was treated as the general slave by every one of her in-laws, and many quarrels could be traced to this state of affairs.

I had begun to notice that my sister, herself hardly twelve, was also becoming a victim to this treatment, and my remaining with her or near her was an embarrassment to both of us, and sometimes irritating to our other relations. I found an escape from these situations by calling on one of my 'grandmothers' to keep house for me in the school village, and this suited my health also.

There is one thing about the school which has left a lasting impression on me. We had a history teacher, a tall, hefty, dark young man, who had a certain skill in drawing maps of campaigns and battles. He used to pin the map on the blackboard and explain in vivid language, the courses of battles. He had a flair for this kind of teaching. We had him only for a few months. But he aroused in me an abiding interest in history. I was a quiet and inconspicuous pupil in that fairly rough school, where the students were given to quite a deal of games and sports. I did not distinguish myself by any great achievement in the examinations.

4

A School Escapade

While I was in the mission school, an incident happened which well might have given a different turn to my life. But it remained an embarrassing episode without altering the course of life to which I was being trained. I went to school after a few days' absence to find that during my absence the teacher had been particularly active and had given several notes and exercises. All the notebooks of the boys were checked by him, and those boys whose notebooks were not found satisfactory were caned. I was told by the teacher solemnly that I should produce my notebooks for his inspection on the next working day. I borrowed the notebooks of one of the best pupils of the class and devoted all my leisure hours to copying the exercises. I was not particularly aware of what I was copying—some of the notes and exercises were above my understanding. I noticed that in the margins there were some corrections and some unintelligible scribblings. I copied these as well. I was ready with the notebooks for the teacher's inspection the next day, and proudly produced them when he asked.

I could see his face turn practically savage. His moustaches were twitching. He frowned on me and asked whether I did all these—pointing out the corrections and scribblings in the margin. Then he accused me of forging his signatures. I did not understand what he meant. All that I could sense was that I was being accused of a terrible crime. He took his cane and flogged me mercilessly in the class, to the consternation of the pupils. From the abuse he was hurling at me, I slowly gathered that I had imitated his signatures and that that was unpardonable and besides, I was a cheat, a rogue, and should be put in jail. After his excitement settled down, being exhausted by his sadistic fury in flogging me, he took me to the headmaster. I could not follow their conversation, but I had a vague impression that the headmaster did not think so seriously of my misdemeanour. But he also frowned on me and advised me that I should never repeat the offence.

I have thought over this incident often in later life. A child of eight has no idea of the criminal implications of forgery. I did not pass off anything spurious as mine own. I was not profiting by it and cheating someone. I copied the notes and I thought that the corrections and scribblings added to the importance of my copying. The notes were to be seen by the teacher and I did not endeavour to cheat him by saying he had already seen my notes and that the corrections and initials were his. I did not even think it was clever and funny to copy the initials and corrections. I was not even aware of the significance of these. A good sympathetic teacher might have explained to me that I should not copy his initials and corrections, and that what I was asked to do was only to make my notebook up-to-date. The severe manhandling I got unnerved me and I made up my mind that I would have nothing more to do with that school or the teacher.

Next day I left for my home—twelve miles away. My wardrobe could not have been much more than what I carried on my body, and collecting the few books and notes I had, I walked my familiar way back through fields, pasture-land, village roads, till I came to Tenkasi, the town only five miles away from my place, from which there was a good road. I walked the distance in about four hours.

When I came home and reported what happened to my father, I got another flogging. What incensed father was that I ran away from school—an unforgivable lapse, in his eyes. He saw all his dreams vanishing. He also took a serious view of my forgery. I seldom opposed father and was always mortally afraid of him. He was short-tempered and prone to violence in speech and action at the least provocation. He was always dreadfully afraid of authority and knew that forgery was a punishable offence.

Treated to merciless punishment both at school and at home, I was disconsolate. The only person who gave me some grudging sympathy was grandmother. This worldly-wise woman understood that I was innocent and that whatever I did was due to ignorance and not even out of childish mischief. But she too thought I should not have run away from school. She advised that I should be sent back to school promptly and that I should seek the pardon of the teacher whom I had unwittingly offended and provoked. At any cost my education should continue.

I was soon sent back to the school with some relation escorting me. But, boiling with rage and angry with the people who had treated me so unfairly, I made up my mind to dodge the school again. There was no question of shame or guilt. I was quite clear in my mind that I had done no wrong, but the world was punishing me for no reason at all. So from my relations' house in the old village, I set out in the morning, ostensibly bound for school. I did not, however, take the straight road, but wandered in a different direction, without any clear idea of what I should do. I left the village, crossing the stream, and began walking in a southerly direction along the road leading to my father's ancestral village. But I did not want to go to my uncles. I had never been there except in the company of others, for a wedding or other functions. I did not want to see anyone whom I knew. Then there was the fear that no-one would sympathise with me or help me after the way father had treated me.

There was the Railway line and a Railway station a mile beyond that village. I might have alighted at that station perhaps once before. A Railway station and the open spaces along the Railway line somehow have an allure for village children. I sat on the bench near the waiting shed and began contemplating the recent events. I had no plans at the time except that I did not want to go home or to the school. A train arrived just about that time and, unobserved by anyone, I slipped onto the platform and boarded a compartment, the door of which was open, and sat on a vacant bench. In those days, trains were not crowded. In a third-class compartment, except on rare occasions, more than half the number of benches would be empty. I did not know whether everyone bought tickets. No-one asked me or stopped me. Perhaps I looked too small and innocent to be wanting to travel to attract the Railway staff's notice. I had no idea even then where I was going and in what direction the train itself was going. Anyway the train was taking me away from the places and people I dreaded. To sit on a bench in a moving train was a relief and a comfort after the experiences of the last few days.

Travelling alone in a train was an adventure in itself and I had heard of young men who had gone by train to faraway places in search of adventure. The sense of mystery and the thrill of adventure began to take its grip on me slowly. Being a quiet and meek child, always kept under strict tutelage, I was not accustomed to rash deeds or thoughts. As I said before, I had not even played the games children of my age and class play in the streets. With that upbringing, the deliberate marching out on an adventure was not in my line. But the sense of wounded pride, and the discontent arising out of injustice, was just carrying me away adrift. I had no fears, however. I was not afraid of what would happen to me. I was disarmingly simple and of appearance innocent, and I had no fear of talking to people. I had a feeling that whatever happened, I would be able to understand things, explain myself to anyone who talked to me, and feel my way through whatever strange experiences awaited me.

After the train had been in motion for some minutes, I sensed that it was moving in a westerly direction, and that possibly it was the train going to Quilon via Shencottah. I had heard of this train passing through my place about 1 p.m. I had not travelled by train more than once or twice before, and I had never been beyond Shencottah on this line westward. I had heard that the train would pass through several tunnels dug through the ranges of the Western Ghats in between Shencottah and Quilon. The thought of seeing and passing through those dark tunnels exhilarated me. I began to take an interest in the journey and thought that I was lucky. I was already feeling hungry after the long walk and the unusual experience of running away from everything. When the train passed through Tenkasi and Shencottah stations, I made myself inconspicuous, hiding behind doors or in corridors. I did not want anyone who may have known me to see me. After the train left Shencottah, I felt safe and free. In the next station, I purchased some eatable with the two pice that I had—that was all that I had—and having satisfied at least partially my hunger, I fell asleep on the bench.

As I was new to long-distance train travel—my previous experience having been limited to half an hour or forty-five minutes only—I was soon feeling uncomfortable. Going up the steep gradient of the Ghat section, the train was making a din and clouds of smoke and soot were drifting down from the engine. The unaccustomed vibration and the smoke, on an empty stomach, brought nausea. I remember now, for several years I had this experience when travelling on this section frequently during the course of my journeys to and from College. But my first experience is still vivid in my memory.

My condition attracted the attention of a party of two men and a woman sitting nearby. They probably noticed I was alone. It was unusual for children of my age to travel alone in those days. They also noticed that I was a Tamilian, and not a Malayalee, from my tuft of hair. One of them spoke to me in Tamil. He was himself a Malayalee and so were his companions. I told them I was travelling alone and that I belonged to Shencottah. They began to ply me with further questions and asked me for my father's name, what I was doing, and where I was going. When I mentioned my father's name, the man who spoke Tamil seemed to recognise it and said that he was one of my father's pupils and had stayed in our house a few years ago when I was a small child. I told him about my experience with my teacher and that I was running away from home. He laughed over the whole matter and treated me with great affection and said he was going to look after me. He gave me food and made me comfortable. He did not mention that he was going to restore me to my parents.

We got down at the Quilon Railway station which then impressed me as the biggest building in the world. We had a hearty meal at a nearby eating-place and boarded a boat later in the evening. My new friend's native place was a village across the lake—or the backwaters—off Quilon. All along the coast of Travancore, there are several beautiful lakes formed by the backwaters of the Arabian Sea. After an hour's pleasant journey by boat, we reached his house, where I slept peacefully after my adventurous day.

This good friend, whose name I do not remember now, was not much of a success as a musician, though he had been my father's pupil for a few months. He had settled down in his native village. He was returning from a visit to Kuttalam, the beauty-spot near Shencottah, where people go to bathe in the waterfalls. He and his companions boarded my train either at Shencottah or at Tenkasi. I did not notice them then, and it was just an accident that they noticed me an hour or two later and it was providential that he knew my father and had the traditional loyalty and affection of a pupil for his guru. Luckier still for me, he was a good man, with a sympathetic understanding of a child's mind. Without letting me know, he had sent a telegram to my father from the Railway-station soon after we got down at Quilon. He expected father to come over to Quilon immediately. I do not know what the wording of the telegram was and whether his name brought anything to father's recognition.

Father got the telegram only the next morning. It was not very intelligible to him or to those who read and translated it for him. He did not know where to look for me or my friend in Quilon, as no address was given. Father had received a report from Surandai the previous evening itself that I had disappeared and that I had not gone to the school. One of our relations must have run up in the night with the news, after causing searches to be made for me in all the likely places round about the school and in the neighbouring villages. Father and the women of the house had a fright; their first fear was that I must have fallen into some tank or well and ended my life. The whole night and the next morning, a number of friends and relations were on the look out for my dead body. Father told me later that he consulted an astrologer. This is an inevitable course in such circumstances. The astrologer said that he saw a watery sign, and the inference was obvious to their tormented minds. In the midst of this conversation, the telegram came. After some deliberations, father rushed to the Shencottah Railway station, where he had a friend in the Railway telegraph office. He sought this friend's help to contact the telegraph staff in the Quilon Railway station. He got confirmation about the correctness of the telegram, and the telegraphist obligingly promised to look out for the man who despatched the telegram, as he was bound to visit the Railway station in anticipation of someone coming there in response to his message.

Next afternoon my friend asked me to accompany him back to Quilon, as he was expecting father to come to take me home. I was not very pleased. My immediate reaction was alarm that I would be thrashed again for my escapade. My friend promised to protect me, and gave me good advice as to how I should pursue my studies and be a dutiful son.

We came by boat across the lake and waited at the Railway station. The telegraph clerk located us and informed us that there had been enquiries about me and that somebody was coming by the next train. We walked along the platform as the train steamed in, and were watching the people alighting. At a distance I saw father, dishevelled and in grimy clothes, keenly looking at every passing face. I hid behind my friend, afraid to meet my father, but my friend accosted him and gave the customary salutation of a pupil to a teacher, which is an exaggerated version of the *namaskaaram.* Father ignored me completely, but embraced his old pupil, and with tears in his eyes, thanked him profusely. I do not remember what he spoke to him. All that I remember of the conversation was my father telling his old pupil that he had lost his son yesterday and that he was receiving the gift of a son from him now. Both were deeply moved. I am quite sure father did not show his customary wrath with me on this occasion. I was made a fuss of—for the first time, as far as I could remember—and endearing words were spoken to me.

My friend wanted to take his old guru to his home and to feast him on the occasion of this reunion—a twofold reunion at that. Father, at no time keen on accepting hospitality if it could be avoided, was keen on returning home with me by the earliest available train. The women in the house, he said, were inconsolable, and would not touch food till they saw me again. Grandmother was on the verge of death with a nervous breakdown. Father himself had not eaten since he heard of my disappearance. So all of us went to a hotel for food, and my friend saw me and father off on my journey back to home and school.

Thus ended my childhood escapade. It was providential that I took that westbound train. Even if I had not met this old acquaintance, sooner or later in Travancore, so close to our home, I would have been recognised and bundled off home. If I had taken a different train and reached a more distant place where the chances of my being identified were remote, my life might have taken a different course—for the better or the worse, no-one can say.

The family were happy to see the lost sheep back in the fold. After a couple of days of feasting and rejoicing, I was again on my way back to the old school. My father accompanied me and tendered his apologies to the Headmaster and the teacher. They welcomed me back to the school, duly impressed by my performance in the interval. The teacher was quite a different person now. He seemed to have realized the unfairness of the punishment and was convinced of my sincerity and earnestness. He also realized that I was highly sensitive and had taken the punishment too much to heart. Thenceforth he became a great friend. He was obviously a kind-hearted person, and the unusual nature of my copy-work had momentarily irritated him. He took to me kindly thereafter, and I remember his visiting me several years later, when I had attained a certain distinction in life. He thought his punishment had helped to bring out the best in me. Strange are the ways of people. I, however, bore no ill-will towards him.

I had to spend only a few more months in this school. My record was considerably better after this episode, and at the annual examination I did well. I was promoted to the higher class and given a transfer certificate and a 'good conduct'. Father decided that it would be best for all concerned that I join the Shencottah English School in

Form I. There were several reasons for this decision. Keeping me away from home was costing him money he could ill afford. Whether I boarded with a relation or was looked after by one of the women of the family, he had to meet the expenses. The state of affairs in my sister's house was such that my presence there was an embarrassment to her. I had also reached the standard in school which would enable me to join Form I in our town school where English was taught. The brief interlude enabled me to march a class ahead of my contemporaries, the boys who were in my class in the Malayalam school. This was an advantage worth the trouble and expense of my migration from my home for a year and a half.

5

Three Years in English School

The Headmaster at the time was a brilliant member of the Travancore Education Department. He was a good disciplinarian and administrator, though not a particularly good teacher by the standards expected by students and parents. A man of culture and wide intellectual tastes, he was not the type of teacher for lower forms, where students require coaching to pass examinations. Handsome and always very neatly dressed, he was never without a smile on his face. He walked with quick short strides, and made his presence felt. He was not sparing with his cane, but there was no sadistic quality about him. He produced no resentment even when he caned bunches of erring boys. He made them take the punishment in good humour. I was attracted to him and felt happy in his presence. My slightly better understanding of English than the other boys, my father's earnestness in educating me in spite of difficulties, and my general demeanour, impressed him favourably. He always spoke to me with sympathy and affection and was the first to put the idea into my head that I should eventually go to College for higher studies.

Most of the other teachers were colourless men. Though at that time school teachers in Travancore were paid better than in other services and their lot was also better than that of their colleagues in the profession in the British Indian province of Madras, very few of them took to their profession with zeal or enthusiasm. Many of them were Matriculates only (the school had no high school classes then), and they had passed their exam after several attempts. Intellectually they were a mediocre lot, and their classes were monotonous.

I have a good recollection of only two teachers—one was the Drawing Master and the other, the Tamil Pandit. The former was neither from Travancore nor from Tirunelveli District. He appeared to be one who spoke Telegu at home. There were a few isolated communities in several towns in the South, where there were Telegu-speaking people, descendants of civil and military personnel of the Vijayanagar Feudatories who ruled over the southern regions for over three centuries, with varying fortunes. This Drawing Master was one of that class—a Naidu. He was a dapper man with a distinct military bearing—perhaps inherited from his martial ancestors.

This teacher not only taught Drawing in a manner to arouse interest even among the most inartistic-minded students, he also showed how art could improve other lessons and the general ways of students. He encouraged pupils to write headlines and paragraph headings in a neat print style when writing up notes or exercises and even examination papers. Students were asked to bring what was beautiful in nature available in the locality—flowers, leaves, fruits, sheaves of corn—and he would explain their anatomical structure and how drawing is not an imitation, but something evolved by the appreciation of the natural structure of the object. He was a painter of some merit and devoted his spare time and his private resources to painting beautiful objects and displaying them in the school hall. His contribution to the study of Geography and History was greater than that of the teachers of those subjects. He made a beautiful relief map of the Himalayas and the Western Ghats, showing clearly the origins of the great Rivers and their passage through various stages to the plains. The relief was executed in clay and coloured chalk on the floor of a room so as to facilitate observation by students.

For all the Drawing Master's labour and talents, his salary was only Rs 40 per month. But he always was cheerful and active. I heard later that he left teaching and joined, as artist, a dramatic troupe where his skill was obviously better rewarded and appreciated.

The Tamil teacher was just the opposite of this good man. He was an orthodox Brahman. He came to class with his tuft of hair hanging loose over the back of his coat. He was constantly handling it as if the hair was perpetually wet and required drying. When he was not fondling his hair he was nodding his head, half asleep even in class. He uttered profanities without restraint, in class and outside in the school verandah, talking to students or to other teachers. His knowledge of Tamil could not have been profound. Memorizing and recitation of poetry was given priority over the proper understanding of the Tamil language and the acquiring of skill in writing an easy style. In class, pupil after pupil was asked to recite lines from the poems in the textbook. No attempt was made to teach their meaning. Failure to recite correctly was visited with gross abuse. He had no hesitation to use the cane also, though the Education Rules vested this right only with the Headmaster. No-one dared to complain against him and therefore he ruled like an obscene petty tyrant.

This man had no hesitation about displaying his contempt for pupils who were not of his caste. He had the intellectual arrogance of his caste, though he himself had no intellectual attainments. If a cultivator's son did not recite the Tamil verse properly, he would taunt him, saying, 'Why don't you stick to your plough?' His general abuse was, why should not the erring pupil take to the barber's razor instead of wasting time in school not meant for him. I had on several occasions been the victim of his wrath. Memory has never been one of my strong points, especially repetitive memory. Recitation therefore was my bugbear and I cannot remember having memorized and recited more than four lines at a time. This teacher produced in me almost a revulsion towards learning Tamil, which took me several years to get over.

The Tamil Master was not an exception in his class. Teachers of Tamil or any Indian language were the least respected among the teaching fraternity in those days, and often they were the worst paid. No wonder then that some of the worst failures in life took to this profession as a means of livelihood. I am not saying that there were not good Tamil teachers. Only, they were rare, and those rare ones were really men of culture and character. There was another special feature of the teaching profession. Most of the teachers were Brahmans who considered themselves the hereditary custodians of learning. They were the first to take advantage of the facilities offered by the British system of education. Therefore they filled Government offices, and the unsuccessful, and in some cases those who thought they had an aptitude for teaching, became teachers. The proportion of the former was generally higher than the latter, at least among non-graduate teachers. Thus they had not culture enough to appreciate that the gift of education which they had in their hands should be given impartially to all their students, and not humanity enough to have sympathy with the underdog. This lack of humanity, and the traditional arrogance of the superior caste, retarded the progress of education of the vast non-Brahman classes for several decades. In the meanwhile, the hatred of the Brahman became almost natural to those classes, with disastrous consequences.

The Brahman students in the school also kept aloof from the others, with few exceptions. They also received specially favourable treatment. Drinking water was provided for them in separate vessels. Those who ate their midday meal—brought with them from their homes—in the school premises, observed segregation. If there was a pupil from a very low caste, his life was made unbearable by petty acts of discrimination and ostracism. In this tyranny against the depressed class pupils, all others, not Brahmans alone, joined. The atmosphere was caste-conscious, more so in a small school like mine. Things were slightly more tolerable in the schools in bigger towns.

I cannot say I was subjected to any particularly humiliating treatment. I was perhaps lucky. I was very thin and short and generally minded my own business. The 'toughs' must have thought that I was too small for them to bother about. Except that I strongly felt and resented the caste atmosphere, and was made aware of the Brahmans' claim to intellectual superiority and social aloofness, there were no untoward incidents. In fact, in rural areas, the respect for the Brahman and tolerance of his arrogance was so deeply engrained in popular tradition, that the non-Brahman students seldom noticed, much less protested against, the display of arrogance and superiority. Anything was tolerated, short of violence, and even when a Brahman boy assaulted a non-Brahman boy, retaliation was unthought of. But I must add that Brahman boys seldom resorted to violence to assert their superiority.

My three years of lower secondary school, from Forms I to III, were fairly uneventful. Life at home for the family was a perpetual struggle to make both ends meet. Father's income as a musician and a teacher of music was never very high, and it was always fluctuating. During the marriage and festival seasons, we were above want. Otherwise, there was perpetual improvisation to give the children their night meal of hot rice and dal and curry.

Those who owned rice-growing lands kept rice in sufficient quantities from the harvest to last till the next harvest. The surplus rice was sold and the cash was used for sundry expenses, supplemented by any additional income the family may have had. That was the domestic economy of the small landholder. There were prosperous cultivating tenants who, without owning land, cultivated on lease the lands of rich landlords, and who also managed their lives likewise. The artisans, skilled and unskilled workers, the salaried employees and shopkeepers who were not themselves landlords—these alone bought rice from the shops according to their needs. In village society, to have to buy rice from a shop for your daily cooking was a mark of disgrace or social inferiority.

We had no rice-lands of our own. We possessed a few acres of dry land, where only maize, pulses, and oil seeds were cultivated. We did the cultivation ourselves, practically all the members of the family taking part in field work. Father purchased paddy with the proceeds of the sale of our crops. So we had rice in the house, as other small land-holders had, and we had not always to buy in the local shop like the masons and carpenters and bricklayers. But we also wanted cash for various other needs and so could not spare enough to buy paddy for our requirements till the next harvest. The family was growing and unforeseen expenses arose frequently, and almost every season we were forced to buy rice from the shop on at least some days. This was a matter of great grief to my father and mother, and they resorted to ingenious methods of raising money to be able to afford to purchase a bag or two of paddy from the local stockist or a well-to-do landlord. These attempts were pathetic instances of our endeavour to maintain respectability.

Leisure and laziness were unknown to us in those days. As a boy of nine or ten, I got up before sunrise and went to the local stream—we called it the South River—for my bath. Our house, and for that matter, most houses in the locality, had no privies or conveniences. Excepting small children, women, and bedridden old men, everybody went out to the fields or the banks of the local tank or stream to answer their calls of nature. After bathing in the river and washing my clothes and my father's clothes, I came home before 7 o'clock. I do not remember to have used a soap on my body till I became a college student in the year 1921. Soap for toilet purposes was rarely used by ordinary lower middle-class people in rural areas. Even richer people thought that the use of soap was harmful to the body, and was a repulsive habit copied by the English-educated from Europeans. Dipping in the flowing water or, when there was not enough water in the stream, pouring a few lotas of it over the head and the body, was sufficient, if one scrubbed himself vigorously with his palms and fingers. I sometimes used the fibre of some plant which had a spongy appearance and a soapy smell. Oil was rubbed on the head occasionally before bathing. The clothes were treated to vigorous beating on a stone, and occasionally a piece of Sunlight soap was used, bought for a single pice.

Returning home, drying the clothes by holding them over your head on hands outstretched, there were small jobs to be done to help the household. Being the only boy in the house, I ran errands, went to the shops to buy our small necessities, and delivered small quantities of milk and buttermilk which we sold to some neighbours, and then had my morning meal. Breakfast consisted of a small quantity of rice kept overnight in rice water which by the morning had slightly fermented, and a little lime pickle or chutney made of dal, tamarind, and chillies. Sometimes a single hot chilli was all that was available to eat with the rice. As a delicacy, sometimes I had a piece of dry fish slightly burnt over the live fire. My sister and mother used to tease me in later life, saying that I used to save a bit of this delicacy and keep it in a niche in the wall to consume with my lunch, which was a repetition of the breakfast in smaller proportion.

We had a cow in our house then, but I do not remember using any of its products with my everyday meal. Part of the daily yield of milk was sold in small portions to a few neighbours, mostly Malayalee clerks and peons working in the Taluk office and court located near our house. The rest was converted into curds. After recovering the butter, the watery buttermilk was again sold for a very few pice every day. Occasionally I was given a little of it with my cold rice—I do not know whether father or grandmother had buttermilk with their rice. The butter was clarified and the ghee was sold to the richer houses for a rupee or two every fortnight.

On the last Friday of every month, it was the custom to observe fast and feast in our house, as was the general custom then. On that great day, I had *idli* or *dosai* for breakfast, with buttermilk to drink. Coffee was given to father alone. We got the coffee habit very much later, not during the years of Great War I. The proper meal of that day was at noon. We sat on the floor with leaves spread in front of us and mother served us with plenty of rice and three or four vegetables prepared tastily. We also had small drops of ghee on our dal or *saambaar* and the last helping of rice was mixed with buttermilk—no curd. Only my father, myself, and grandmother, sat together and ate. The other children and women partook of their holiday feast after we finished. My grandmother, though an old widow, was allowed to sit with us, for, being the mistress of the house and an imperious personality besides, she was given honours usually reserved for the master of the house.

Such was the even tenor of my childhood life. The poverty of our circumstances forced itself on me, sensitive child that I was. There was one incident which marked the extent of our difficulties and the struggle everyone was engaged in, in overcoming them—that was the death of the cow which was an important earner of cash for the family. When I returned home late from some errand after school I saw my grandmother crying loudly. I was afraid there had been one of those violent quarrels between her and father which frequently disturbed the uneasy peace of the house. When I went to the backyard I saw her sitting near the carcase of our cow.

The cow had been out to the nearby hills in the morning to graze as usual. A village cowherd collected several cows, calves, and oxen also (in the off season) from the street for a small monthly wage, and drove them to pasture in the hills in the mornings, and brought them back in the evenings. The grazing grounds were three or four miles away and the return trip in the evening was completed in about an hour's time. Casualties due to attack by wild animals, snake bites and the like, and physical accidents were not unknown, but were infrequent. That day our cow was stung by a poisonous spider or scorpion and this was immediately noticed by the cowherd. Men working in forests generally knew something of herbs and roots, handy remedies for serious ailments. The cowherd applied some herbal remedy, but did not want to risk the cow dying on his hands. He arranged with someone to drive the cow home slowly. Frothing at its mouth, its tongue hanging out, the cow reached home and died soon after at grandmother's feet.

I did not even then understand why grandmother and the other women should cry. Perhaps I asked someone. Grandmother told me that the cow was like a mother; it gave us all so much for so little. The cow had been with her since it had been a calf, the mother cow having also been in our house. Two generations of service to the family, so much of ready cash by the sales of her produce almost every day—if that did not bring out lamentation, human hearts must be made of stone, grandmother said.

It was pointedly brought home to me that in our strained domestic economy the contribution of that cow was by no means negligible. We could not afford to purchase another cow. It took us several years before we had the purchasing power to buy another cow.

Personally it mattered little to me, for I was never a big consumer of milk and milk products. But grandmother's and mother's attachment to this particular cow was deep and well deserved. I did not wonder after that why in Hindu households the cow was a sacred animal.

In the evenings and during holidays I went to our little piece of land which is about a mile to the north of the North River. During several months in the year, there was always something to do. It was either just to see that cattle had not strayed in to eat the growing crops or that someone had not come to cut the grass away from our borders. Our own womenfolk used to cut this grass periodically and sell it in bundles for a few annas, for fresh green grass was the best feed for cows as well as young draught bulls. I have helped them in the task of cutting grass and carrying it. As a boy going to English School I was not expected to indulge in such plebeian occupations, but I thought there was no harm doing it occasionally to help out my mother or grandmother or aunt.

The job that I fancied most was the chasing away of crows and birds from the ripening corn during the two or three weeks before harvest. We constructed a small scaffold with rough bamboo, twigs, and leaves of the palmyra palm, and on its raised platform, about six or seven feet above ground level, a child or a boy could stand and shout at the birds or swing pebbles at them with a crude catapult. One of the old women of the house used to perform guard duty in the field during the season. Sometimes a part-time workman was engaged for a few weeks. But most evenings I used to be there, enjoying this work. The completely rural setting, rich cornfields wherever you looked, birds of all hues and different sizes hovering so near the heads of corn, and the evening twilight, and the gentle breeze of the countryside—these were a delightful change for the little boy from school.

During the harvests of both seasons, I was there if the school was closed, assisting in my small way in the operations. My special privilege as an educated person was reckoning wages and perquisites and calculating the amount of produce which we could carry home. In spite of the solemn protests of my parents and the workmen, that as an educated boy I should not meddle with those pursuits of the unlettered, I continued to interfere and enjoyed myself in the process. It took me some time to realize that in Hindu society, manual labour was always regarded as undignified and no-one with any pretensions to education would perform such labour even for his own benefit. This explains the craze people have for office jobs. It is gratifying that of late we are beginning to realize that there can be dignity in manual labour.

In order to supplement the family income during this period father was engaged in village money-lending in a small way, with the small capital he had saved up. There is an institution which is now known as Chit Fund and organized in a fairly big way even in cities. In those days, the Chit Fund was typically a village institution—a form of co-operative credit. The organizer had to be someone of integrity in the locality, with some means—property or house of his own. He brought together generally twenty to twenty-five men known to him in the locality, who would subscribe a fixed sum—from two to five rupees if it was a monthly chit, and a proportionately bigger amount if it was a three-monthly or six-monthly chit. There were two kinds of chit fund. One was the raffle fund and the other was the auction fund. The raffle fund was a simple proposition. The names of the subscribers were written on pieces of paper and a lot was drawn. The winner of the lot was entitled to the full amount of the total fund, representing the month's subscription. In this way, every month someone got the whole amount, the name of the preceding winners being eliminated from the lottery, but all continuing to pay their subscriptions. The last month's collection was left as remuneration for the organizer, his name not being included in the drawing of lots.

The auction Chit worked on the discount principle. Instead of drawing lots for the beneficiary, the members bid every month for the total amount in the chit pool. Twenty-five subscribers subscribing Rs 2 every month meant a collection of Rs 50 every month and theoretically, each subscriber was entitled to this amount only at the end of the twenty-five-month period. But needier persons might be willing to cash in their rights at a discount in advance, and their sacrifice (bid) would generally be the amount which at the ordinary rate of interest, would yield Rs 50 at the end of the chit period. The very importunate borrower might be prepared for even a higher sacrifice. The higher his sacrifice, the more advantageous it was for the other subscribers. There would be acute bidding in the earlier months when all the more needy men were satisfied. The organizer would be given the option of the first month's bid, or the collection of the last instalment. Those who had bid successfully would continue to pay the full subscription in succeeding months and the others would pay a proportionate share of the difference between the month's bid and the full subscriptions of successful bidders.

Such chits were frequently organized and shrewd and competent organizers, who chose their men correctly and were able to collect the monthly dues regularly, made profits. They had not only their legitimate profit, being the entire proceeds of one unit, but they also had varying amounts of money lying with them for temporary moneylending at exorbitant rates of interest for short periods. Their responsibility was to collect the monthly dues and pay out within a stipulated period to a member whose turn it was that month. There were always defaulters and the chit fund organizer, being a man of substance, was bound to honour his obligations without default. Otherwise his credit was at stake and the whole system would collapse.

Father, first in partnership with a friend and then by himself, began organizing these small Chit funds and soon ran into difficulties. He was no shrewd moneylender and his selections of members were not always well advised. One of his friends (who turned often against him) to whom he owed money filed a civil suit for recovery, and suppressing due services of processes, brought an attachment order on our moveable property.

This diabolical schemer chose the most sacred holiday of the Tamils for the execution of the attachment order. I was studying in the Second or Third Form at the time. The day was Pongal Day, which falls on the first day of the Tamil month *Thai*, corresponding roughly to the 15th of January. This is regarded as the pre-eminent Tamilian festival, when worship and offerings are made to the Sun God. In our front courtyard, a brass lamp was burning. The pot (copper vessel) in which fresh rice was cooked and ceremonially offered to the God was placed on a green plantain leaf spread before the lamp. Various fresh vegetables, fruits, coconuts, sugarcane, and flat rice offered in worship were still on the leaf before removal inside the house and distribution to the family. The process server presented himself with the attachment order and began attaching the moveable property. We did not know any means of preventing this inauspicious action on that holy day. Father protested and pleaded—but the order was executed. Besides a few utensils, the tall brass lamp burning in the bright morning sun was also removed. A great gloom descended on the house. There was no more rejoicing for us. Though father succeeded in depositing the money involved in the civil suit—it was a small sum—in a few days, and brought the lamp and other articles back, all of us were convinced that evil days were ahead and that this was only a warning. In that house which had not much cheer at any time, there was positive gloom and the dread of the unknown in the shadow of which we had to live, till destiny unfolded itself.

The next few months were disastrous months. There were two deaths in the house and a third in the extended family. There were other miseries besides. Grandmother and father as far as I could remember were never on very friendly terms. She was an ambitious person, suffering from several disappointments. Her greatest regret was that she was not born a man. She thought she could make a great success of father. It was under her inspiration that father launched on his several business enterprises. It was their belief that from small beginnings, with hard work and clever management, fortunes could be made within short periods. The stories of such fortunes made by a lucky few fired them up to repeated endeavours. Unfortunately, father was not a businessman. He came out of every venture of his poorer than before. This was the prime source of conflict between the two. Grandmother was a domineering type and would not brook disagreement or failure. Her wishes had to be respected without question. Father himself was a proud person. He was always impatient and hasty and would be quick to blame others for his failures. Mother and the other women in the house did not count at all and were treated as so many chattels by grandmother and father.

Father used to return from his trips or visits in a great hurry. A vessel of water had to be kept ready outside for washing his feet, and hot water in the backyard for his bath. He always bathed in hot water even at mid-day in summer. After washing his feet, he would walk through the house to the backyard for his bath. No sooner was the bath over—he seldom took more than two minutes over it—than food had to be served. He liked his rice and curry hot and tasty. He would shout in rage if these wants of his were not complied with promptly. He would not wait; he would not forego any of these things; he would not excuse the women of the house delays, however busy they might have been in other pursuits at the time. His arrivals and his requirements had to be anticipated. All this was a tall order in a house where women and children were toiling perpetually—where leisure and laziness were unknown.

Father would throw anything he could get hold of on the head of his offending chattels. He firmly believed in the patriarchal right to chastise his dependants in any manner he chose. He would not do any work, even of the most trifling character, in the house. If he wanted his pan box, and even if it was only a yard away from where he sat, he would shout to someone to get it for him. His wrath was seldom pacified unless he gave physical expression to it. All his brothers and relations were afraid of him and avoided him. Strangely enough he made good friends from outsiders, and some were immensely devoted to him. Men in higher walks of life always treated him deferentially and he commanded some influence in official and social circles. The reason for his impatience and perpetual anger with his family was somewhat of a mystery to me. Even as a boy I had thought about it often. I had asked him sometimes why he was losing his temper for trifling reasons, only to be rewarded by a resounding boxing of my ears. He was impatient because of his poverty and the failure of his attempts to raise himself to a higher level. He was naturally discontented and brooded over things. It might have struck him that his having too many dependants was dragging him down. His perpetual state of irritation overshadowed his really kind heart.

That he was soft-hearted I had no doubt. He would rush to rescue people; suffering touched him. He gladly suffered even people who cheated him. If he had been affluent, he would have liked to live well, and see that his children were well clothed and well groomed. He would starve, but he would like his children to get good food. He was particular about bringing something—some fruits or some trifling articles of use—when he returned home after his trips.

Father's thrifty habits were very irritating to the family. He might lose money which we could ill afford on his ventures, but if mother or grandmother had given a little more to the mason or the carpenter for petty repairs to the house, he would lose his temper and break someone's bones.

It was in one of his fits of temper that he kicked grandmother. She was already shrivelled up and shrunk with her perpetual cough and ailments and she began vomiting blood. Thereafter he was contrite and nursed her tenderly. The old lady had seen life and suffered immensely. She bore her last illness stoically and died a couple of weeks later. Her last wish was that my education should not suffer, whatever might happen. As she had no son, father performed the last rites for her like a dutiful son.

The house was empty when she died. The void she left could hardly be filled. With all her failings, she was a great woman. She had brains, ideas, the gift of conversation, and personal magnetism. She was our pillar of strength and our sustaining influence. Father himself felt like an orphan after her death. Life at home was gloomier still without her forbidding presence.

Two other old ladies followed her to the grave soon after. The other bereavement that affected father was the loss of his own father. The old man who was living in Pavoor was struck with paralysis. Till then he was independent of his sons. Father, mother, and I went to see the old man. My uncles demanded that father also gave his share towards the expenses of his treatment and for his maintenance. The old man partially recovered and expressed his desire to live with his son (my father) in our house for a change. He was brought over and well looked after for a few months. He went back to his village and died after some time. He was well over seventy and had lost his wife, who was very devoted to him, a couple of years before.

To his funeral we went. None of father's brothers spoke to us, for what reason I could not fathom. From the burial ghat, father and I returned to the Railway station to return home immediately. All the sons and near relations return to the dead man's place and observe mourning till the 16th day. We should have also, in conformity with practice, gone to my uncles' houses. But their attitude even in the presence of death was far from cordial and we felt we were not wanted there. This affected father more than his bereavement. We decided that we should not join the brothers for the final ceremonies and observed these rites separately in our house. The support the rest of the family gave father in this matter gave him great solace. The relations between father and his brothers, which were never very intimate, now practically ceased. We were not on visiting terms for several years.

The development that gave us most worry at this time was the estrangement of my married sister from her husband and in-laws. Though she was only sixteen or seventeen, she had been married for several years. She was tolerated and even fussed over as a child wife. But when she grew to woman's estate, troubles began and there were frequent quarrels over petty things. One day we found her suddenly coming into the house with a bundle in her hand, crying. There had been a quarrel with her husband, and her mother-in-law had thrown her out of the house and shut the door on her. She was stripped of her jewellery and asked to go back to her father. Her lamentations and importunities were of no avail. The poor girl ran all the way, nearly 12 miles, hungry and lonely, to seek protection in the house of her birth. It was not usual for girls of poor families to travel alone. Part of the way, the path runs along deserted tracks. Waylaying and other dangers were constant even at mid-day. The poor girl remained with us for several months before we could effect a reconciliation. This was the first of the many misadventures the poor girl had in her sad life before she died after a severe illness at the young age of twenty-two. She hardly remained with her husband for more than a year without one of these violently upsetting quarrels.

It was in this atmosphere of poverty, quarrels, and domestic miseries that I was finishing my education in the English school. I was in Form III—the highest form in the school. I had neither domestic peace nor leisure nor conveniences for proper study. Electricity had not arrived, but kerosene-burning hurricane lamps were just coming into vogue. But people were averse to burning these lamps inside the house lest the fumes poisoned the air. The living room in the house had only a door leading to the narrow outer verandah which led to the front yard. There were no windows. A tall ornamental brass lamp was kept in the corner, bearing a screwed-in little tray for holding oil. Wicks made of white cotton rag were kept in the oil, the ends of which, opening out of a beak in the oil tray, were kept burning. As the cotton end burnt out, the wick was gently pushed a quarter of an inch forward. This was the only illumination in the room. A similar, but smaller lamp burned in the kitchen, and when the women went about the house, they carried a small oil lamp in their hands to guide their steps. We had a hurricane lantern, but it was constantly in demand elsewhere when father went out at night. So my reading was generally done squatting on the floor by the oil lamp in the house. There were by this time my younger sister and brother. The sister was four years my junior, and like girls in our class, she was not sent to school. The brother was eight years my junior and at that time was the baby of the house. These two would also be in the room playing or quarrelling while the women were busy about their household duties. Father, if he was at home, sat on the narrow verandah outside. If any one was sick, the sickbed was near the oil-lamp.

However my studies progressed satisfactorily, though I was by no means the top student of the class. I managed to pass all my examinations, scoring just a few marks above the minimum. Nevertheless my proficiency in reading and writing was considerable for my age and class. Many neighbours brought their letters for me to read and explain. My services were in demand to write letters for them in Tamil and Malayalam. I had even written letters and petitions to high officials in English for some neighbours. I passed Form III and the problem arose of how I should prosecute my education further. There was no question at any time, however, about my stopping my studies. The family resolved that I should pass my school final examination at all costs.

6

Change of Name and School

In my younger days I was called by several names and for some time I was not sure what my correct name was. The old ladies of the house and our neighbours referred to me as Thangam or Thankia. This is a fairly common pet-name and a good many people bear this as their proper first name also. Presumably this was a term of endearment as it meant 'gold' and as I was the first male child in the house the ladies bestowed this golden appellation on me. My father's relations invariably called me Muthiah. This is also a term of endearment as Muthu signifies pearls, and as pearls were traditionally associated with the southern districts, this term in its several modifications was used either by itself or in conjunction with other names, generally of deities, in naming children. Muthu, Muthiah, Muthuswamy, Muthukumar, Muthukrishnan, Muthu Raman, etc. are familiar names in the South. As long as I could remember, father used to call me 'Sami' or 'Swami', probably a pet-name given to sons in some rich households. When I was first enrolled in a departmental school, my name was entered as Muthukumaraswamy, which was an embellished version of the derivative name Muthu.

In my father's village there was a family shrine dedicated to a village patron deity known as Venni Muthu. He was not a god known to the Hindu pantheon, nor was he one of the popular deities of Dravidian folklore or legend. He was the local patron deity of the tribe. The story goes that when one of my early ancestors, several generations ago, was returning from a business travel along a deserted countryside track at night, a spirit appeared before him and said in a ghostly voice that he should build a shrine for him at the back of his home and offer him worship, in return for which he would protect the family for all time.

There was a legend associated with that particular spot where this vision appeared. A gallant soldier in the service of a local chieftain fell in love with the master's beautiful daughter. The love was reciprocated, but the chieftain would not think of giving his daughter away in marriage to this humble knight; but as the suitor was persistent, in accordance with the code of justice administered in those days, the chieftain ordered the soldier to be hung by the feet with the head down, from the gallows outside the village gates, till he died. The soldier did not die, as was expected, within a few days, in spite of the torture, but exclaimed to the chief's messenger that his life would not depart unless his beloved came out dressed as a bride, in silk, with flowers and jewels, on the coming Tuesday, and offered salutation to him by walking round his hanging body thrice as around the marriage altar. The girl heard of this and wanted to do this last service of love to her lover. In these strange circumstances, the chieftain had no option but to allow this. The girl did this penance and when she completed the third round, the valiant lover, with a loud laugh, gave out his last breath. The girl performed the funeral rites for him and committed suttee on her lover's funeral pyre.

Legends similar to this are numerous, and have enriched the folklore of the countryside. Bards have sung the romance, love, and sacrifice of such heroes and heroines, and the worship of these heroic spirits in village shrines has been a colourful feature of rural life in our districts. My ancestor dutifully built the shrine, and the worship of Venni Muthu and his heroine has been observed without break through generations. Every firstborn child and every first male child bore the deity's name or a variation of it. No marriage or auspicious social function would be celebrated without appeasing this deity initially. One male member of the family was generally dedicated in every generation to officiate as his priest. He did not have to observe any vow of celibacy, but for a week before the deity's annual festival, he had to observe the vow of cleanliness and purity and perform all the *Pooja*s and offer blessings in the name of the God to the devotees.

My father was the ordained priest of his generation, and even after he left his village to settle down in Shencottah, he had to continue this duty. I have heard my relations assert that the deity's spirit would not be appeased unless father was present. Even on occasions when father refused to go to his village, in view of his feuds with his brothers, at the time of the festival, he was seized with a mad frenzy and would rush away, running all the ten miles to perform his duties before the titular deity. After some time father started propitiating the deity by offering *Pooja* to him at home, and someone else, a male member of the next generation, took over his duties in the village.

I remember father offering *Pooja* to his family's patron deity several times in our house. This was done only on a Friday. For a week prior to the day, father would abstain from eating meat and fast (i.e. abstain from eating more than once a day). The house was swept and cleaned spotlessly. The big lamp was lit near the south-west corner of the room, and before it several broad plantain leaves were spread. The deity was represented by a big copper *chombu*, with its mouth covered by a coconut. Turmeric and sandal paste were applied to this, and it was covered with flowers, preferably red flowers. A large quantity of cooked rice, vegetables, chicken curry, and sweet rice was heaped on the leaves. No salt was to be added to these edibles. No portion of the cooked dishes was to be kept apart. Every thing cooked was offered intact and in full. Incense and camphor were offered and all the customary rites of Dravidian worship were gone through. Father as officiating priest was wearing a wet dhotee (soon after bath) and his mouth was covered with another piece of cloth. After offering incense and camphor, all of us prostrated ourselves before the *Pooja* arrangement. If the deity was appeased and if the *Pooja* was acceptable, father used to be 'possessed' as it were by the deity. I have seen his whole body shake and shiver. Sometimes he would shriek some weird sounds and then say a few words of advice, warning, or blessing to the family. It would take some time for him to calm down and become normal. We kept breathlessly silent and when father said the *Pooja* was over we got our share of the offerings. Strange as it may seem he gave up observing this *Pooja* later on—but he always had a guilty feeling that he was remiss in his duty. He had great belief in his patron deity and in the traditional method of appeasing him. In my earlier days, when we suffered from poverty and other trials of fortune, this ritual was regularly performed and father derived great satisfaction from doing this.

On the few occasions I had been to my ancestral village, my uncles and cousins had taken me to the family shrine and I had been impressed by their solemn statement that I was bearing the name of the deity. My mother and my people at home were always vague about it. I had not questioned my father directly on this, but I had an impression that it was taken for granted that as the first male child, I was, in accordance with time-honoured tradition, named after the titular deity, without, perhaps, a formal naming ceremony. My father's devotion to the shrine was unquestionable and he would not deliberately deviate from tradition. I was strengthened in this belief by the fact that my elder sister was called Muthamma, also after the shrine, in accordance with the tradition of the family. But if the firstborn is given the name, there was no need to name the second child also after the deity. This perhaps was the reason for the uncertainty over my name, and apparently no serious thought was bestowed on the matter.

My mother used to visit K's family occasionally. I remember accompanying her as a child. K died when I was studying in Form III, as I have already mentioned. He had five sons, the second of whom, S.K., was held to be the most important of them. He was a graduate, the first from the town, and was endearingly referred to as 'B.A.' K. Ordinarily, no-one mentioned his proper name, 'B.A.' K was so popular. He and his wife treated mother sympathetically—but with a certain degree of condescension. One occasion, when we stayed long in the house, we were treated to a good midday meal. Mother was asked what my name was, and I have a vague impression she said that I bore the name of the respected K. It was becoming fashionable to bear that name in view of his stupendous success. So that family was given to understand that my name was 'S'. I do not know whether grandmother and mother wanted me to be called by that name, or whether there was a controversy about it. But no-one thought of enrolling me in that name when I was admitted to the Government Malayalam School at the age of six.

When I finished Form III, father was advised to have me admitted to Form IV in the High School at Ambasamudram, a place twenty miles away. This High School was chosen for two reasons. It was the nearest and it had a reputation for high standards. Boys from Shencottah in those days generally went to Quilon or Trivandrum in the state of Travancore. The educational system was different in British India. Parents preferred their children to have continuity, and were apprehensive about changing over to schools in British India. Quilon or Trivandrum would have been more expensive for us as we had no relations with whom I could board. Living in students' lodges or hostels would entail expenditure beyond our means. Near Ambasamudram, we had relations with whom I could board more cheaply. Even then, school fees, expenses of boarding, and other incidental items would amount to about Rs 12 to 15 per month. This amount father could ill afford, as his income was dwindling at that time. The family council decided that we should approach K's sons who were rich and had a reputation for generosity and private charity.

Mother took me to their houses, and waiting for suitable opportunities, explained her mission individually to the brothers who were living already in separate houses. K's son—the B.A. gentleman on whom the mantle of his father had fallen in many ways—was the most sympathetic. He wanted to be sure that I was deserving of his patronage and would not turn out to be a wastrel. He called on the Headmaster to make confidential enquiries about my character and attainments. From the Headmaster he found that I did not bear his father's name—but nevertheless the Headmaster gave me a good chit. Next time when mother and I called on him, he expressed his disappointment that mother should have led him and his family to think that I bore a different name to that actually entered in the school register. Mother was apologetic and blamed someone for carelessness at the time of first enrolment and assured him that the mistake would be remedied. He offered to help but not fully, and said that we should get some contributions from his brothers. The brothers were also sympathetic, and with their promises arrangements were made for my admission to the famous school in Ambasamudram. At the time of my departure, I received small amounts from three of the brothers, totalling Rs 15—with this fund, my High School education started.

There is a small village, Brahmadesam by name, about a mile and a half to the north of Ambasamudram which is a taluq headquarters town on the Railway line. My father and mother accompanied me on this momentous trip and we went to some relations in Brahmadesam. This was the village to which my grandmother came as a bride more than fifty years ago. The old man whom she deserted married again and had several children. He had several cousins, one of whom lived in a big house. This man was the leader of the community and had some landed property. He was requested to lodge me in his house and to feed me and generally look after me. Father offered to pay Rs 5 per month as a small compensation for all these services. The old gentleman was very happy to be able to look after the boy—the first in the community to reach high school stage in the district. This problem settled, we called on the Headmaster with an introduction from a local pleader whom father knew. The transfer certificate was produced and father requested that my name be changed. He was apprehensive that without this the benefactions from the K family may not continue. The Headmaster agreed to do this on a written application being presented by father. So I entered Form IV with a new name which became my proper name ever since.

The Ambasamudram school was housed in impressive buildings in a spacious compound on the northern outskirts of the town. It was a model school, not only because it had a Teachers' Training section attached to it. The students proudly claimed that it was one of the best-equipped schools in the whole of South India. After the small school in Shencottah, I was impressed by the large school buildings, furnishings, and equipments. It had a History Hall and Geography Hall, besides the Science laboratories. The Geography Hall was specially equipped with an impressive array of maps, models, globes, and an apparatus for demonstrating how eclipses are formed, the movements of the sun and the moon. I took a great deal of interest in Geography as a consequence. The standard of Tamil taught here was higher than I expected, and with the aversion to this subject engendered in me due to the habits of my old Tamil Master, I found this subject alone too exacting for me. There was nothing unusual otherwise, and I spent a pleasant year.

In the house at Brahmadesam village, I ate with the family and slept with the younger members in the verandah of the house and read my lessons by the common lamp or the kerosene lantern kept near the old grandfather. There were several boys of my age in the street and for the first time in my life I moved with them, as in Shencottah this freedom was denied to me. Very few boys, however, had been to school beyond the Second or Third standard in the Tamil elementary school. Apart from a slight acquaintance with the Tamil alphabet, they had no other book learning. They helped their fathers in agriculture and other pursuits. The music profession was popular and the village had at that time a few skilled musicians, playing the pipe as well as the drum, and they were fairly affluent. The women observed the Hindu fast and feast days and followed the conventional life of the Hindus more fastidiously than the women in my house. Their general standard of living was not better than ours, but they seemed to be happier and more cheerful. I mixed freely with them and had no difficulty in getting an occasional anna or two annas from any one of them when I happened to be in distress.

I went out to the fields, neighbouring temples, and to places of interest in the neighbourhood with the boys and with some of the families. I noticed with some curiosity that several of the men had two wives. One or two of them had mistresses, women belonging to other castes. One middle-aged person had a Muslim mistress who lived in a hut next door to his own father's house. The Muslim lady freely visited the house and those of the relations. The children of the mistress and the wife were friendly. Another elderly gentleman had a mistress from another caste who lived with him in a house on the street alongside his sons, all of them middle-aged, with families. The wives married to the same man lived together like sisters, except for occasional quarrels. There was one adventurous girl who eloped with a man of another caste, and after sojourning for years elsewhere, returned to the village. All the boys and girls from our street went to see her and she seemed quite cheerful and delighted to see her relations. Though the orthodox Hindu is very vehement about the Tamil's great tradition of chastity and high moral code, laxity in the villages was quite common and the Hindu conscience did not appear to have been very much disturbed. Brought up strictly and with high ideas of religion and morality dinned into my ears, these sights I saw in the village were somewhat disturbing to me, but soon I began to understand the ways of life in the village.

Though there were only two vacations in the course of the school year, one in September and another in January, I went home at least once a month. The railway fare was only 5 annas (30 p) and these frequent trips were necessary for obtaining money for my monthly expenses. In spite of the promises of my rich patrons, it was difficult to persuade them to send me money orders; never could they give me enough to last for two or three months. The two days I spent on each occasion in Shencottah were partly occupied in waiting in the verandahs of my rich patrons' houses. They knew why I had come and it would not have been too much trouble for them to give me their contributions without my waiting for hours. After I had stood for an hour or two, they would say, come tomorrow; often they would walk into the house without speaking a word to me. I would be told that the master had gone for his bath or lunch and would not come out till evening. I would then wearily walk to another brother's house, if it was not already too late. My morning time, from 8 to 12 noon, and again evening from 4 to 8 p.m., would be taken up waiting at the doors of my benefactors. Boys like me were not expected to sit.

In those days I seldom wore a shirt. I had only my loincloth, and even if I had the customary towel which people carry on their shoulders, I was not expected to put it on my shoulders or cover my body with it. It had to be tied round the waist or carried on the arm. Otherwise it would indicate lack of respect and I stood the risk of being chastised. I never took that risk. No-one would ask me to sit on the benches generally provided in the verandahs, and to sit unasked would have been a crime. Standing for hours together, often on an empty stomach, could never be a pleasant experience for a boy. Beggars, if they were Brahmans, would seat themselves unasked, and would cover their bodies too, even if they were of no better status. Because I was poor and a supplicant for favour, I had to humiliate myself.

Waiting and walking from the house of one brother to that of another, I would manage to collect, after two days' effort, anything from Rs 5 to Rs 7. I remember seldom to have managed to obtain more than Rs 5 from any one of my benefactors at any one time. It was only 'B.A.' K who gave an occasional five rupee note. Father managed to find the balance of my requirements somehow or the other, and with my monthly amount thus secured, I would go back to school. After paying for my boarding, and school fees, I had never more than Rs 2 for all the miscellaneous needs of a schoolboy. Pencils, pen and ink (no fountain pen, please), paper, exercise books, soap, oil, and an occasional article of food—all these had to found within that meagre balance. If in any particular month, there was any additional expenditure, by way of purchase of books or something unforeseen, obtaining an additional rupee or two from father was not an easy job. If I wrote him a letter, a postcard, all that I could expect was a virulently abusive reply that I was wasting money. During my periodic visits home for collecting money, I had no end of trouble rendering account to father of my previous month's or term's expenses. Often I would be abused and beaten for my audacity, if he was not satisfied that every pie literally was properly and usefully spent. Even when account was properly rendered, his satisfaction was only grudgingly extracted. I must add here that in those years there were no scholarships or concessions for students from Backward Classes or even for poor students.

After 5 or 6 months boarding and lodging in the village of Brahmadesam, I moved over to another relative's place in the town itself. This house belonged to the most successful person among those practising music as a profession in the district. He hailed from a village with the beautiful name Sundarapandyapuram, near the village where my sister's home was. When he became affluent, he felt the need for having a town residence. It was convenient for his business as well, as it gave him better contacts. The annual income of the better-class musician in those days was hardly Rs 700 or Rs 800. But this man's income was well over Rs 2000 even when he was a young man of thirty-two. He was the only one from that district whose services were in demand for marriages and Temple festivals outside the district. Steadily his income rose and was between Rs 3000 and Rs 4000 for nearly 12 years before the inevitable decline set in. More about him I will have to say later.

This musician bought a nice house on the bank of a canal running through the centre of Ambasamudram. He too had two wives and the younger of the two was stationed there. He used to be away for two weeks to a month at a time. But his wife was there with her four children—all girls. Only one was married at that time and even she was with the mother frequently.

The mother was my mother's step-sister, daughter by the second wife of the old man deserted by my grandmother. She was a very charming lady, by the standards of the women I knew then. Even though unlettered, she had grace and was well informed on all matters a woman was supposed to know. She ran the house competently during her husband's frequent absences. She it was who suggested to me that I would be more comfortable with her than in the village. Father, however, insisted on paying her also for my boarding.

I had an attack of fever when staying with her and as the fever persisted, I was taken home. Then I was in bed for over two weeks and I was thoroughly shaken up and reduced to almost skin and bone at the end of it. I was attended to during this illness by the village medicine man, an elderly barber. His medication consisted of herbs and extracts of roots mixed in some pungent red powder of his own alchemy. The main feature of the treatment for fever was starvation. After the first few days, as there was only a low fever, starvation was far too taxing for my delicate system. I took to purloining eatables from places where these were kept hidden from the prying hands of children. Mother had made some spiced fried rice balls (*cheedai*). These last for more than a month. A considerable quantity was kept in an earthen receptacle in a dark room where stores were kept. I learnt of its existence and when no-one was about, took handfulls of the little balls and secretly chewed them. This was discovered after I had practically exhausted the stock. Mother thought that the persistence of my fever was due to my secret violation of the rule of fasting. This propensity of mine for eating rice-balls became a standing joke against me in the family ever since.

After the fever was over I went back to school. I had lost several weeks and missed many lessons in the last term, so important from the point of view of the examination. Nevertheless I worked hard, though my people and several of my friends thought that I would have to stay in the class for another year. The thought of failing in the promotion examination was repugnant to me and I managed to avoid that shame. The year in High School was over and with pride and jubilation over my narrow success I came home for the summer holidays.

Meanwhile some developments were taking place in Shencottah which were to affect my educational career directly. That was the year when the people of Travancore celebrated the jubilee of the old Maharaja of Travancore (Sri Moolam Thirunal) attaining the age of sixty. There were festivities in every town and village. The principal ceremony was the Durbar in Trivandrum, at which the Maharaja announced various charities and reforms. The occasion was availed of by leading citizens for announcing various public benefactions of their own to mark the occasion. In some cases, these philanthropic and charitable deeds might have been motivated by devotion and loyalty to the old ruler. Not infrequently, shrewd businessmen took this occasion to thrust themselves into public notice. Any announcement of a public benefaction on this occasion would be appreciatively noticed by the Maharaja and his Government. Such notice would indirectly and directly benefit these persons in their various dealings with Government Departments.

The public of Shencottah, or to be more precise, some of its vocal citizens, used to talk of the advantages of having a High School there. The old Headmaster of mine, a very ambitious and energetic person, carried on a propaganda in favour of raising the middle school to the status of a High School. I was not however aware of any keen or persistent demand for it. The territory of the Travancore state that would be served by a High School in Shencottah was small. The middle school itself did not have the average strength of pupils of similar schools in other parts of the state. Several schools I knew had two to four divisions or sections in each class. The Shencottah school did not have more than a single division in any class. The local people were not education-minded to the degree one noticed elsewhere in Travancore. Nevertheless, for those who were so minded, a High School would be an advantage.

Mr 'B.A.', shrewd businessman that he was, saw the opportunity to achieve popularity, to place the people of the town in eternal obligation to him, and to secure royal favour, by one single act of educational charity. In the Durbar held at Trivandrum, he announced a donation of Rs 25,000 towards the founding of a High School in Shencottah which would be both a memorial to his father who had died a year ago, and commemorate the ruler's jubilee as well. The Government accepted the donation and immediately announced that steps would be taken to raise the Middle School to the status of High School from the commencement of the following school year. The people of Shencottah were jubilant that there would be a High School and that poor parents who wanted High School education for their children need not incur heavy expenses. When I came home for the summer holidays, there was talk everywhere that the school would have Form IV from June. That was no consolation to me as I had already completed Form IV.

During the summer holidays I had another spell of fever and my health at the time was giving my parents anxiety. But the continuation of my education gave them greater worry. At that time there was no thought of my studying beyond the matriculation or S.S.L.C. But even that meant two more years outside, with all the expenses involved. A couple of weeks before reopening, I approached 'B.A.' K again. He peremptorily suggested that I study in the new High School even by joining in Form IV when it was due to be formed. I did not like the idea of studying in the same class, forfeiting the advantage of having passed that class already. He then suggested that I stay at home for a year and join Form V the following year. The High School had naturally to be built up form by form in successive years. There was one technical objection to a break in High School studies. The Rules of the Education Department required that studies in the higher forms should be continuous. But 'B.A.' offered to obtain special dispensation from the Director of Public Instruction to waive this requirement. This dispensation was obtained and I was by circumstances forced to stay at home for a whole year. I felt very disappointed that my poverty should have led me to this break in studies. The consolation, however, was that I was only thirteen then, and would have finished High School by fifteen; this enforced break would enable me to do so a year later. As I was the youngest boy of my class, and a couple of years younger than the average age of the class, there was no serious loss.

7

A Year without School

The year was however not wasted in idleness. I began reading books—whatever I could get hold of. I helped the household in various ways. I was lucky enough to get a job giving private tuition to a boy—much older than me, but studying in Form II—for the princely sum of Rs 2 per month. My solid achievement was the study of the *Ramayana* and the *Mahabharata* and other books on Hindu mythology in Tamil. I also began reading the works of Swami Vivekananda and formed one close friendship, with a boy who eventually rose to be a distinguished Mathematician.

My father, though an unlettered person, knew many of the stories enshrined in the great epics of the Hindus. His knowledge was astounding, as most of it was acquired by hearsay. He was interested in having these stories read to him, as there was now one who could do that easily in his own family. He began looking out for books—several cheaply-printed books on the legend of Vikramaditya, and on various episodes from the *Mahabharata* and the *Ramayana* were available. I read these, but the quest for knowledge of the epics was not satisfied. I procured a complete prose version of *Kamba Ramayana* and of the *Mahabharata* by Villiputhur Alwar and completed reading them. Father then suggested that I should read a chapter or a few pages of these epics every day in the evening so that all the family could listen and also those neighbours and friends who may be interested.

There has been a tradition in Tamil Nad for these epics to be similarly read in some of our Temples and in the houses of some rich philanthropists. There was almost a ritual around this practice. The reading was done by a scholarly pundit from the original text in a musical style, and after every verse, he would expound the meaning in simple prose with his own embellishments. I had neither the scholarship for reading and interpreting the poetic texts, nor did I have a singing voice or the talent to recite poetry in the traditional manner. I therefore had to be satisfied with reading the prose text as clearly as I could and as I had already studied the texts, I was able to explain any difficult passages and to annotate the discussions and references to previous or subsequent incidents. A simple *pooja* before the picture of Rama was performed before the commencement of the reading, and when the reading came to some of the celebrated episodes in the epics, a bigger *Pooja* was offered. On occasion, twenty or more listeners gathered around me for the performance of the *Poojas*. I had to go over in the morning to collect flowers from distant gardens on the banks of the rivers and tanks in the neighbourhood.

The best part of a year, I was occupied in this edifying task on most evenings. I became thus proficient in our ancient lore even at the age of 12 or 13, and this interest in the epics sustained me all through my life. The various beliefs and tenets on which the Hindu ways of life and worship are based are enshrined in the epics. The study of Mythology and of the learned dialogues between saints and kings, on every conceivable subject from metaphysics to statecraft and magic, with which the epics are interspersed, has always been the solid foundation of the learning of the orthodox Hindu. This lore is cultivated by successive generations in good Brahman families. But other Hindus have generally neglected these studies, except professional Pundits and scholars. I found the study very educative and interesting. No amount of reading of fiction in later life gave me that much emotional and intellectual satisfaction. There was always some story or episode in the epics on which I could fall back, to illustrate a point in daily conversation or to point a moral for guidance. Purely as the raw material of literature, these epics were an inexhaustible source. I felt lucky that my enforced idleness at that early age gave me this great opportunity. In school and College, and later in life, I found I was richer and better for this experience than most of my friends and contemporaries.

Surprisingly enough, these studies did not make me superstitious or bigoted. I was able to analyse the supernatural elements with logic and reason and felt that under the layer of the miraculous and supernatural there were substantial truths. The supernatural method was used by the ancient authors to convey metaphysical ideas in a manner which the ordinary man would more easily comprehend. It was symbolism used extensively, and with some thinking, the nature of the symbolism was comprehensible.

I carried my learning in other directions also. It was the year 1918–19, when the first world war ended. I was too young to understand the course of the war. During my early school years, I had heard from my teachers and from educated acquaintances that there was a war in Europe between England and Germany. A year previously, when the German submarine 'Emden' cruised round the Indian seas, people were alarmed and some said *Kaliyuga* was coming to a close. When the tide of the war turned in favour of the Allies, many older villagers were heard to say that the English had succeeded in discovering the heavenly weapons of the Pandavas, kept hidden when they went on their heaven-ward journey, and it was only by using those weapons that they were able to defeat the Germans who were none other than reincarnations of Ravana's *Raakshasas*. The discovery of aeroplanes and their use in the war did not surprise these old villagers. These, they said, were only the *vimanas* of Rama and Krishna, similarly discovered by the English. When the war was over there was general jubilation.

Till then I had not heard of the Congress or the nationalist movement or of Gandhi. But now in 1918–19, I heard for the first time that there was a movement for self-government. The concept of Independence was not known then. Some of the lawyers and the younger teachers were heard discussing self-government and what it meant. These discussions were always hush-hush and considered very rash.

But the ordinary man in the street thought the British were in India for good and had no doubt that British rule was the best the country had had for ages. In spite of this, there was a curious revivalism. The younger generation, including some sections of the students, were beginning to take pride in things Indian, in India's early history, in Indian philosophy and religion. The beginnings of nationalistic pride, I sensed even then.

For us young boys, the most important single inspiration for kindling patriotic pride was Swami Vivekananda. I had vaguely heard of him and now I began making acquaintance with his literary legacies. I have no distinct recollection of how I came to be introduced to the Collected Works of Swami Vivekananda. But I managed to borrow volumes from some acquaintances and their study was then almost an absorbing passion. For a boy of thirteen who had read only up to Form IV, study of Vivekananda's speeches was a difficult exercise. But I was carried away by the jingling music of his words. Their meaning escaped me often. But I read them over and over again and got infinitely thrilled. I began to feel that it was something to be proud of, to be born in India, that after all we have a legacy of wisdom and achievement. I knew then what was meant by patriotism. For years I read Swamiji's works repeatedly, read all I could get hold of, on Ramakrishna, the Brahmo Samaj, and other liberal movements. But my acquaintance with the political movement was still very vague.

It was during this period I met another young boy somewhat older than me in years, to whom I felt drawn even from the beginning. He was my companion in the reading of Swami Vivekananda. He was a sceptic in matters connected with religion and mythology, but he had even then evinced a thirst for higher knowledge. What attracted me to him was his undoubtedly superior intelligence and critical faculty. He thought I impressed him by my common-sense and practical outlook. Though younger, I was treated by him with the affection and respect due to a leader. He followed my advice on all worldly matters and I admired and respected him for his superior intellect and wisdom.

His name was Sivasankara Narayana Pillai. I called him 'Sankar' for short. I was always teasing him for his simple and sometimes eccentric ways and soon my form of addressing him was the familiar and endearing 'whoy'. He was the only son of his father who lived in neighbouring Vallam. His mother died when he was a small child, leaving some landed property of her own to the child. The father enjoyed the produce of the land as the child's natural guardian, and after a couple of years of widower-hood, married again. The step-mother did not like the child and at an early age the child left his father's house to live with an aunt. At the age of 10 or 11, he left even the aunt, came to Shencottah, and started his studies. He boarded and lodged in a local eating-house and sometimes used the house of a friend or a distant relation as his temporary lodge. A kindly brahman schoolteacher looked after the boy's lands and kept accounts of his income and the expenditure arising out of the cultivation.

I met him by accident and was soon seeing him frequently, mainly to discuss Swami Vivekananda, Hindu religion and philosophy, and the National movement—rather highbrow stuff for boys of our age. He was of simple habits, avoided luxuries and extravagances of any kind, and was kind at heart and as pure as one could be in thought. His two passions even then were Mathematics and Beauty. He saw beauty in Mathematics, in the structure of numbers, in the harmony of forms, and in Nature in general. He saw Beauty in Creation, in the thoughts of the ancients, in poetry, and he also was quick to perceive and appreciate Beauty in human form. Our conversations on Beauty were our private secret and boys of our age would wonder what two simple boys like us had so much in common to talk about.

There was another friend, a Christian boy of my age, the son of the local Protestant catechist. The Protestant Mission operating from Tirunelveli had recently built a school and appointed a teacher who was also the local catechist. His wife also helped him with the school. They had a son, a year older than me, who was studying in Form IV in our new High School. He would be my classmate next year when I was expected to join the Fifth Form. I made his acquaintance as we admitted my younger brother, eight years my junior, in the elementary class of the school run by the catechist. I was a frequent visitor to the school and learnt much from the kindly catechist about the story of Christ. I read the New and Old Testaments, both in English and in the Tamil translation. Like all converts, the catechist was a zealous Christian, but he was strangely not bigoted. He had some understanding of Hindu religion. His grievance against Hinduism was in respect of its social order—the caste system. In that we were in agreement. His young son developed a great liking for me and became a good friend. He was a strange contrast to my other friend, Sankar. The Christian priest's son was very worldly in his ways and outlook, enjoyed life, and had a cheerful loud laugh at every turn of conversation. He thought Sankar serious, thoughtful, philosophic, and simple as he was, eccentric, and not to be taken seriously. I was amused when later in life this cleric's worldly son became an ordained priest himself.

During this year I developed another interest which has abided with me all my life—love of theatre. There were no cinemas in those days. Periodically a dramatic troupe visited our town and, in a temporary shed of corrugated iron sheets and thatch, performances were given on alternate days. The season lasted a month or two, according to the response from the public. People came to see the performances from villages within a radius of 15 miles. The show commenced at 9 p.m. and generally terminated at 2 or 3 a.m. No play was repeated, unless it was a tremendous success. The role of heroine was played by a man, but some troupes had women in the cast and then the shows were more popular. The price of admission ranged from four annas to a rupee. The popular seats—benches—were eight annas. Most of the village's young men and students patronised the floor seats for 4 annas. I could not afford to spend even four annas and my parents would not hear of my wasting time seeing Dramas. But they had no objection if I got free admission, provided I did not make a habit of it. There was one easy way of getting free admission. For the publicity of the Dramas, printed notices were distributed in the streets of that place and in the neighbouring villages. A band of clarionet and horn players was engaged to play hybrid tunes outside the theatre to attract the crowd. I made friends with this band and managed to sneak into the theatre with them. On several occasions, I have managed to slip out of my mat bed in the verandah of my house, quietly returning after midnight. I would slip back into bed, without any of the other sleepers on the verandah being aware of my nocturnal disappearance. In this way I saw most of the Dramas and had the opportunity of seeing many of the famous professional actors of the day. My knowledge of mythology gave me an additional interest, as most of the plays were based on epic themes.

8

Two Years in High School

A year passed soon and I joined Form V, newly constituted in my old school which was fast getting transformed into a big High School. The same sympathetic headmaster was there at the time of my admission, but soon he was replaced by an elderly and more experienced headmaster. All my teachers were new; the older ones whom I knew had either been transferred, or confined to the lower forms.

At the commencement I approached 'B.A.' K and his brothers for help with the school fees. They said that as I was living with my parents and had no special boarding expenditure, my father should be able to pay my school fees, which were only about Rs 5 per month or less. There was no chance of my getting any scholarship. There was only one merit scholarship, given to the pupil who stood first in the Third Form examination, and he obtained this for all the three years of the higher forms. I failed to get this when I passed the Third Form. There were no scholarships for poor students, or fees concessions, except for Muslims and students from the Depressed classes. Father therefore had to find the money for my books and school fees.

I felt somewhat self-conscious for the first few days, as some boys who were my juniors in the lower forms had come up to be with me now, as I had lost one year. Surprisingly, a few boys of my class in the Malayalam school, whom I outstripped in the lower forms due to my short-circuiting by going to the mission school in Surandai, also caught up with me. There were therefore several familiar faces and I did not have the dread boys experience when going to a new school. Very soon I came to be liked by several boys who were impressed by my wider general knowledge and better understanding of English. Though in examinations I did not always stand high, I came to be recognised as one of the abler students.

I remember vividly the visit paid by a European Chief Inspector of Schools. He entered our class when a Geometry lesson was in progress. He asked several boys in succession as to the use of learning Geometry and Mathematics. Some said, we can become astronomers, engineers, builders, accountants. A few boys blankly said, to pass examinations. Somehow I felt that the answers were not adequate and that the inspector was not satisfied with the answers. When my turn came, I answered, with some diffidence, that the study of Geometry and Mathematics enables one to exercise his thinking capacity. The class teacher felt that I was eccentric and scowled at me; but the inspector appreciated the answer and delivered almost a speech, lasting for ten minutes, elaborating my answer. I felt very happy and this incident gave me a great deal of self-confidence. My optional subject was not Mathematics, I had taken only History, and some of the cleverer students of the class, who invariably took Mathematics as optional, used to tease me for being only a History student. They were now feeling crestfallen and wondered how a History student's answer, on a question relating to Geometry, came to be appreciated. In the school in those days students taking History as optional were looked down upon, by the Mathematics group and even by Masters, as inferior specimens of humanity. The Mathematics group professed that they would become engineers and doctors, whereas the best that a History student could do would only be to become a teacher or a clerk. I used to ponder over these remarks and sometimes felt sorry that I did not take Mathematics myself. But I knew I had no great aptitude for the study of Mathematics, and must make the best of History—a virtue of necessity.

I was unfortunate in my History master. A fresh graduate from Trichy joined the school about the middle of the year as History Master. He was a vain person and thought highly of his education in the Jesuit college of St Joseph's, which had then a great reputation. He talked pompously and took great delight in speaking in a loud squeaky voice. His sources were some of the standard books which good college students read in those days. These books were in the school library and I had read them very thoroughly. It was my habit to make copious notes from books that I read, and I have kept up this habit all through life. Lane-Poole's book on Muslim India and Lyall's on British India, and Tout's and Green's books on English History were my favourites even in High School. The new master had read them in college for his graduate classes and could never have thought that in a newly-started High School in a small town, any student would have gone so far as to read these standard reference books. Our ordinary textbooks were of lower standard and students hardly mastered even these.

Even during the first few classes, the Master spotted that I knew more History than most pupils of the class. Perhaps I was also vain and must have tried to show off. This is a fault in young students. He did not like the way in which I answered his questions in class. I sometimes corrected the mistakes in facts that he occasionally made, and also showed my familiarity with the books he had read in preparing his lessons. He soon showed his dislike and I was often ordered out of his class as a punishment. My friend Sankar was also one of his other victims. We retaliated by arranging rags. His classes were often noisy and the Headmaster came to restore order. He pointed me out to the Headmaster as the arch-villain and as the source of all the trouble in his classes. The Headmaster was surprised, as I had a reputation as a good and well-behaved student. The reputation was not well deserved, however. I was occasionally impish and was often carried away by my conceit arising from my superior knowledge and my popularity with my fellows. The Headmaster, however, properly warned me against indulging in any show of disrespect towards the Master.

The History Master's treatment of the class in general, his pompous ways, and particularly the abusive language he used when he lost his temper, made him the most unpopular master in school. The next year, when I was in Form VI, this teacher was away for a week to get his degree at the Convocation annually held in Madras. This was the first time the students had actually seen a teacher being away for a Convocation. There was considerable excitement when he appeared in class after his return, and some of the curious students asked him questions about it. Instead of explaining the Convocation and satisfying their innocent queries, he behaved even more haughtily. The resentment mounted up. There were several small incidents, calculated to annoy him.

One afternoon when the students were waiting in the class—it was the first after the mid-day interval—there was a spontaneous desire to play a practical joke. Without much discussion, the boys had their plans ready and executed them in a few minutes. His chair was placed on the top of his table. A few bricks, stones, and thorns were hastily collected from the compound and these were heaped on the table and chair. In large neat print the blackboard was covered with the name of the teacher. The entrance door was closed and gently bolted. All the boys were seated quietly in their accustomed places. I played the leading part in organizing the rag and a brahman boy, brother-in-law of another teacher, assisted me. We sat on a rear bench in class as usual.

The teacher, as was his custom, arrived a few minutes after the bell, and finding the door closed and perfect silence inside, felt that there was something wrong, went back to the common room and returned with a peon. The peon pushed the door open, and the teacher entered the class with the peon, and the boys stood up, as was the regular practice. The teacher saw the reception and the decoration on the table and for a minute could not open his mouth. He shivered and perspiration lined his face. He rushed out of the class and came back with the Headmaster. The Headmaster ordered the stones and thorns to be removed. The chair and the table were properly arranged. The Headmaster delivered a homily to the class and called upon the offenders to come forward and confess their guilt. He threatened them and the entire class with severe punishment. Not a word was uttered by anyone. The class sat in mute silence, without any sign of response to the Headmaster. They left the room after some time, as the teacher was in no state to handle the class.

The boys dispersed one by one during that idle hour, but no-one thought of betrayal. This was remarkable, as only three or four boys took active part in this cruel joke, with me. The others were silent witnesses. There was no appeal by us to our fellow students for protection. The agreement however was spontaneous and unanimous. The reason was partly my popularity; the dislike of the teacher was universal. There were several boys from rich houses, sons of prominent citizens of the locality. Opportunists and dissidents are generally found among this lot, as they represent the ruling class and vested interests. The Headmaster subjected all the boys to vigilant interrogation during subsequent days, with a view to obtaining evidence against the offenders. There was no betrayal; however, suspicion turned round on me and my good brahman friend. This had its sequel at a later date. This was the first time I had taken part in a serious rag against a teacher. This must have been a surprise to my fellow-students, who always took me to be a well-behaved boy. This was a new experience to me—the thrill of mischief and the risk of punishment. Thereafter the boys knew I was capable of mischief and would not tolerate anything meekly. It was heartening to find from subsequent events that my popularity stood me in good stead and saved me from the consequences of a betrayal.

It was the practice in the school before it became a High School to celebrate the birthday of the Maharaja of Travancore. Since the High School was started, there was an additional annual celebration, to commemorate the Donor's anniversary. The annual *sraardham* or death anniversary fell on a day in January–February, and the K family bore the entire expenses of the celebration in the school, which had a local holiday for the purpose. The portrait of the old gentleman was taken in procession through the main streets of the town, and after sports and light refreshments for the boys, a public meeting was held in the school premises.

I was not present for the first celebration, as I was not studying in the school at that time. Before the second celebration, during my

Fifth Form year, the Headmaster asked me whether I would read out a speech on behalf of the students. This was the first occasion on which a student was asked to speak at such a function, and I was delighted. I prepared a neat little speech in Tamil, extolling the Donor's benefactions, and when it was read out the impression produced was very flattering to me. I was the recipient of several congratulations. I repeated the performance in the following year. The speech then was in English, and these two public performances heightened my reputation.

During these years, my father was taking small P.W.D. contracts or sub-contracts with the Forest Department. The Forest Department jobs consisted in arranging for felling trees, having the timber cut to size and produced for acceptance. I kept accounts for father. The other contracts were for the disposal of fish production in government irrigation tanks. The rights were auctioned to the highest bidder, and before a particular date, which generally coincided with the commencement of the monsoons, the available catch of fish had to be collected and sold off. We had several such contracts. The work relating to them came up during the summer holidays. I visited several villages in the taluk and supervised the sales and kept accounts. Every summer we made a net profit of a few hundred rupees. These jobs gave me valuable experience in handling money and observing the life of people of various castes in the villages.

It was during one of these visits to a neighbouring village, about eight miles away, that I came into contact with a Swamiji or recluse from among our relations. He was a widower; he had several nephews. He had a coconut grove outside the village where he lived in a small neat cottage. He looked after the grove, watered the trees, and sold the proceeds. One of his nephews went in the mornings and prepared a simple meal for him. He ate only once a day, at about 11 a.m. He spent most of his time in meditation. He had numerous disciples from several villages. There were daily several visitors; some brought him gifts of fruits and grains. Those who had come to see him were fed with him, irrespective of whether they brought gifts or not. He talked to them of numerous things and advised them on all matters.

He did not hold any spiritual discourse as such, but we felt his presence consoling. I saw him on several occasions and often spent hours with him. He was greatly interested in me and appreciated my heroic attempts to complete my studies.

This contact with the Swamiji, following my intimate study of the great epics, aroused in me an abiding interest in religion and philosophy. I was not of the conventionally religious type, though in those days I visited Temples occasionally. I was sceptical of most of our religious beliefs and practices, but I began to appreciate the Hindu religion for its attempt to reconcile various strata of spiritual development. The deep symbolism and poetic allegory behind our myths I came to understand gradually.

During my last year in school, I made another strange friend. He was a brahman boy considerably older than me. He was the son of a hotel-keeper, had been in different parts of Malabar, and eventually came to Shencottah when his father opened an eating-house there. The boy had failed in the S.S.L.C. examination twice already and was studying in the same class for the third year. He was the only one whose mastery of spoken English was superior to mine. His general knowledge was also vaster. How he began to be regarded as a somewhat undesirable person, I could not then understand. He had two unmarried sisters. In those days, brahman girls were married before they attained the age of thirteen. When girls remained unmarried after that age, public opinion gave them a bad name. The boy was talkative, and treated teachers with scant courtesy. He often came to my house to see me, talked to my parents, and even partook of our food—a thing a brahman would be excommunicated for doing. He knew of our poverty, but he was far too liberal-minded and large-hearted for questions of caste and wealth to influence him. I derived considerable pleasure from his company and I cannot say he did me any harm, though my schoolmates and teachers apprehended that my association with him would only end in my ruination. This coincidence of my association with the school's bad boy, I remembered too often in later life, for I had the felicity of forming close friendships with people of diverse tastes and stations in life, and this trait in me was regarded as peculiar in one of my educational and social attainments.

Two years passed quickly enough and the S.S.L.C. examination was approaching. I had no doubts about my chances of passing the examination. Not being a student of Mathematics, I could not hope to get the merit scholarship awarded by the state to the best pupil from each school, on the basis of the Public examination marks. As the examination was approaching, the question—what next?—also began to worry me and father. In this state of anxiety I wrote the exam and by the middle of May 1921, the results were known.

Much to my regret, my good friend, the brahman boy who participated in the rag on the history Master, failed. When I went to the school to obtain my certificate from the Headmaster, I found my good friend Ramachandran standing outside. He wanted to leave the school and had come for his Transfer Certificate. The Headmaster wanted a confession from him about the authors of the rag and virtually put him through the Third degree. He was kept waiting for days, before he got his T.C.

When I entered the Headmaster's room he gave me the certificate and began addressing me on the importance of character and discipline for a college student. He was quite convinced that I was the mischief-maker, but he could not punish me as my crime could not be proved. I would be coming into contact, he said, with European Professors and great scholars, and unless I improved my ways, he could not see any future for me. He hoped that I would be a changed person and realize my responsibilities.

In silence I took my leave of him. My school life was over. I felt I had come of age. I had had much more experience of the vicissitudes of life than many students of my class, though I was perhaps younger than many. I had attempted to do, and succeeded in doing, things which many of them would not. The struggle I had to endure to make education available to myself, made me realize my position. All this also contributed to give me a zest for life and a sturdy spirit of self-reliance and independence.

9

I Feel My Way

When I was in High School, there was at first no idea of my trying for a College education. It would mean at least four years in a distant place—Trivandrum, Trichy, or Madras—and a minimum expenditure of not less than Rs 400 a year. This was definitely beyond our means. The difficulties we had had when I spent a year in Ambasamudram were still fresh in our memories. These difficulties would be nothing to what I would have to endure if I attempted College education. Nevertheless, during my Sixth Form year, the comparatively good progress I was making, and the appreciation I won from my fellow-students and from my teachers and a few elders in the town, kindled the spark of ambition and I began to think seriously of College.

Father and I discussed the problem often, without coming to a satisfactory solution. The alternative to college was service. Ours was a small place, and profitable employment, even for an S.S.L.C., was not available then. Our political and official contacts were with Trivandrum, the capital of the Travancore state. The only opening for an S.S.L.C. was either a small clerkship, or the post of a teacher in a lower secondary or elementary school. Graduates alone were entertained as clerks in bigger offices. The easier course would have been to take to teaching. But a boy of 16 would not be much use as a teacher. The minimum age was 18. In any event I would have to live apart from the family in distant places. Even then the prospects of getting employment before the age of eighteen were slender. Instead of wasting two years waiting for opportunities of service, we thought, I might begin at least by studying for the Intermediate Examination.

We approached our only patrons—the K family. 'B.A.' K continued to take an interest in me and appreciated my performances during the Founder's Day functions. He had occasionally requisitioned my services for translating or transcribing official papers. I had run some errands for him now and then. Father, mother, and I approached him and put our proposition to him. He made detailed enquiries of father about our financial position and father's earnings. He agreed that I should be given a chance to study in College, and made two propositions. Father should take employment with their family as some sort of supervisor of the agricultural operations of the common property of the family, which each brother looked after in rotation. The salary and perquisites in kind would be adequate for the maintenance of our family. The other proposition was that he would contribute every month some amount towards my college expenses, and I should get some token contributions from the other brothers also from time to time. If these were not adequate, I should get father to make good the disparity. The K family had a house in Trivandrum, and in the outhouses and sheds, there was plenty of accommodation. So the problem of lodging was solved. Initially I could board with a boy of the family who was also proceeding to Trivandrum for studies; a cook was being sent to keep house for him.

The arrangements appeared very satisfactory—in fact we thought they were too good to be true, and we were pleased with our luck. Employment on a permanent basis for father, meant that he could say goodbye to all the heart-breaking and uncertain jobs he had been undertaking from time to time to provide the minimum sustenance for the family. I was to be looked after, and to begin with I was to board and lodge with a nephew of the Ks. In great jubilation I made preparations for the journey to Trivandrum—not realizing fully the hazards I had to meet in those five long years ahead.

We had no claim on the K family except a moral claim. Grandmother always used to say that in her younger days, monies belonging to her were appropriated by the old gentleman, and one or two small properties, which were intended to be purchased for her, were actually purchased in his name. Even father was trapped into surrendering a bit of property in this manner, to my knowledge. He had lent some money to a Muslim in a neighbouring village. Since the Muslim defaulted, his property was attached and a court decree was secured, transferring the property rights to father. Father could not, however, evict the debtor and in despair, he approached 'B.A.' K for help. 'B.A.' suggested that father transfer the ownership to his (B.A.'s) name, and he would compensate us for the value of the property. The transfer was made just about this time, but to date, we did not get the compensation. Father was afraid to press for this in view of our obligations to him. The help we sought was not very much, for people of their means. They have been known to give away, in charities and festivities, very much more. Given the background of our old family contacts, our approaches to them for help in connection with my College studies were not unreasonable, and they did not also at any time repudiate their moral responsibility.

Before I started for Trivandrum, for several days I was waiting at their doorsteps to receive whatever they were willing to give. As I would be coming home only once in three months, it was necessary for me to obtain, once in three months, whatever help I could, to sustain me through the term. Only he who has waited for charity outside the doorsteps of people can understand the feelings of frustration and humiliation I experienced. Standing for hours without any notice being taken, and then being told, after one's feet and heart had begun to ache, that one might call again or try one of the other brothers, could not cheer a person. Only 'B.A.' K gave, after two or three visits, a ten-rupee note. To get anything out of the others required endless endurance. 'B.A.' K used to visit Trivandrum almost every month. I managed to get some money out of him on those occasions. The total bounty I received in the first two years (during my Intermediate classes) did not exceed Rs 200, and the number of hours of waiting in silent supplication would have been at least a hundred. I acquired considerable experience in standing and waiting, and also developed patience to a degree that my nature normally rebelled at on occasion.

In later life, I followed a rule which I would not like to be departed from even by my children. I did not like any one to wait either in my house or at the office, and I loathed supplicants for favour who believed in wearing out your patience or your decision by indefinite waiting. I liked anyone who came to see me to tell me his business straightaway. Many do not do so, and will linger on, waiting for what they consider the proper mood or an opportune moment.

I have often in those days thought of charity in the abstract. Charity is ranked among the highest of man's virtues. Charity has all the attributes of mercy as described by Shakespeare. Properly given, it ennobles the giver and morally uplifts the recipient. But I cannot say I received my charities in this manner. I was often bitter and sometimes the mental torture I underwent almost brought my patience to breaking point. Often I had thought of throwing up the sponge, and saying goodbye to college. But there was a dogged persistence, and I began to develop a high sense of my moral obligation to the family. I had seen their pitiful existence and how much hope they had placed in me. I could not let them down. I had to give them a chance of a better life, for all their suffering. Poverty can be a great spur to ambition.

The scion of the K house, who also joined college with me and with whom I boarded for the first two months, was a good lad. He was two or three years older than me, but he took to his studies with quiet indifference. He married his cousin, and soon the bride also came up to live with her newly-married husband. I had to shift for myself, for it was obviously impossible to live with a honeymooning couple.

I made arrangements with a Hotel for my food, though I continued to stay in one of the rooms on the premises. For two meals, one at 9 a.m. and another at 8 p.m., I had to pay Rs 10 per month. My usual routine in those days was to get up in the morning and have a bath, drawing water from the well in the compound. Then I studied for two hours. About 9 a.m. or a little earlier, I left the house for the main street in the town, where my hotel was. The distance was about a mile and a half, and after taking food, I went to College by 9.45 a.m. During the noon interval, half a cup of coffee and a little eatable, for a total outlay of two annas (about 12 paise) or a little more, served as tiffin. I walked to the hotel late in the evening for dinner. Sometimes I varied the routine and had a light breakfast at 9.30 a.m. and the regular meal at noon.

College fees and food and my minimum expenses cost me about Rs 25 per month. Father sent me Rs 10 or Rs 15 per month, according to the state of my other finances. I had to write to him by the commencement of the month a detailed account of my receipts and expenditure for the previous month and my forecast for the current month. The report was subjected to a meticulous audit, and if I had asked for an additional couple of rupees, I did not get the amount without further interrogation. I did not blame him, though I got irritated at the tone of his letters. Often he had to pawn or pledge household articles to find the money for me. If during any month 'B.A.' K did not pay his customary monthly visit, I would be in trouble.

My wardrobe consisted of two handloom dhotees, two shirts of cheap material, a banian or two, two coats, and two handloom towels. In our College, students were required to wear a coat. I did most of my washing, except the coat, and occasionally, a shirt was given to the dhobi. I did not possess a pair of chappals till I took my degree, nor did I possess an umbrella of my own for several years. I did not have even the meagre bed-roll of a thick dhurrie and a pillow, during all my five years in college. Any mat that was available in the house served my purpose. Later I purchased a leaf or grass mat for a few annas, and a pillow. I had no table or chairs. I sat on the floor, or wherever possible, and read by the light of a hurricane lantern which of course I had to have. There was an ancient steel trunk in our house, but it was too big for my needs. I had made a small box out of a deal wood packing case, and this served to contain my books, my meagre clothes, and all my belongings, all the five years in college. I bought a steel trunk with my earnings in 1927. All my train travel during the years of my study was undertaken without even the inevitable tin trunk.

With all these shortcomings, my days in College were pleasant. I liked the study of History, read voraciously, and was one of the best students in the class. Soon I was getting the first or second place in examinations, and the professors began to take notice of me. There were several pinpricks from some of the K family people who came to Trivandrum, mostly of a petty kind, but I learnt to endure them stoically, as long as my studies gave me satisfaction.

During one of the vacations which I spent at home, I experienced one of these pinpricks, which almost broke my resolve. There was some social function in a village about 5 or 6 miles from Ambasamudram, to which most of the members of the K family from Shencottah went. I also went with them. We went by train up to Ambasamudram, and from there, some went by bullock carts, and the humbler ones walked. There was a river to cross, and there was neither a causeway nor a bridge. On our return trip, there was the same crowd—some in bullock carts and the others walking. One of the K brothers, the waster of the family, whom even his brothers did not treat properly, stepped out of the bullock cart near the river and, to wade across the water, slipped off his chappals on the sand, and hesitated for a few seconds. Then he took his chappals in his left hand, tucked up his dhotee, and waded through the shallow water. I was immediately behind him and there were a few other camp followers, tenants and servants of the family. As we stepped on dry sand on the opposite bank, he turned on me fiercely and asked why I did not pick up his chappals when he slipped them off. I was flabbergasted. It did not strike me that he expected me to carry his chappals, and I did not think that I should have humiliated myself to that extent. But at that time I did not have the presence of mind or courage to give him any rational reply. All that I could say was that he did not ask me to do this menial job for him, and therefore I did not. But what he wanted was that I should have come forward and picked them up when he slipped them off.

He said something about my conceit arising out of my English education and in silence I reached the railway station and boarded the train.

The offended gentleman complained to his brothers about my conceit and lack of courtesy. After a day or two, one of the family—a younger member whom I considered to be the most considerate of them all—upbraided me for my lack of courtesy to his uncle. My mother and father were told about it and an apology was demanded. This created a crisis in my affairs. Father blamed his lot. He had a high sense of personal dignity himself and in ordinary circumstances would not have thought of blaming me. But he could not afford to incur the displeasure of these people on whom we were dependent for our livelihood and for my education. I do not know whether this episode reached 'B.A.' K's ears, but he did not speak to me about it. But several members of the K family were visibly annoyed with me. We had to eat the humble pie and apologize to the gentleman concerned. There were several people in the K family who did not very much like the idea of my getting a college education, and if we had not borne this humiliation submissively, serious impediments would have been placed in my way. It took them a long time to get reconciled to me. Nothing succeeded like success.

Even before my College days, I had begun to take an interest in politics and to follow the progress of the Nationalist movement. Our town was always backward in its political consciousness. As it was a fairly prosperous place, with several landlords and rich men, the atmosphere was conservative. Besides, the people in the Indian states were less politically aware than those in British India. Having imbibed the deeply nationalist ideas of Swami Vivekananda early in life, I found myself taking a keener interest in the nationalist movement than many of my contemporaries.

During the summer holidays after my S.S.L.C. examination, I heard that some great National leaders were touring Tinnevelly District. That was the triumphal tour of C.R. Das prior to establishing the Swarajya party. He was accompanied by Phookan of Assam. From

Madras, C.R., as Chakravarthy Rajagopalachari was then known, and A. Rangaswamy Iyengar of the *Swadesamitran* accompanied them. I, along with another boy, went to Ambasamudram to hear C.R. Das speak. That was the first occasion when I heard a political speech by a great leader. C.R. or Rangaswamy Iyengar translated these speeches sentence by sentence. I got in close touch with some of the party, and travelled with them to Tenkasi, where again there was a public meeting. After two days' absence, I returned to Shencottah, reluctant to part from them. I was emotionally touched by C.R. Das's oratory. He was tall and handsome and his presence was winning. In those days the crowd attending political meetings was not so large as in later days. Listening to C.R. Das's and Phookan's speeches, I was emotionally transported to a different sphere altogether, and was able to share their innermost feelings, and the identification momentarily was so complete that I experienced the same intense emotional experience the speakers were interpreting. I could not take an objective view of these speeches; the experience was subjective. I had the same feeling when I visited some temples where the religious atmosphere was sufficiently intense to attract my complete mental surrender.

About that time, the Vaikam Satyagraha and other agitations for temple entry and the abolition of untouchability were in progress in Malabar. I read about the part played in these movements by E.V. Ramaswami Naicker and P. Varadarajulu Naidu. These were great names in the South then—greater than Satyamurthi or Rajagopalachari. The agitations in Malabar for winning the right for untouchables to enter the streets where temples were located drew wide attention, and batches of *satyagrahis* came even from the Punjab. It was then that I heard of the Akalis—the Sikh volunteers.

Gandhiji came to Malabar to see what was going on in the Vaikam Satyagraha. He was invited to Trivandrum by some citizens. The Maharaja avoided complications by inviting him as a state guest and he stayed at the Guest House. Along with a few students, I went and saw him at close quarters. Among the official classes, there was considerable criticism about the conduct of the Maharaja in inviting

Gandhi to be a State Guest. Gandhiji stated before he entered Trivandrum that he was not going to speak on political or controversial subjects as long as he was within Travancore territory, and that his mission was confined to work connected with the removal of untouchability—a purely social mission—among the Hindus. He kept his word and the Maharaja was therefore also saved from embarrassment.

Gandhiji addressed a mammoth public meeting—the biggest I had seen and perhaps the biggest in Trivandrum till then. Many came from distant places, and there were a large number of women. Perhaps even in Gandhiji's experience this may have been the first occasion when he had seen such a vast assemblage of women in any public meeting. I still remember the compliment he paid to the women of Kerala. He said, 'I have fallen in love with the beautiful women of Travancore and I am charmed by their simple white clothes. Their white dress is a symbol of their inner purity.' For days afterwards students talked only of Gandhiji. The words he uttered about the women of Travancore I remembered all my life and I have repeated them in some meetings I have addressed and in my private conversations.

There were two other notable visitors during this period—Rabindranath Tagore and Sarojini Naidu. Tagore was accompanied by his daughter-in-law and by C.F. Andrews who was then his private secretary. Most well-informed students who had taken an interest in the National movement and in the renaissance of Indian literature knew the *Gitanjali* and there was a great demand for Tagore's books. The visit therefore was a great attraction. As Tagore was collecting funds for the Viswa Bharathi University, admission to his lectures was by ticket. In the meeting I attended, he read out an eloquent essay on the Forest Gurukulas of ancient India. The Students Union invited the Tagore party to visit the College so that all the students could have an opportunity of seeing him at close quarters. He walked along all the verandahs of the college, peeped into lecture Halls, and was introduced to the Professors. Tagore's daughter-in-law was dressed in a simple Bengali saree and had her hair hanging loose, spread on her back, as women do after they have had a bath. For students, this was their first look at a Bengali lady. One of the Professors remarked to a class later that he was more impressed by the elegance and grooming of Tagore's beard than even by the lady's sartorial get-up. Tagore was very particular about his gown, the grooming of his flowing white beard, and his general appearance, and by his side, even his daughter-in-law looked rustic. C.F. Andrews, by his identification with the Indian National movement, his part in the South African agitation, and his personal devotion to Tagore and Gandhi, had made himself very popular with Indian students, and we considered ourselves very lucky to have had an opportunity of seeing him at close quarters.

Sarojini Naidu had a tremendous reputation at that time as the unquestioned leader of the women of India. She also came to the Malabar Coast in order to whip up enthusiasm for the Vaikam Satyagraha movement. A public meeting was arranged in a theatre-hall. She was scheduled to speak at 5 p.m.; students however began to rush in even at 1 p.m., and at 3, when I tried to enter, there was hardly standing space, and thousands were waiting outside. Electricity had not become so common then; even street lighting was done by gas or kerosene lamps. This hall was used for cinemas of the silent days, and had some primitive electric installation—but no fans. Sarojini Naidu came in about 5.30, and after the tumultuous welcome and introductory speeches, began her speech about 6 p.m. The electric lights were on, but they suddenly faded out a few minutes after she began her speech. After a few minutes' confusion, the lights went on again, and Sarojini Naidu resumed her speech by quoting from a German poet and translating the verse into English. It meant that the people cried for light, light, and then it came. She took it as her theme and began elaborating the birth and growth of the patriotic movement in India. She must have spoken for over two hours. There were no loudspeakers in those days, but Sarojini did not stand in need of one. She had the most magnificent voice of any one I have heard in my life. In spite of its loudness, it was sweet and musical. She spoke as one would sing, in singsong periods. Her words jingled like bells. I have never experienced the thrill and the magic of the spoken word as I did listening to her oratory.

My heart responded to the call of the great patriots to the youth of the country. I felt intensely a craving to be in the thick of the fray and take part in the various struggles the leaders were launching. Nothing then would have pleased me more than an opportunity to serve in the political agitations. But I was then developing a strong consciousness of my obligations to the family. It was becoming increasingly clear to me that I had my duties to perform, and the path of duty at that time lay in finishing my education and in doing something to improve the hard lot of my own kith and kin. I often thought then that if my economic position had been better, the best thing for me would have been to become a lawyer and then a politician.

At that time, perhaps for the first time, the thought of a brilliant official career by passing the I.C.S. examination began to take root gradually. I never thought of it as a High School student. In my junior class in college, we had a young lecturer who took a First class Honours degree in English. He looked very small and young, but was regarded as an outstanding scholar. He appeared for the I.C.S. competitive examination held in Allahabad in 1922 and on being successful, he left for England the next year for training. A little later, N.R. Pillai, who had just returned from England after admission to the I.C.S. visited the college. He was received with respect and affection by his old professors and taken round. N.R. Pillai's visit, and the success of Sivaramakrishnan (the young English lecturer), made me think of the I.C.S. as a career. I could hardly mention this to my friends. They would have upbraided me for my audacity and shunned me as an eccentric person. Admission to the I.C.S. was regarded as so difficult. People did not believe that merit alone counted; some influence of the highest kind was mysteriously referred to as leading to the success of the few men whose names we knew then.

I was then not an outstanding student. I had not obtained any merit scholarship. I had no money and I had no influential connections. But I used to ponder why I could not succeed in getting into the I.C.S., if others like Sivaramakrishnan could do so. These occasional thoughts had one result. I began taking a greater interest in my studies. After the first one or two terms, I was easily topping the class in History and English. In the final examination of the first year, and in the Second year class examinations, I was heading the class. My answers were read out by some lecturers as the best and model answers, and my method of answering questions was appreciated. I began reading voraciously, borrowing from the libraries. I came to be sought after by all the good students in class. There were always a few of them with me when I went for my evening walks. I began to acquire confidence in myself.

During these two years there were some unhappy developments at home. My married sister had a year before developed an abscess in her breast, a month or two after she gave birth to a child. She suffered a good deal even after the abscess was lanced and cured. Her relations with her husband and his family were never very happy. She lived most of the time with us, sharing our hard lot. About the time of my final intermediate examination, she had an attack of some virulent type of fever. It might have been Typhoid or a severe type of influenza. We could not afford medical attention by doctors. She was treated most of the time by village *vaidyam*. During the recess before the examination, I went home and saw her in bed. We hoped that she would somehow recover. She was young and sturdy. But she had suffered in mind from her unhappy marriage and perhaps had not the will to live.

I was notified of her death on the day previous to my examination in Logic. This news upset me more than I thought it would. Life had been unkind to her. Married at the age of eleven, when she did not know what marriage meant, all her young life she had been unhappy. As she was only four years older than me, she was my friend and the companion of my childhood days. She was frank and open hearted, and took her misfortunes in her stride. She did not indulge in continuous moaning, as some would have done, but she went about her tasks cheerfully. She was fond of me and said often that her days of misery would end when I grew up and began to earn. I always promised her that I would make her happy when I started earning. The news of her death at the age of twenty-one, plunged me in grief and I could not answer my Logic examination well. I almost feared I would fail and all my dreams would be shattered.

I finished my examinations and came home. My parents were in great grief, as she was their firstborn. Our grief was aggravated by the conduct of my brother-in-law. As soon as her burial was over, he took possession of her motherless child—hardly two years old—and left for his village. All the importunities of my parents, and others who had come for the funeral, would not change his mind. He was always a stubborn person and he did not realize that he was denying the child the opportunity of living, by his rash action. In the absence of the mother, no-one would care for the infant orphan better than the maternal grandmother. The wretched child survived the mother about a year and a half, and with the death of the only issue left behind by my sister, all our contacts with her husband's home were severed. Neither my father nor I have visited that village since. One of the persons whom I wanted to make happy, into whose life I desired to bring a little cheer, denied me that opportunity—one less to whom I was bound by ties of blood and duty.

10

I Graduate

The summer vacation of 1923 was a period of anxiety. It began with my sister's death. I already had misgivings about my examination results. As I did indifferently in the Logic paper, I was not likely to get a First class. I had built some hopes on this First class. I wanted to study for the Honours examination, either in History or English Literature. Without a First class, admission might not be easy, and I might not get the necessary encouragement and monetary support. I was anxiously awaiting the results—I passed, but without a First class. I learnt however that my marks in English and History were quite impressive and, but for my poor performance in Logic and Tamil, I would have secured a First class. Several boys who appeared for the Inter examination that year with me did not make the grade, and so I was the recipient of many congratulations from the notables of the town.

I had, without consulting any outsiders, applied for admission to the History and Literature Honours courses, as well as to the Pass course. Only father knew that I had applied for admission to the Honours course. I had to approach my financial supporters very cautiously. There was great surprise when I mentioned to these gentlemen that I wanted to join the Honours course. Only 'B.A.'K. was sympathetic and wanted to know my reasons for preferring a three years' course to the ordinary two-year degree course. Even to him I was afraid of mentioning my secret ambitions. I explained that a pass degree would enable me at best to get a clerical job at Rs 40, and even clerical jobs in Government offices in Travancore and Madras were difficult to get, but an Honours degree, if it was a Second class even, would enable me to secure a College lecturer's job at Rs 100, and my prospects would be better still if I secured a First class. He agreed and promised to make more satisfactory arrangements for money. The contributions I got during the previous years were irregular, and on the whole, only about half of my minimum request came from this source, and on several occasions, I had to rush to father almost at the last minute. It was now decided at the K family council that money should be remitted to me at the rate of Rs 25 per month from their salt factory which was managed as common property by one of the brothers in rotation. For my initial expenses, for buying books etc., 'B.A.' K gave me Rs 50. This was the largest largesse I had received so far, and I regarded this as an earnest of his goodwill.

My original desire, when I joined College, was to study Law, so that I could combine the practice of law with politics. Gradually I had to give up this thought, in view of its risks. After having seen a few of my seniors in College competing successfully in the I.C.S. examination, I wanted to follow their example. I was also convinced that a good Honours degree was essential for this purpose.

When I joined College in June 1923, some of my professors who knew me well, were very pleased to see me in History Honours. The younger lecturers gave me considerable encouragement, and discussed my chances in the I.C.S. competition. However I kept my own counsel, and went about my studies quietly. I bought a few of the standard textbooks. Soon I realized that an Honours student was in a privileged position and could have the free run of the library, especially that portion of it set apart for Honours students. If he was favoured by the professors, he could take any book at any time. I thought in the circumstances I could do without textbooks and promptly sold the few books I had bought. During the three years of the course, I did not buy a single book and did not treat any single book as a textbook. I read extensively, and took notes.

In K's Bungalow in Trivandrum, where I stayed, a small colony of students had grown up. During my first year we were only two regular students. There was another gentleman, a distant relation of the

Ks, staying there. He must have been about 27 or so at the time, though he looked very much older. He had practically made studying for examinations a leisurely, but full-time, occupation. He had failed in the Intermediate examination about three or four times before I met him. He appeared for the examination with me also, and failed. However, he continued to write his examinations, but regarded himself as superior and senior to us. Several boys from Shencottah, who came to Trivandrum for higher education, obtained free lodging in the sheds and outhouses in the compound. In 1923, we were four, and soon the number became seven. There were three bare sheds which we shared between ourselves. We studied and slept there, living in the most unsanitary conditions. There were no bathrooms or closets, and the open compound, with its several shady trees, served all our purposes. Bathing was communal—drawing water from the well. However, our evenings and nights were spent pleasantly in conversation and political discussion. Some of us went for long walks to the Botanical Gardens in the evening, before going to the Hotel for the night meal. I formed several good friends who frequently came over to our place for talks.

During 1923–4 the Government decided to start a separate Arts College in Thaicaud, quite close to our residence, and the Senior Professor of History, K.V. Rangaswamy Aiyangar, was designated Principal. He left during the middle of the year to organize that college. There was a Training College for graduate teachers attached to it. Many of the History students had great respect for the Professor. He was a very learned man, and could talk for hours on any branch of History, Politics or Economics, to any class, without prior notice. He had occasionally walked into our intermediate classes during the absence of the lecturer, and lectured to us. It might be Pericles or the Magna Carta or Julius Caesar—it made no difference to him. He had a phenomenal memory for dates and facts, and a tremendous flow of language. During our first year in the Honours class, he did not take any regular classes for us, but occasionally he talked to us on some special topics. I came to know him rather well and felt sorry that he was leaving us.

The other Senior Professor was a man of a different type altogether. He was educated in England and had a sophisticated air about him—K.V.R. being the old-fashioned conservative brahman in dhotee and turban. Chandrasekhar (the other Professor) talked with what we then thought a refined accent, and his lectures were carefully prepared. He had not his senior colleague's versatility. I attended his lectures on English Constitutional History, which he delivered to the Pass course students. He had a sense of humour, would joke with students, and did not mind if a student gave an intelligent repartee. We had a textbook on Constitutional History, written by Miss Chambers, which he closely followed in his lectures. During one of his lectures, I was sitting at the back of the class, somewhat unusually, and the professor noticed my talking to the neighbours. He addressed a question to me, and being caught unawares, I fumbled. He then asked whether I had got my 'Chambers' with me, and quickly I replied that by mistake, I had left her behind in my chamber. The whole class burst into laughter, and I thought I was in for trouble. But joining the class in the laughter, he proceeded with his lecture good-humouredly. In view of his more liberal outlook and polished ways, and his reputation as a specialist in Political Science, I was equally attached to him.

Chandrasekharan expressed his unwillingness, if the Arts branches moved out to another College with K.V.R. as the Principal, to work under him in that College, and Government, appreciating this position and respecting both the professors for their different qualities, agreed to retain him in the old College (since named the Science College), as Professor of English. When I heard this I felt sorry. I would have K.V.R., but would lose Chandrasekharan. Before we went home for the summer holidays I had a long talk with Chandrasekharan, and received many valuable tips from him.

Though there were several boys from Shencottah in our residence, I did not form any intimate friendship with any one of them. During the second year, I persuaded my great friend Sankar to come and live with us. I spoke to 'B.A.' K, who kindly gave the permission. Sankar was my junior in school by one year, and passed the S.S.L.C. a year later. He did not however gain admission to the Maharaja's College, Trivandrum. He studied at the Scott Christian College, Nagercoil, and passed his Inter examination a year after I did, and he joined me in Trivandrum during the second year of my Honours course.

When he was in Nagercoil, I had occasion to visit him there. I was receiving my remittances from the salt factory at Thamarakulam. These remittances were seldom regular. Once when the managing brother was camping there, I decided to go and see him. Thamarakulam is about 10 or 12 miles away from Nagercoil. I went by bus to Nagercoil and spent an evening with my friend in his lodgings. As was usual with him, he had his food in a hotel, and lived in a small room in a neighbouring house. In the adjoining rooms, I saw, for the first time, the famous singer and actress, K.B. Sundarambal. She was only twelve or thirteen years of age, and looked even younger and smaller in her petticoat and jacket. She had already established a reputation as a rising stage star.

On the way from Nagercoil to Thamarakulam, I visited several places of historical and religious importance. My friend and I leisurely toured these places, discussing their history and mythology. We visited the famous Suchindram temple, and reached Cape Comorin by the evening. We bathed in the sea, saw the beautiful sunset, and visited the temple. The idol was decked beautifully for the evening worship. Its beauty, and the excellence of the make-up and the glittering jewellery, made a profound impression on me. I thought the idol looked more like a young girl than like a stone image. There were no electric lights inside or outside the temple. The place was illuminated by numerous tiny oil lamps. The *devadasi* system was very much in vogue and the procession idol was being taken round the temple corridors, with a party of *devadasis* dancing in the traditional style before the idol. There were several of them dressed in the orthodox style and they were dancing solo as well as in groups, with the attendant band of musicians swinging to their tunes behind.

We slept that night in the choultry and the next morning, we visited Thamarakulam. I accompanied the Boss to the salt pans. This was my first introduction to the salt industry with which, several years later, I came to be officially connected. After receiving my remittances, we returned to Nagercoil on foot and the next day, I returned to Trivandrum.

I continued to correspond with my friend, and during holidays, we were always together. Often he slept in our house and ate with us. Though, as a Saivite Vellala, he was of higher caste, he was a radical even as a boy, and had no scruples about distinctions of caste. I was therefore very happy to have one with whom I had so much in common to stay with me. We continued to argue, quarrel, and laugh together. He had quaint whims and peculiarities, and our other associates took him to be eccentric, and wondered how a normal and rational person like me could be so friendly with him. Sankar would bathe, but would not dry himself with a towel. He would wear his loincloth and go about, water dripping from his head all over. He would wear a shirt for going to class; otherwise, wherever he went, he would have only a small piece of cloth over his shoulders. He refused to wear a shirt, except for conformity during college hours. *Khaddar* had come into vogue, but in Travancore, it was not so popular with students. But Sankar took to *khaddar* from 1921, and did not change for a long time. He neither bought nor read a textbook. He kept a tuft of hair, as all of us did in those days, but his tuft was always unkempt. He shaved once a month. He loathed using a razor, though he had a liberal growth on his chin. He had several fads about food. Some vegetables he would not touch and others he ate in large quantities. His ways of eating aroused considerable mirth in the hotels, but our regular Hotel keeper knew him and his simplicity, and liked him. He was stubborn and unyielding in arguments. Very few students cared to have friendly discussions with him, as he took everything seriously, and his naivete was such that he believed sometimes what he was told even in fun. If later he found he was let down, he would not spare the person who had spoken to him light-heartedly. Once Sankar, myself, and a friend went out for a long walk. We thought we would go to the sea, but halfway there, I and the other friend got tired and wanted to return. But as we were afraid to tell

Sankar, we told a casual lie about not knowing the road. He insisted on our accompanying him, and physically dragged us along till we had no choice but to go with him.

Honours classes in those years were always small. In my class there were five boys and two girls. In the second year, a third girl joined as a postgraduate student. Contact between the boys and the girls was very limited. During the first year we hardly spoke to the girls. In the second year, things improved, and I was on talking terms with all the three girls. They were good students and in later life, distinguished themselves in different ways. One became a High Court judge—the first woman High Court judge. Another became a politician, and a third renounced the world to lead a life of meditation and service.

Among the boys, there was one bright student who had been with me in the Inter classes. Very hard working and methodical, he had a reputation for steadiness. He sought admission first to the English Literature Honours, and after discussion with the Professors, changed over to History. The Professor had told him that the History Honours course, as organized then, comprising History, Economics, and Politics, gave a good student better opportunities for liberal studies and a more satisfactory field of subjects for selection for the competitive examinations. It was therefore known to the students and the staff that he was an aspirant for the I.C.S. I did not encourage any such advance publicity. Before long, we were rivals for honours and there was a healthy competition between us. He was a fine lad and we were good friends, notwithstanding our keen rivalry. The other boys were mediocre and, except for one, did not leave any lasting impression on me. The exception was a simple likeable brahman boy from a village near Tirunelveli. He was also the son of a poor brahman and depended on some well-to-do uncle for support. Viraraghavan was lighthearted, fond of music, and took things always easy.

My best friend in College was a Brahman boy in the English Literature Honours class. In his batch, there were five girls, and he was the only boy. It must have been a strange experience for him. He came from a prosperous Brahman village, Monkompu, near Aleppey; he was the son of a pleader. Krishnan was tall, fair, and handsome. There was one unusual feature about him—a prominent fleshy lower lip. He had a long tuft of hair, almost as long as a girl's. He had an artistic and highly emotional temperament, and was fond of all the good things in life. He lived in private quarters near the main street of the town, with an uncle of his. We made our acquaintance early, in College, and became good friends. He was constantly with me in Thaicaud, and on holidays and in the evenings, we were inseparable companions. Sometimes the light-hearted classmate of mine, the boy from the Tirunelveli village, joined us. We used to be known as the inseparable Trio in student circles, as we were seen in College corridors, in the streets, and in Hotels. Viraraghavan sang, Krishnan talked, and I listened and criticised. That was the general set-up. As these two boys were Brahmans, inevitably, discussions arose about the caste system. I was a vehement critic, Krishnan often agreed with me, and Viraraghavan, though not orthodox, often supported the caste system. In spite of our heated arguments, we seldom quarrelled or came to personalities.

This kind of argument about caste was common among students. The society was caste-ridden, and in Trivandrum, there were everywhere evidences of Brahman superiority or favouritism in all walks of life. During my first year in Trivandrum, some of us went to the famous shrine of Padmanabha, the patron deity of the state. At the entrance, we removed our shirts, and tied our upper cloths round our waists. The priests who were guarding the gate asked us whether we were Brahmans, Malayalees, or Tamilians. When we replied that we were Tamilians, but not Brahmans, they wanted to know whether we followed *Makkathaayam* or *Marumakkathaayam* (inheritance by male line or matriarchal). Even after the questions were answered we were not allowed to go beyond a certain stage and we could not have a look at the sanctum. One amongst us was a Yadhava, and not of a particularly peaceful disposition. He asked the priest if his God did not incarnate as a Yadhava cowherd, and if such a God was worshipped in that shrine, why a Yadhava could not enter the temple. But argument was of no avail. We returned disgusted. Of course things improved in later years.

There was another temple, dedicated to Subramania, in the neighbourhood. We visited this temple occasionally. Admission was easier, but Non-Brahmans were not permitted to enter beyond a certain limit. From where we stood, we could, however, see the sanctum and the performance of the *pooja* by the priest. But what irritated us in this temple was that the priest would not give the prasad—the sandal paste or holy ash—in our hands. He would throw it on a stone and the non-Brahman devotees had to pick it up.

The place was a paradise for Brahmans. Attached to the big temple were great massive buildings known as *voothu purai*, or feeding shed. Brahmans were fed free here twice a day, and literally thousands of them—not all poor—were living on this free food. Many Brahman students received free food, obtained free lodging also, and were able to prosecute their studies. Large numbers of low-paid Brahman clerks, and numerous visitors and pilgrims, benefited in a similar manner.

In all eating-houses, there was an inner apartment exclusively for Brahmans, and an outer hall for all others. The Brahmans would walk through the outer Hall, but others dared not peep into their Hall. It was forbidden for others even to see Brahmans eating, as the food was supposed to get polluted by such unholy sight. Most people took these distinctions for granted, but in the wake of the national movement, some had begun to think rationally, and discontent was growing.

During my second year in the Honours class, we had two new Professors. One was Gopala Menon, who returned from England after taking a commerce degree in the London School of Economics; another was Tampi. He was a scion of the Royal family, and had spent seven years in England, studying for an Oxford degree and the Bar. Gopala Menon was Professor of Economics, and Tampi taught us Constitutional History and Politics. Both lived very close to our residence—Tampi was next door. I was frequently invited to their houses and I benefited from my close association with them. There was another Professor, Krishnamachari. He was an orthodox person, but an excellent teacher and conversationalist. He taught me Moghul History. He had a flair for story telling. He never delivered set lectures, but spoke in a conversational style, describing events like battles and court intrigues, as one would comment on a sports event. It was a pleasure to listen to him. Even in private conversation he was extremely interesting. Gradually I became the favourite of all my professors and was treated more like a friend than like a student. They encouraged me to read extensively, and guided me with sympathetic interest. Their rooms in the college, and their houses, were always open to me.

I became the first secretary of the History and Economics Association, and organized many lectures and group discussions. I wanted to become the Secretary of the College union, but my principal and all the professors dissuaded me from standing for election. I was annoyed at first, but they convinced me that as an Honours student and an aspirant for a First class, I should not fritter away my energies, and that as secretary of the college union, I would have little time left for serious study. Nevertheless I continued to take a certain interest in the affairs of the union, in addition to managing the History and Economics Association.

These activities brought me in contact with prominent citizens and I called on the Dewan of Travancore also, once. The Dewan commanded almost the same prestige that a Governor did in the Provinces. I was very thrilled when I saw him by appointment at his official residence, and my status among students went up from then. It was during this time, when I had earned a reputation for leadership among students, and a name as an outstanding student, that I met Viswanatha Iyer, the High School teacher of History, who had predicted an evil end for me. He was deputed for training in the Teachers College, before confirmation as a teacher. I met him in the corridor of his College, where I had been to see a Senior Professor. He certainly did not seem pleased to see his old pupil. Having heard of me, he was most anxious to avoid me. To a mutual acquaintance he mentioned that he was surprised I should have made so good in College.

Another event, of some importance locally, took place in 1924 or early '25. The old Maharaja was ill for a long time, and there was a general apprehension that he might die. As the next Prince in the line of succession was a young boy, there would have to be a period of regency, and as there were two Maharanees, there would be some contest for this honour. The Principal of our College was a personal friend of the old ruler, and held him in great esteem. He made a touching reference to him in class, and wished for his recovery. The poor old man died. Students in large numbers flocked to see the funeral procession, and for the first time, I saw the young prince, a boy of 12 at the time, clad only in a white loincloth, his body above the waist being uncovered. He was thin and short for his age, though quite handsome. His aunt, the senior Maharanee, was installed as the Regent by the suzerain power, and a new chapter in the History of Travancore was heralded.

The old Maharaja was an institution by himself. Orthodox and conservative, he believed in personal rule. In later years, he bowed to popular demand and instituted some constitutional reforms. But he was reputed to be well-informed, and all Heads of Department were to report to him directly, besides the Dewan. Nothing of any importance could take place without his personal approval. In his earlier days there were favourites and court intrigues, but in later years he functioned as a model ruler, and introduced many constitutional and administrative reforms in the state. Travancore enjoyed a reputation as a progressive native state, and the standard of literacy and higher education was of the highest amongst the states and Provinces of India. Naturally the demise of such a ruler was considered a great loss.

Among my activities in the History and Economics Association, I must mention two events. For the first time in the history of the College, I convened a mock Parliament, and the subject was 'the impeachment of Aurangzeb'. I took the story of Aurangzeb and made as valiant a defence of the Great Moghul as was possible. The session attracted considerable interest. Unfortunately I could not hold any more such sessions, as the strain involved was considerable. Another innovation for which I was responsible was speaking in Tamil. In the College unions and other associations, English was the only medium of speaking. We never had any one speaking to us in Tamil, and for students to have discussions in Tamil was unprecedented. Though there were several good speakers among the students, none dared speak in Tamil. I was myself not very proficient in Tamil, and my Tamil scholarship was limited. Under the auspices of the History Association, with Prof. Krishnamachari in the chair, I spoke in Tamil on Moghul heroines. During my term as Secretary, the Association did good work, and in my final year, when I could not carry on as Secretary, the enthusiasm flagged.

My friendship with Krishnan (the likeable English Honours student) involved me in a peculiar situation. Romantic as he was, he imagined himself to be in love with one of his girl classmates. She was a tall, well-built, good-looking girl, by name Chellammal, from a non-Brahman family of Nagercoil. She was considered the beauty Queen of the college, even in that land of good-looking girls. I did not know whether she reciprocated Krishnan's attentions in the beginning. He was often composing sonnets and poems, and after a year of romantic imagining, began to lose interest in his studies. His distraction became noticeable, and he confided to me that he was madly in love with that girl, and would marry her in spite of his parents' orthodoxy. He began meeting her outside college also, occasionally, and had long conversations with her. My impression was that the girl did not take him seriously and was perhaps only amused and flattered by his lovelorn-ness. His uncle was very worried and the task of weaning the boy out of his calf-love was inevitably entrusted to me, as the only person who had any influence over him. We had long conversations on the subject, and for days together, we were discussing romantic love and the realities of practical life. I spent several nights in his room without going to our place. I thought I was doing a good service by reforming my friend, and succeeded ultimately in his agreeing to marry a girl selected by his parents. During the holidays, he was married to a brahman girl, and so the problem of his love and marriage was settled practically.

At home my younger sister (my only sister now) became a big girl, and was staying indoors. She was never sent to school. The thought of her remaining unlettered did not please me at all. I was so full of idealism and of a sense of duty that I thought my education was wasted on me if I did not bring a little culture and enlightenment into my family. During the holidays I took up the task of teaching her the Tamil alphabets. I did it in the traditional style, in the manner in which I learnt it in the village school. Using sand and the finger, and then slate and pencil, I taught her the alphabet and the numerals. During the long summer holidays, I devoted several hours every day to teaching her to read simple books, and by the end of a year, she was able to read Tamil magazines and storybooks. She did not practice much writing, and so could not write as well as she read. However, I opened the doors of learning for her, and left it to her to improve her education. I also took great pains to explain to my parents events that were happening in the outside world, and made them more knowledgeable. Since they were not able to read books or newspapers, their knowledge was confined to the limited requirements of the small peasantry. I thought again that it was my duty to transmit a part of my knowledge to those nearest and dearest to me, in this manner.

It also became my responsibility to look out for a suitable bridegroom for my sister. I wanted an educated person to be my brother-in-law. There was only one other boy in our community who was studying in College. I knew him when I was in Ambasamudram. He studied in Tinnevelly for his intermediate, and would have continued there for his degree examination also. I invited the boy to visit us during the summer holidays and persuaded him to come over to Trivandrum for his B.A. studies, and made arrangements for his lodging with us in our extensive sheds. He was perhaps a year older than me, but of bigger build. His father was an associate of the premier *naadaswaram Vidwan* of our district, in whose house I had boarded for a few months in Ambasamudram as a Fourth Form student. At that time, he was my junior in school, and he finished his intermediate also after I did. He was very happy to be taken notice of by me, and his father too agreed to my proposal that he should stay with me.

In Trivandrum, in the sheds of K's Bungalow, we were six students, belonging to different communities, but we lived like a family. All of us messed in the same hotel, to which we used to go in a batch, and in our spare time in our rooms, we amused ourselves without any discord. We used the buckets near the well for drawing water in turn for our communal bathing, and there was a general air of gaiety and frivolity, associated with all young boys.

Almost within a month of his coming, the young lad, Sundaraswamy, began to act as if he was of superior social status, and frequently passed disparaging remarks about our easy communal ways. There were amongst us at least two boys from fairly rich families, and they did not like his ways. In that atmosphere of easy friendly camaraderie, he became a misfit and I was the first to take him to task, though he was my protégé then. He did not hesitate to scold me. My friend Sankar, with his scholarly but eccentric ways, could not understand this lad. Occasionally we boys used to cook some delicacy ourselves on a holiday, picnic-fashion. Frying plantains or ripe jackfruit was our speciality. We gathered firewood from the trees, made a fire, and did all the work ourselves. This lad, on one occasion, sat on a window-sill near the picnic kitchen and solemnly declared that he had never done such work in his house, and could not understand how we managed to do all this manual work. We took turns in cleaning our rooms and keeping the place tidy, but he would not give a helping hand. In the hotel where we were messing, he became unpopular with the hotel staff for similar conduct. I began teasing him, and in the end I drove him out of our compound. He was easily the vainest and most unsociable young man I had met in school or college. With all my eagerness to help him for personal reasons, I could not tolerate his presence. Thus ended my first attempt to find an educated bridegroom for my sister. My parents were not surprised that I found this young man so unsatisfactory, for it seems he had a bad reputation already, and his parents were also an equally unfriendly lot.

Thereafter the family council met and decided that the nephew of the famous *naadaswaram Vidwan* would be a suitable person. He had no English education, but he was of suitable age and social status, and he was practically regarded as the adopted son of the gentleman who, in spite of his three wives, had only four daughters and no son. When I was in Ambasamudram, he had had two wives, of whom one was related to us. She had four girls, and the old gentleman, egged on by some relations, had married a young girl a few years before in the hope of getting male issue. Till 1924 she too had no issue. Just about this time, his nephew was looking after his household affairs. During one of my holidays, I heard that this husband of three wives had had a stroke of paralysis, and was bedridden. My parents had already seen him and I also wanted to see him, as I knew him so well. His wife, the mother of the four girls, had died a couple of years earlier, but the other two wives lived with him. My parents advised me to see the nephew also and negotiate for his marriage with my sister.

I paid two or three visits to their village (Sundarapandyapuram), and on each occasion, stayed for a week or more. My presence was a great consolation to the sick man, and I also introduced a Muslim quack *vaidyar* to try some oils and herbal remedies. The patient made slow progress and was for some time able to sit up with help on the charpoy and hobble about with someone to lean on. During one of those visits, a niece of the patient, living in the house opposite, a girl of fifteen, took a lot of interest in me and did various small acts of service, in a manner not usual with village girls in her sphere. My friend, the Muslim *vaidyar*, and a few others, ragged me on her account. I took all this in good sport. However, the wives of the patient and his grown-up daughters behaved rather strangely, and treated me with cold indifference. Except for the patient's insistence, I could not have stayed there at all. I had my books and notebooks, and in the quiet of the village, continued my studies, when not attending to the patient or settling the details of the negotiations.

Eventually my sister was married to this young man. The wedding ceremony took place in Sundarapandyapuram itself, as the patient wanted to witness the happy event himself, and the bridegroom was his favourite nephew, in addition to being his assistant. From the K family, the eldest gentleman alone came as a distinguished guest to honour us. The wedding cost father a good deal more than he could afford at the time, and he incurred a debt of Rs 1000. My sister went to live with her husband soon after, and with my job done, I went back to Trivandrum for the final year of my studies.

My friend Krishnan was also married by that time, and his personal problems ceased to distract me. The lad from Ambasamudram, having been boycotted by us, and having lost interest in us with my sister's marriage, left our college and joined another college elsewhere to continue his studies. My good friend Sankar alone was my boon companion, though I continued to spend several evenings with Krishnan, and the happy-go-lucky Viraraghavan.

Sankar was by now concentrating on his unaided and unguided researches in Mathematics. He had been reading Higher Mathematics and had been attracted by the Theory of Numbers. He had studied some of the problems in the field and had begun working on his own on a few unsolved aspects of these. He would sit in contemplation for hours, occasionally scribbling on sheets of notepaper, and sometimes he would scribble mathematical notations on his own dhotee and upper cloth. Though he took little interest in the textbooks and did indifferently in college examinations, his Professor—a very enlightened man, R. Srinivasan—withstood his gifted pupil's peculiarities. He asked him often to his room and encouraged him. Though not a brilliant mathematician, he was interested in developing the latent potentialities in his pupil. He was however not able to guide him in the details of his work, owing to his lack of research experience, but he gave him books and magazines. Sankar had decided by then that he must dedicate his life to the study of Mathematics and to begin with, he wanted to do research with proper guidance. He tried to interest me in his work and took great pains to explain what he was trying to do, but my basic knowledge being inadequate, my understanding was limited. However, it gave me great pleasure to see my friend and companion for several years, chalking out a future for himself in the realm of pure science.

I had no doubt at that time that he would one day become a celebrated Mathematician. Though most of our contemporaries scoffed at him for his unworldly ideas, and thought poorly of a person who had no desire to make a living as a clerk or a teacher, I always stood by him. In fact even at that time, when I had distinguished myself as a successful student, I was scoffed at because I could be nothing but a teacher, even with my Honours degree. The glamour of petty Government service was so much that those who sought other careers were looked down upon.

About the middle of my final year, I sheared my long tuft of hair and appeared in class with closely-cropped hair. I was met with thumping of desks and catcalls by the students. In my own class of five boys, only one had cropped hair—and he was a Christian. The Hindu boys kept their tufts. The proportion of cropped heads among Hindu boys in the college was about 5%. What was peculiar about my action, as it struck my fellow-students, was that I should have cropped my hair in the middle of the year. They thought it was one of the preliminary steps for equipping myself for the I.C.S. Even the girls, who were now on talking terms, joked about this, and several of my friends began teasing me. Even the Professors noticed this sudden change, and could not suppress their smiles. My rival also soon followed suit.

Having limited my extraneous diversions, I concentrated on my studies and relaxed only on the eve of the examination. I read about 14 to 15 hours a day, for nearly 5 months. I had one difficulty. I could not keep awake at night for long. Beginning my reading at

8.30, after the night meal in the hotel, I would nod my head in sleep uncontrollably, and I adopted several stratagems to keep awake. For nearly half an hour, I battled with sleep, and then carried on comfortably for an hour or two. My falling off to sleep with a book in my hand, even as early as 9 o'clock, excited considerable amusement among my friends. They kept awake easily up to eleven or twelve p.m. In the earlier months of the year, I succumbed to sleep, but read for two or three hours in the mornings before getting ready for College. But during the last three or four months of the year, I required more reading during the night hours. In spite of all my efforts, I could not get over the tendency to fall asleep at 9 or 9.30, much to the amusement of my room-mates.

One night I retired to an empty room and spreading my mat and pillow, started reading with a candle light near the pillow, as the hurricane light was being used in the other room by my friends. I must have slept off, and suddenly woke up at 11 o'clock to find sparks of fire flying all over the room. My pillow was half burnt, and the cotton inside, being released by the burning of the cover cloth, was flying about. A portion of the mat was also burnt. I ran out, shouting to my friends, who brought water in buckets to put out the fire. The hair on my head was smelling of smoke. My friends teased me a lot and I decided thereafter that I would read only sitting at a table, and made courageous attempts to get over my 9 o'clock sleepiness. But at no time did I sit up after 11 p.m., and as the examination drew near, I closed up my reading by 10.30 and slept more at night, so that I was fresh and active during the day.

The girls of my class often asked me to help them out in their preparation for the examination. Miss Saradamma was the cleverest of the lot, and she asked for my advice occasionally on one or two subjects. Miss Anna Jacob, the lady who afterwards became a High Court judge, borrowed notes. Both of them invited me to their houses, a concession never normally extended to boy students in those days. Miss Mary Mascarenhas, the postgraduate student and future politician, was not as good as the others in studies. She lived in a private hostel for women students in our neighbourhood, and implored me to give her at least half an hour's talk every morning. I did this for several weeks, and left with her all the essays on political and historical subjects I had written in class. As the examination drew near, she was increasingly nervous, and I could not refuse the little help she asked from me.

My competitor in class was, I heard, already cracking up. Even on the first day of the examination, he was nervous and he told me later that he had not answered well. On the day we had had the paper on Public Finance, he entered the Examination Hall 25 minutes late. He seat was just behind mine, and almost with tears in his eyes, he implored me to help him. I mumbled my answers as I wrote them, much to the annoyance of the good lady who was the invigilator in the Hall. I do not know whether he benefited from my slow mumbling, but he persisted in whispering to me to help him.

The examination was over, and with that, five years of life in Trivandrum. My professors expected me to get a First class, and I too was quite hopeful.

I came home heaving a sigh of relief. Father was not at home, as he had gone out of town in connection with some work. He had ordered a bench to be made, and the carpenter delivered it at the house on the day I reached home. He wanted Rs 7 as his wages for carpentry. Mother said that father had offered only Rs 6, but the carpenter would not agree to this, and so there was no harm in paying him off. I paid the carpenter Rs 7 out of the money left with mother. Father returned the next day, and noticing the bench outside, asked mother what she paid the carpenter as wages. When he heard mother's reply, that she had paid Rs 7, he flew into a temper, and one of the worst domestic scenes that I had witnessed ensued. I felt very sad and irritated and frustrated. Father did not even ask me how I had fared in my examination. I really expected him to express his relief and pleasure at the termination of my period of studies, and to congratulate me on my satisfactory performance in the examination. I was no longer a little boy. I was twenty-one, and would soon be a respectable citizen. The sort of domestic scene I had just witnessed was not exactly the kind of reception I had hoped for. I expressed my grief and sense of frustration to father after he quietened down. I could understand his state of mind. He knew the value of money, having earned every pie the hard way. He was economical, as any one would be in his circumstances, and he must have been thinking about how to beat the carpenter down, and perhaps if he had settled the bill, he would have saved a rupee. His chagrin at the loss irritated him, and in his fit of temper, nothing else was seen or felt by him. With this homecoming began the next phase of my life.

11

Searching for Employment: Madura

The summer holidays of 1926 were soon over for me. I paid a visit to my sister's place. A small incident indicated a change in attitude on the part of some of my brother-in-law's cousins. As my sister's house was small, I used to sleep in the upstairs room of a house that belonged to my brother-in-law's rich uncle. During this visit, his daughters refused me the key of that place, and I had to shift for myself elsewhere. The birth of a small boy to the third wife of the sick man, on the day of my sister's marriage, perhaps caused the change. There was a slow estrangement between the wives (two surviving), and the children were also taking sides.

In spite of my good performance in the examination and my hope of a First class, this was a period of anxiety. I was no longer a student, and it was imperative that I begin to earn soon and help the family. Father was still in service with the K family, and his independent nature and tendency to short temper did not make him feel happy in his position. I began seriously thinking of a choice of career.

My ultimate aim was Superior Civil Service through competitive examination. This would involve waiting for a minimum of at least a year, and I could not afford to be jobless that long, whatever may be the demands on my time for preparing for the competitive examination. The only profession that would give me some income, in addition to facilities for the preparation for the examination, was a College lectureship in a major town. Even before my results were officially published, I wrote applications to a few Colleges, offering my services. I mentioned in the application that I hoped to get a First class in my Honours examination, and to demonstrate my confidence, I gave my examination number also in the application. As soon as the results appeared, I received a call, from the Principal of a college in Madura, for a personal interview. He was impressed by my self-confidence and had noticed the First class against the number given in my application.

There were three First classes in History Honours that year, but only one (myself) from our College. My competitor got only a low Second class, but Saradamma, the girl student, got a higher Second class. All my other classmates got only Third classes. In Literature Honours, all my contemporaries, including my friend Krishnan and his girlfriend, got only Third classes. The Professors of my College were very pleased with my success, for a First class had come from the College after several years. I received several letters and telegrams from my friends and the professors.

Several people in Shencottah who took little notice of me in the past were surprised at my academic success, and my stock went up. 'B.A.' K offered to get me a clerical job in the Travancore Government, but I declined. Even to him I did not disclose my plans fully at that stage, but only said that I wanted a College teaching job. It was only a little later that I disclosed to him my idea of writing the I.C.S. examination. He was not very enthusiastic, though he did not discourage me. Even he did not think that merit alone could help a man get into the I.C.S. He thought that financial status and various other factors also counted. His brothers and other relations were frankly sceptical about my plans. One of them quoted a Tamil proverb which meant, a pheasant, however high it might fly, will not become a skylark. I kept my counsel and did not discuss matters frankly with anyone except Sankar, my Mathematician friend.

I went to Madura to be interviewed by the Principal. He was a Brahman gentleman with considerable experience, having served in the Pachaiyappa's College, Madras. It was the first time I had travelled beyond Tirunelveli on this Railway line, and so Madura was the first big Railway station I had seen so far. After tidying myself at the Railway station, where I also had my food, I met the Principal. He was impressed by my academic record and by my conversation, and straightaway gave me the order of appointment. I was to be a Lecturer in History, to take both Inter and B.A. classes. My salary was nominally Rs 100, but I would be paid only Rs 80. I had no option but to accept the appointment, as I needed one badly. I thought that it would be risky to decline this and look for a better-paid job in another College, though I had had a call from another College—Alwaye in Travancore. Madura appeared to be a more suitable place for my purpose, and communications were easy, as it was on the main Railway line to Madras.

I returned to Shencottah with an appointment secure in my hands. A visit to Trivandrum was necessary, as I had to procure testimonials from my professors, and make arrangements for my I.C.S. application. The application was to be sent through the British Resident in Travancore, as I was a state subject, and a certificate of age had to be signed by the Resident. Completing all these arrangements, I returned to Madura to take up my first appointment, about the end of June 1926.

I had no clothes for my role as a lecturer. It was the custom for young lecturers to be dressed in the English style. I had to procure shoes, socks, and ties, things I had never known before. All this required a cash outlay. I arrived in Madura with less than Rs 30 in my pocket, borrowed by father specially for the purpose. The Principal allowed me to appear in class wearing a dhotee only for two or three days, provided I had a coat and tie or bow. Within a few days, I was able to get together my minimum sartorial equipment.

The other problem that confronted me was accommodation. I spent the first night in the Third class waiting room at the Railway station. This was not so crowded as it is nowadays. Some of the better eating-houses had rooms to let, and in the Bazaar and in some streets, rooms were available for rent. It would have been convenient if I could secure a room in an eating-house, for then both boarding and lodging would be together. The eating-houses run by Brahmans would not take non-Brahmans as lodgers. Similarly, rooms in the Brahman quarters were also not available. After considerable wandering, I found a decent room in a non-Brahman locality. It was already occupied by an Indian Christian from Madras, who was employed in the Postal Department. I shared the room with him, and he introduced me to the eating-place patronized by him. This was run by an elderly non-Brahman lady.

Having settled my boarding and lodging satisfactorily, I was able to devote my attention to my work. I discussed with the Principal the College lecturing arrangement, and desired that I be given such subjects as would facilitate my preparations for the I.C.S. examination. I did tell him even at the first interview that I intended taking the I.C.S. exam in December 1926, and he did not raise any objection. But now he was reluctant to help me in the choice of subjects I should teach. I did not press the matter, as I thought that I would be able to manage, since my knowledge of the I.C.S. subjects I had chosen was fairly good.

Within a week of my joining this College, the Principal sent for me to ascertain how I was getting on with my work. He asked me about my boarding and lodging arrangements. When I mentioned where I was staying, he expressed surprise that I should be staying in that locality. I told him that I could not get suitable accommodation elsewhere. He asked me whether I was not a Brahman, and was thoroughly amazed when I said I was not. I then understood the meaning of his previous question. He appeared however to be nice about it, and tried to remove any impression that I might have formed about the communal aspect of his question. He confessed that he never suspected I would turn out to be a non-Brahman. My academic record, my self-assurance, and my style of talking both English and Tamil, led him to believe that I was a Brahman. Honours graduates, and especially First class men, were rare among non-Brahmans. The College Council consisted of Brahman lawyers and landlords, and the staff had always been Brahmans. He advised me not to disclose my non-Brahman origin to everyone, and cautioned me that I need not call on the President or Secretary of the College Council.

This conversation perplexed me a good deal. I knew that non-Brahmans had not made much progress in Education, but to presume that a person must be a Brahman because he had a good academic record, was an indication of the Brahmans' conceit and their superiority complex. I did not form many friends among the members of the staff. Some of them probably knew that I was not one of the heaven-born tribe.

There was one brahman young man—a Vaishnavite from Madras, who became friendly with me. He was orthodox like the others, but was cultured and broadminded enough to treat me on a footing of absolute equality. He invited me soon afterwards to share his room with him in the College Hostel itself. So within a month or six weeks of my arrival in Madura, I left my Christian friend and his old lady, and took up boarding and lodging in the College Hostel. I was not very keen on non-vegetarian food. I had not been eating fish or chicken for several years, and even mutton I ate occasionally and sparingly. I therefore preferred the Brahman vegetarian food in the hostel.

My application for the I.C.S. examination had been routed to the Madras Government by the Resident. The procedure was that the Madras Government arranged for the medical examination and after being medically certified, names were recommended by the Madras Government to the Public Services Commission for admission to the examination which was at that time held only in Delhi in November–December. I was expecting a call from the Madras Government for the medical examination. In the application form and subsequent correspondence, the College address was given, and so I expected the letter to be delivered to the College.

In August there were six holidays consecutively. My friend, the Madras Ayangar, and I were coming to the College every evening to collect our letters from the clerk or darwan who was on duty. Almost every day, either my friend or I had some letters. After the holidays, on a Wednesday it was, I was lecturing to a class, when the Principal's peon delivered a long heavy postal envelope to me. I immediately opened it—to find the Madras Government's letter, asking me to appear for a medical examination at 9 a.m. that very morning. On verifying the postmark, I noticed that the letter had been delivered to the College on the Thursday previous, i.e., the first of the six consecutive non-working days we had had. I was thoroughly nonplussed and could not continue my lecture. Leaving the class, I came to the Principal and told him that great misfortune had befallen me, and that by the late delivery of the letter, I had forfeited my chance of appearing for the I.C.S. examination in December 1926. I asked the Principal how it was that this letter alone had been kept back from me, while almost every day, I had been given my other personal letters. Very coolly, the Principal answered that he himself had noticed this particular envelope on Thursday, and thinking that it might be important, had it locked up.

I had met the Principal several times in the hostel and in the College during those six days, and he did not mention that there was a service postal letter for me. I suspected mischief and felt that the Principal had deliberately suppressed the letter, perhaps after clandestinely reading its contents. I showed my annoyance in unmistakable terms, and said that it was none of his business to distinguish between my important and unimportant letters and that there was no justification for keeping only this letter back. He neither expressed his regret nor tried further justification, except to repeat that he did it in the interest of the safety of the letter.

It was the bitterest experience of my life, and for days together, I was without cheer. The one great hope of my life, which had sustained me through years of hardship, suffering, and humiliation, was shattered. There was no good friend or relation to whom I could turn for solace or advice. I could not write to my father as he would have to turn my long letter over to someone else to read and reply, if my sister was not at home. I nursed my grief and disappointment in solitude for several days. I then regained part of my cheer, as I reassured myself that I was still young and could take a chance the next year, or even the year after. I could have gone straight to Madras and met some high official who might, in the circumstances, have arranged for my medical examination. But I was far too inexperienced and had no influential friends. Even the idea did not strike me then—as I was a backward boy from a backward area.

I began taking some interest in my classes, having set aside intensive preparation for the examination. In my History classes occasionally, I used to question the students, either before the commencement of the lecture or after the end, for a few minutes. I found this useful as a means of getting to know the students better. In the junior Inter British History class, after the lecture one morning, I put a question to a student in the first row. The desks were arranged on either side of a central passage. Having begun the question with a student on one side of the passage, on the front row, I continued questioning the other students on the rear rows on that side. Just by accident, I ignored the other side of the class altogether. It so happened that all the students in the two or three rows failed to answer the questions. I dismissed the class when the bell rang, but asked all those students who had failed to answer to look up their books and bring their answers written up for the next class. Several students complied with this, but about 6 or 8 students did not. I asked them to write out their answers twice before the next class, and continued with the lecture.

Asking students to write answers to questions more than once in this manner was known as imposition, and was regarded as a punishment. This was not generally resorted to by Professors, except in dealing with recalcitrant students. I apprehended that these particular students were trying to defy me, and that was the reason for the imposition.

The next day too, these students did not carry out the imposition. I ordered them out of the class and further told them that I was not marking their attendance for that period, till they complied with the imposition. They were also told that the imposition was doubled. The defiance went on from Monday to Friday of a whole week. On Friday, only one student persisted in his defiance; the other five or six boys submitted their imposition, which was by now eight times over, and were admitted to the class.

I expressed my displeasure at the conduct of the recalcitrant students, and explained the value of discipline as an important factor in education. The one defying student was still outside the class, in the verandah. Some of his friends asked me whether I would have any objection if some of them went out and wrote the imposition for that boy, and whether I would admit the boy to the class in that event. Though it would have been proper to insist on the offender doing his imposition, I did not object to this offer from his friends, and permitted four students to leave the class to complete the task. They returned with the offender after a few minutes, with the imposition completely written up. After a brief moralizing, I resumed my usual lecture. I felt there was strong resentment among a section of students, but ignoring their angry looks, I left the class when the time was up. It was the last hour of the working day, and so I walked out straight to my room in the hostel.

The sequel to this I heard later that night in the hostel, when the Principal dropped in to see another lecturer. When I left the class, the students stood up at their seats as usual, and the moment I was out on the verandah, the offender among the students shouted some abuse at me, calling me 'sudra fellow', and threatened that I would be taught a lesson for treating college students in the way I did. I mentioned earlier that there were rows of desks on either side of a central passage, and that I questioned students sitting on one side of this passage. I did not know then that there was a deliberate communal division of students. On the questioned side, there were only Brahmans. On the other side were the others. I was not aware of this and it was just accident that I had questioned one side instead of taking the desks length-wise across the class. The Brahman students perhaps thought that I deliberately punished only one side. When I was abused with reference to my caste, the other students got offended, and their leader struck a blow on the cheek of the offender. A fierce fight ensued for a few minutes, the brahmans were vanquished, and all the students ran out when they saw the Principal coming towards them, attracted by the noise.

The Principal obtained details of the incident from a few students whom he detained for questioning. However, he wisely refrained from taking disciplinary action or holding a formal inquiry. The incident however proved an eye-opener to him, as it brought to light the communal tension among the students. While relating this incident to my fellow-lecturer, the Principal did not find any fault with me. On the contrary, he appreciated my sense of discipline, while regretting the final outcome. Among the staff of the College, this incident produced some impression, and thereafter some of them treated me with a marked deference, slightly tinged with coolness. I did not know what the Principal's real impression was. Though he did not discuss this incident with me thereafter, I had a feeling that he was not very happy about my presence in that College. In course of time, I was not left in any doubt about this.

When I went home for the Xmas holidays, some of the K family members asked me whether I had written the I.C.S. examination. I did not like to tell them about the incident of the delayed delivery of the letter. Even if I told them, they might not have believed it. I simply said that I did not appear for the medical examination, and so I could not take the I.C.S. examination. Some of them immediately jumped to the conclusion that I had some unmentionable disease, perhaps venereal disease, and that therefore I was afraid of the medical examination. One of them openly suggested this to my face. I did not care to offer any explanation. The extent of jealousy among some people leads them to unlimited pleasure at another person's discomfiture.

My parents wanted to take advantage of my stay in Madura to visit the Holy City and to pay a visit to Ramesvaram. I engaged a couple of rooms in the house of a friend, an employee in the Revenue Office, and shifted there from the Hostel. I took my parents, sister, and brother-in-law to the Holy places, and after their departure, continued to live in these rooms. I had my food in a hotel, and for some time, my mother's aunt came over to keep house for me.

Thus nine months of my stay in Madura came to a close. I gained some experience in lecturing, and considerable insight into the social life of our people. It was a period of mental adjustment for me. In spite of my suffering from the prejudices of Brahmans, I continued to be a robust nationalist. There was a Justice Party ministry in power in Madras, but the Congress movement was gaining in strength and popularity. I heard lectures by the Raja of Panagal, the then Chief Minister of Madras, and E.V.R. I heard Satyamurthi and Annie Besant, and attended some Congress public meetings. My non-Brahman friends were annoyed that I continued to be ultra-nationalistic in my outlook and views, and not embittered by communal politics.

12

Some More Job-Hunting: History Repeats Itself in Trichy

During my nine months in Madura, several of my friends impressed on me that I should try for suitable Government appointments. The position of a junior lecturer in a private college was no good career for a person with academic distinctions. Pay was unattractive and prospects depended on several factors, the least important being your merit. Unless one became a Chief Lecturer or Professor, one could not hope to see more than Rs 250 a month. The position of a Professor could not be reached before you were at least forty years old.

The appointments which were popular at the time were those in the Revenue Department. Graduates considered themselves lucky to enter as Revenue clerks, even in Deputy Collectors' offices. To be directly recruited as a Revenue Inspector was even luckier. There were some vacancies of Revenue Inspectors in the Collectorate of Ramnad, which had its Headquarters' offices in Madura. The initial pay of the post was only Rs 50. I was persuaded to apply for this by some of my friends, much against my will, some time after August. As I was then in a despondent mood, I thought no harm was done in applying.

I was called for interview along with seventeen others applicants, and I presented myself before the Collector. He was an Indian I.C.S. officer, who rose to considerable height in service later. All my fellow applicants were sure that I would be selected, in view of my high academic record. The Collector spoke to me for a longer period than was usual, but I gathered the impression that he thought I was too good for the job. I was not selected. My friends thought that my non-selection was due to my lack of influential support. Honestly, I did not think so, and I felt that the Collector did not like to blight my future by offering me a small job.

Soon afterwards there was a recruitment for the post of Deputy Tahsildar. There were three vacancies in the Province, and the recruitment was done by a Staff Selection Committee, which was the precursor of the Public Service Commission. The starting salary of the post was Rs 150, and there was a three-year training period. A good officer could reasonably hope to become a Deputy Collector in about 10 years' time, and may with luck rise to a higher position. This was one of the best appointments in the State for young graduates, and I applied for this selection.

Several months later I was called for interview. There were about twenty candidates called for the selection. All of them were lined up in a Hall, in the presence of a Board of three officers of whom two were European I.C.S. officers. All those who were members of the University Training Corps were asked to step two steps forward. This training scheme had been introduced only a few years previously, and I had not the benefit of it, as it was not introduced in Travancore. There were several applicants who were not members of the U.T.C. The U.T.C. men were briefly questioned about their educational qualifications, and their certificates were cursorily examined. The interrogation of the others followed thereafter. The entire interviewing was over within half an hour. The candidates were not individually interviewed. No attempt was made to make an intelligent assessment of their capacities and talents.

It struck me at that time that this selection hardly differed from that adopted for the selection of Police Constables. I thought the Board would be impressed with my academic record. I was the only Honours graduate, and a First class, medallist, and Prize-winner at that. All the others were ordinary graduates. The Commission did not show any interest in my educational qualifications. When I left the Hall, I felt very disappointed, though I still had faint hopes of selection. There was a Justice ministry in power then, and there were loud professions of encouraging the Backward Classes. Though I did not seek any preferences on this ground, for an appointment of this category, merit should have counted. The method of selection I saw did not appear to be designed to assess merit. I began to agree with the worldly-wise people that these selections were mere window-dressing, and that actual appointments were fixed up otherwise, on other considerations.

Towards the summer of 1927, there was an announcement by the Madras Government that two scholarships would be awarded on the basis of merit, for young Honours graduates, for studies in the U.K. I had heard of one or two First class Honours graduates in recent years who had gone to England on these scholarships, and who eventually entered the I.C.S. I applied for these scholarships, and was hopeful that here at least, at the higher level of Government, a First class Honours graduate, from a very backward community, would receive encouragement.

The application was addressed to the Director of Public Institutions. It was suggested to me that if I saw the Chief Minister, I might have some chance of my application being considered on its merits. I sought the help of a gentleman belonging to our Community, who was in the legislature. This gentleman became a politician, and later became a minister. He, along with one or two others, saw the Chief Minister, and also arranged for my interview. Dr Subbarayan was the new Chief Minister. After several years, the Justice Party was unable to form a Ministry under Dyarchy, and Dr Subbarayan, an Independent, formed the Ministry, with the active support of the Congressmen, who were then averse to taking office.

I had a very pleasant fifteen-minute talk with him. I was thrilled, because for the first time in my life, I was meeting the highest political official of the Presidency. Dr Subbarayan came to his high office at a comparatively early age, on the crest of an immense wave of popularity. His freedom from previous entanglement in party politics, his high education, and reputation as a social reformer, made people expect big things from him. I did not, however, get the scholarship, but I do not blame him for this. There must have been various influences at work, and perhaps a better man got the coveted scholarship.

An amusing incident took place while I was waiting outside his room in the Fort St George. A young man came out of his room, walking with springing steps, with an envelope in his hand. He gave the slip of paper which was inside the envelope to me, and asked me to read and translate it for him. I was amazed, for this was a testimonial given by the big man to this young man, who was apparently his chauffeur. After extolling his skill and smartness, the certificate wound up with a sentence somewhat as follows: 'can be trusted with anything except where women are concerned'. I hesitated to translate this, but the man had read it himself. His knowledge of English was sketchy, and he wanted to make sure of the meaning from someone who knew English better. When I gave him the translation, I saw him walk back into the room unhesitatingly. I saw him come back with a twinkle in his eyes. Perhaps he had now got a better chit. This gave me my first insight into some aspects of high life that I was not familiar with.

The summer of 1927 was a period of frustration. My position as lecturer in the Madura College would terminate soon. I was unsuccessful in getting a better job in Government service. Unless I secured a college teaching job, there was no hope of my being able to take the I.C.S. competition. In fact it was necessary for me to have a job, for I could not afford to be unemployed. During the previous eleven months, I had been living on less than Rs 35 per month, and I had been remitting Rs 40 to Rs 50 to my father. All my boarding and lodging, clothing and incidentals, I had to meet within this, as father insisted on my giving him at least half my salary. I decided to go to Madras about the middle of June, to look out for a job. It was during this visit, I think, that I saw the Chief Minister.

My friend Sankar was now in Madras, and I shared his room. His company and advice were always welcome to me. He passed his B.A. exam in 1926, but did not get a First class in Mathematics. He was never one for examinations, and cared very little for textbook studies. Even during his college days, he was working on certain mathematical problems without guidance, and had secured some commendable results. His Professor, Mr Srinivasan, knew this, and though not a research worker himself, he recognized in this obscure and eccentric young man great talent. He suggested his applying to the Madras University for a research studentship. The university awarded this studentship only to First class M.A.s or Honours graduates, but Sankar went and formally saw all the Professors who constituted the Board of Studies in Mathematics, and impressed them by his sincerity and learning. He was offered the studentship and began his research studies in the University. He had no other ambition but Mathematics, and was quite happy that he had the chance to develop his genius in its special field. Staying with him in his humble lodgings, I began my search for a job.

I was informed by a friend that there were vacancies in the National College, Trichy, the Sri Meenakshi College, Chidambaram, and the Theosophical College, Madanapalle. I applied for the latter two colleges, and was called for a personal interview.

I visited Madanapalle first, more for the pleasure of seeing this quaint town, which had a reputation as a Health resort for consumptives, and as a centre of Theosophy. The place was about 150 miles from Madras on a Branch Railway line, and after a tedious journey in the hottest part of the year, and walking eight miles from the Railway station, I reached the town. The food in the hotels was different from what I was used to. For the first time in my life, I tasted chappatties made of coarse flour, and preparations that had more hot chillies than vegetables or pulses. The Principal was a kindly, wise gentleman, with the culture and gentleness that Theosophy bred in its devotees. He preached universal religion to me, and hoped that I would become an ardent Theosophist. He invited me to join the staff, and gave me two weeks' time to make up my mind. I had Madanapalle as a last resort, for it would be most inconvenient if I were to prepare for the competitive examination, and travelling to and from my place would take more money and time. However, I was profited and pleased by the visit, and returned to Madras more cheerfully.

My next visit was to Chidambaram. This is the famous pilgrimage city, attracting visitors from all over the world to its shrine of Nataraja, the Hindu God in the pose of the cosmic dancer. The city itself was small and squalid, and at the time of which I write, had no modern conveniences like electric lights or sanitation. The Railway station itself was an unpretentious building. The Chettiars (or money-lenders and bankers of the South) always patronized the place, and spent enormous amounts for the improvements of the Temple and the performance of its festivals in great splendour.

The leading Chettiar of the time, a great philanthropist, departed from the traditional form of public charity, and endowed a college. The college was housed in a magnificent pile of new buildings, a couple of miles away from the town, and was fast becoming popular because of its rural setting, good hostels, and cheaper all-round cost. It was also well understood at the time that the Chettiar intended to convert the College into a university. The necessary legislation for establishing a university was before the Legislature. The Principal of the College at the time was Neelakanta Sastri, a brilliant M.A. in History, who had even then acquired a reputation both as a teacher and as an administrator. Later, he distinguished himself as a great research scholar and historian of South India.

He received me kindly, and was impressed particularly by the testimonial given to me by my own Principal, a great historian himself. Sastri was an admirer of K.V.R. and would have liked to have a pupil of the latter to work in his College. In the course of the interview, he asked me whether I intended to appear for the I.C.S. or any other competitive examination. When I replied in the affirmative, he mentioned that during the last few years, several brilliant graduates who joined his staff had wasted time in preparing for these exams, and one by one, they eventually left. This was unfair to the College, and he would not entertain me unless I gave him an undertaking that I would not appear for a competitive examination. I protested against this stipulation, and pointed out that the I.C.S. examination was the coveted objective of many of the better class of graduates, and that it would not be fair to impose this condition on those who were in temporary need. It should be possible to see that they did not neglect their College duties in the pursuit of their personal objectives. The Sastri was adamant. I stood up and said good-bye, adding 'There are fresh fields and pastures outside Chidambaram, and I will seek my fortune in the wide open world.' He was aghast that I should quote poetry to his face, and stared at me a long time. He was known to be a stern person, and perhaps for the first time in his life, he was replied to in this fashion by a young man.

Back in Madras again with my friend Sankar for a few days, I sent off an application to Trichy, which was my last hope. Within three days, I got a telegram, appointing me straightaway. I had only two days more, and I sent a telegram, promptly accepting the appointment.

I had not been to Trichy before, and my Iyengar friend from the Madura College promised to give me all the useful information and help me in finding my way about the place. A relation of his was a postgraduate student in the St Joseph's College, and I could accompany him. This Iyengar friend, with his tuft and caste-mark, looked very orthodox, but a more liberal-minded and helpful person I had not seen among Brahmans so far. He took me to the house of his sister, who was married to a rich person, and he made me completely at home. It was extremely rare in those days for Brahmans to take their other friends to their houses, and to feed them and entertain them. In his sister's house I was treated as a member of the family, and I was made to forget all differences of caste and orthodoxy. I lost touch with this good friend after some years, much to my regret.

We (my friend's relation and I) landed in Trichy early in the morning. This is the third biggest town in Madras State, and was noted as a great centre of education. The Jesuit fathers were running a college with both science and arts courses, and the teaching was of such high quality that it attracted students from all over the South. The College authorities ran several hostels for its students. Even in the hostels, there were separate Brahman and non-Brahman messes. The Jesuit fathers very scrupulously refrained from interfering with caste prejudices. In fact, even among the converts to Catholicism, the caste system was perpetuated. They boasted of several Brahman converts—but then Christian Brahmans lived in a separate street of their own, they had reserved accommodation in churches, and scrupulously observed their brahmanical traditions and customs, and they continued to boast of their Brahman heritage, and preserved their separate identity.

In addition to the Jesuit College, there was a Protestant Mission College, and the National College. The part of the city known as Teppakulam was a student city. In the streets, in shops and temples, one saw only crowds of students. There were several eating houses, primarily catering for students. These were managed by Brahmans. Food was served only for Brahmans, and rooms for Brahman students were also available. Many students who preferred the freer atmosphere outside the College-controlled hostels, patronized these houses, which were known as lodges. Many of them displayed boards 'For Brahmans only'.

My young postgraduate friend, who was my guide, took me to his room in his lodge. He explained to me that I would not be given a room there and it may even be difficult for me to have my food there, but he chuckled, saying that we would manage somehow. We left our chappals outside, and I was quietly sneaked into his room. He sent for some eatables to his room, for my breakfast, and I was soon ready for my interview with the Principal. In that lodge, there were two boys, students of the National College, who were friends of my young friend. These boys came over to meet me, and introduced themselves as my future students. They were sons of a pre-eminent lawyer in a neighbouring District, and came of a very influential family of Theosophists.

Saranathan, the Principal, was a bachelor. He lived on the first floor of a house close to the College itself. We walked into his sitting-room at about 9 in the morning. After a few formal words of greeting, he asked me, 'Are you an Iyer or Iyengar?' I was taken aback somewhat by this abrupt questioning, but I recovered my aplomb and answered back, 'I am neither, but does it matter?' Saranathan was equally self-possessed. He laughed outright, and remarked, 'Not that it matters now, but I assured the College Committee at the time of your selection that you are an Iyer and not an Iyengar.' He then explained the circumstances. The College Committee consisted of an equal number of Iyers and Iyengars, but the Chairman was an Iyengar, and the Secretary was an Iyer. In view of this competition, the Iyer block always accused the Principal, who was himself an Iyengar, of preferring only people of his clan for staff appointments. On this occasion, anticipating this criticism, the Principal assured them that I was an Iyer and not an Iyengar.

When he explained this to me, I naturally asked him why he presumed that I should be a brahman, as my name was not a distinctly brahman name, and I never used the caste surname at all. He was quite nice about it, and told me that my academic distinctions led him to believe I must be a brahman. When I retorted that First class Honours was not necessarily a brahman prerogative, he asked me to mention the names of any other Tamil Non-Brahmans who had secured a First class Honours or Postgraduate degree. I had no reply to this, as to my knowledge there were no Non-Brahmans till then with such distinctions. In fact in most colleges, there were very few Non-Brahman students in Honours or Postgraduate classes. The whole conversation was carried on in a light-hearted vein; nevertheless I got the impression that I got the appointment due to the mistaken belief about my caste. The last bit of advice he gave me confirmed this. He said that I need not pay the customary courtesy call on the Chairman and Secretary of the College Committee.

The presence there of several students, some of them of the National College itself, led eventually to some embarrassment not anticipated either by Saranathan or myself. As some of them were

Theosophists, freer, comparatively, of caste prejudices, the whole episode was broadcast, with some embellishments, in all the student hostels and messes in the Town. I found myself almost with a Hero's reputation, and as Saranathan was not a particularly popular person, the students became great admirers of mine. Before long, Saranathan came to hear about this, and developed a prejudice against me, which manifested itself in several petty ways during the eight months I spent in this College.

PART TWO

The Dravidian Movement in Tamil Nadu and Its Legacy (1981)

(Three Lectures Delivered at the University of Madras)

PART TWO

The Dravidian Movement in Tamil Nadu and Its Legacy (1981)

(Three Lectures Delivered at the University of Madras)

Preface

I must at the outset express my deep sense of gratitude and appreciation to the authorities of this oldest university in the South for extending an invitation to me to deliver these series of lectures under the Periyar E.V. Ramaswami Endowment. Not being closely associated with the affairs of the University, I was under the impression that only academics, scholars of eminence, and people who have distinguished themselves in several fields are extended this honour. It is not a mere expression of formal humility when I say that I don't seem to fall under any of these categories. I am a retired Civil Servant who spends his time (when it is not necessary to earn a living) studying current affairs. About fourteen years ago, I started writing articles on political, economic, and historical affairs for several newspapers in India. I also had occasion to study certain aspects of our social and political system, when I was called upon to Chair the Tamil Nadu Backward Classes Commission. Since then, I have taken a sustained interest in the Backward Classes agitation and counter-agitation in recent times. The range of subjects from which I was given a choice for the present lectures falls very much within my sphere of interest and study. I therefore welcomed the offer.

I have a personal interest as well. I knew Periyar fairly well for about ten years before his demise. My first contact with him was in the middle 1930s when he visited Bombay, attended by two of his distinguished disciples—both of whom are alas no more. He was staying with a friend of mine in Dadar, and the saintly bearded appearance of the prophet of atheism and the *sishya*-like demeanour of the two disciples attracted the attention of the neighbourhood Hindu ladies, who took him to be a great Swamiji from the South. The ladies spoke to his host and wanted a *darshan* to be arranged. The *darshan* was arranged for the next morning with the stipulation that it was Swamiji's day of silence. The ladies arrived with trays of flowers, fruits, and sweets, and placing them around the great man, sat by his side in silence. He nodded his head several times in appreciation and waved his hands as if in blessing. The ladies departed thoroughly happy and the Swamiji left Bombay the next day.

I wrote this up in a newspaper article in 1967 or 1968 and the veracity of the episode was accepted by Periyar who sent for me after being told about this article. I used to see him thereafter fairly frequently. He had a tremendous sense of humour and was quite childlike in his appreciation. I used to tease him by saying that coconuts will be broken on the various statues which were being erected all round the country, and *pooja* offered to the godless prophet. He used to burst into laughter and his mirth was uncontrollable when I suggested that even Brahman ladies would break coconuts on his head. Such matters have already come to pass!

I am grateful to the University for giving me an opportunity for paying my tribute once again to him, who has done so much for the common people in so short a time. His work will bear the stamp of immortality.

LECTURE 1

The Dravidian Movement in Tamil Nadu and its Emergence as a Political Force

Origins of the Movement—Was it Dravidian?

The most outstanding event in South Indian History in this century is the rise and spread of the Non-Brahman movement, better known as the Dravidian movement. For the first time in Indian History, caste, not religion or race, entered into politics as a major force. Though the Dravidian movement is quite a modern chapter in Indian History, scholars already have divergent views on its origin. It is now almost a matter of historical research. The widely-held impression is that the movement originated in the early years of this century in what was then the Bombay Presidency, especially in its Maharashtra region, and spread to the South. It is worth remembering that in those years the region south of the Vindhya was divided into two large administrative units, the Bombay Presidency and the Madras Presidency; and in between lay a few large and small Princely States. But we cannot give a date for the commencement of what is essentially a socio-religious and ethnic movement. Dates can be assigned for something connected with a personality or a historical or physical event. If it is regarded as a movement of the castes other than the Brahman, against the Brahmans, it might have existed in some form or other since the days of the Aryan settlement, and Buddhism and Jainism may even be called anti-Brahman movements. But these were not certainly Dravidian in any sense. In any case these movements were largely religious and social reformation movements, and were not directed against the Brahmans as a *Varna* or Caste. No hatred was preached against the Brahmans. Any agitation or movement, of the castes other than those exclusively Aryan, can be described as Dravidian only if all these castes were exclusively of Dravidian origin and there were no Kshatrya or Vaisya caste of Aryan descent. The modern Movement is not Dravidian in that sense. It was and is definitely Non-Brahman.

Socio-Religious Reforms in Historical Times

The Brahmans were sometimes rulers, and often the power behind the throne, ever since the Aryans settled in India, right up to the Muslim invasion and rule in the ninth and tenth centuries. Throughout this period there were no agitations as such against Brahman political and administrative dominance or influence. The movements that surfaced from time to time were for social reform and relaxation or simplification of the Brahmanical rituals. There was no direct attack on the ritual superiority of the Brahman caste in the social scale. Mythology asserts, through the Parasurama story, that the Kshatryas who raised their head were put down. From time immemorial, the epics and *Puranas* through preaching the doctrines of *Karma*, *Punarjanma*, and related concepts, made the vast masses accept their inferior socio-religious and economic lot.

No Wholesale Aryan Migration

There was no rational attempt systematically made to denounce these concepts. As far as South India, and particularly Tamil Nadu, is concerned, there may be some truth in the assumption that all castes other than Brahmans are Dravidians. As modern historians like N. Subrahmanian have very laboriously tried to convince readers, what happened in South India was not a wholesale migration of the

Aryan Brahmans from the North, with their entire caste system—there was only the introduction and subtle implementing of the caste framework or caste culture. The local tribes and occupational groups were assigned places in the ritual *Varna* social scale according to the Aryan concept of the caste structure, and needless to say, the Princely dynasties were given Kshatrya status and genealogy. Some of the trading castes assumed the titles of Vaisyas, and all other occupational groups with their local variations were allotted places in the large Sudra fold. There is no evidence which can stand the test of critical scrutiny to indicate that there was any protest or revolt against this cultural adaptation by the indigenous Tamil people in ancient days. Sangam literature and early post-Sangam literature give no indication of any unwilling acceptance of the Aryan cultural concepts. Sanskritic mythology and ideas spread in the land, just as the local gods and rituals were also sanskritized with Aryan religion and mythology.

References in Early Tamil Literature

A modern scholar has tried to find anti-Brahmanism even in the *Thirumandiram* of Thirumoolar, generally believed to be of the fifth or sixth century AD. The scholar has referred to the description of the holy thread and the *Sikha* (tuft of hair), in some stanza in the second tantra, as derisive, and claimed that Thirumoolar was ridiculing the Brahmans, thereby generating anti-Brahmanism. What Thirumoolar has given there is the Tantric symbolism relating to the holy thread and tuft of hair. In an earlier stanza Thirumoolar has extolled the Brahmans, by saying that Brahmans, by reciting the *Gayathri* in the ordained manner, obtained Shiva's grace and conquered *Maya*. After having paid such tribute to the Brahmans, he is unlikely to preach hatred against them. Thirumoolar was one of the earliest Siddhas who were masters of Tantric art. They did not think it necessary to conform to the external forms of religion, nor did all of them ignore idol worship or the employment of priests. Siddhas were neither anti-Brahman nor anti-Aryan.

Brahmans continued to enjoy their privileged position, and even in temples under the Saivite Mutts (established during the period of the Nayanmars), officiated as the chief priests, as they do now. I think it is the height of chauvinism, to say the least, to give antiquity to Dravidianism or Non-Brahmanism, by relating it to Thirumoolar and the Saivite Cult that developed in the seventh and eighth centuries.

It is very surprising that a sociologist of great eminence, Dr Ghurye, has excelled even the scholar referred to earlier, in attributing to anti-Brahmanism an even greater antiquity, in his latest edition of *Caste and Race in India*. The absence of Sanskrit words or translations from Sanskrit in the Sangam age, and the development of Tamil language and literature independently of Sanskritic influences, are cited as instances of anti-Aryanism or anti-Brahmanism. Equally uncritical, if not absurd, is citing the presence of many Vellalas and even Parayas amongst the Alwars and Nayanmars, and the fact that a Vellala, Sekkilar, was the author of the *Periya Puranam*, as illustrations of Non-Brahmanism. The learned sociologist describes the chauvinism of the Dravida Kazhagam and Dravida Munnetra Kazhagam pamphleteers of the 1930s and 1940s, as only revivals of the anti-Brahmanism of the earlier ages. The Pallavas, the Cholas, and the Pandyas who ruled Tamil Nad never showed anti-Brahmanism. In fact they were responsible for importing Brahmans in batches from time to time from the North and settling them round the temples they built.

Anti-Brahmanism: A Modern Phenomenon

Anti-Brahmanism or Non-Brahmanism, under the guise of Dravidianism, is definitely a phenomenon of the British Administration, raising its head towards the end of the nineteenth century. The British, to consolidate their administration, had to rely on the upper caste in the Hindu hierarchy, the Brahman, who had the tradition of learning, and whose aptitude for administrative work was well recognized for centuries. Further, because of their ritual superiority, they would command respect and obedience from the ordinary people. Petty Brahman officials are obeyed and respected, because they are Brahmans. Valentine Chirol, writing in 1910 (in *Indian Unrest*), compared their position as Government Servants to the Filtration theory, and further stated: 'British education in India became closely associated and connected with religion by which the higher education of the Hindus was in the hands of Brahmans and mainly intended for them.' This process was quite pronounced all over the two Southern presidencies and the Princely States also. Towards the end of the nineteenth century, 80 to 90 per cent of all jobs available to Indians were occupied by Brahmans, and they were dominating other professions also. It is needless to quote statistics of the number of Government servants, lawyers, etc. of the period, as these are often quoted in several reports and publications.

A Movement of Protest by the Higher Non-Brahman Castes

What I would like to emphasize is that the present Non-Brahman movement, actually miscalled the Dravidian movement—a point more fully explained in a later context—is a modern phenomenon, arising at about the same time, and for identical reasons, in Maharashtra and the Madras Presidency. There is no evidence that it was imported into Madras from Maharashtra, though there was contact between the leadership at a later stage. It was a protest aimed at impressing the British Administration. It was not essentially anti-Brahman as such in the beginning, though it assumed a hate complex at some later stage. The movement embraced Muslims and Christians, and strange to say, there is no evidence of the depressed classes (as they were then called) being involved in it. It was, however, essentially a movement of the higher Non-Brahman castes, the top people outside the Brahman caste who were always aspiring to take their place, not ritually, but in social and political and official importance. Even historically, under the Pallavas, Cholas, Pandyas, and even the Nayaks, higher offices, especially in the Court and Field Administration were held by Vellalars and Mudaliars. As Velirs in the early Chola days, they were not only big land-owners, but feudal chieftains, raising and keeping troops. They married their daughters with the Royal families. Their pre-eminent position was maintained even under the later Pandyas and Nayaks—as Dalavoys. With the Telugu Cholas and Nayak rulers, the Naidus and Reddiars also came up as landlords and claimants for top positions and eventually these three groups dominated the non-Brahman people. Only under the British rule they lost their position and in the beginning of the twentieth century, they wanted to regain their historic position as leaders of the Non-Aryans or Non-Brahmans. Under the circumstances, it would not be correct to say that the Non-Brahman movement in Madras was an offshoot from the Maharashtra region of the Bombay Presidency. The only thing that can be said is that similar movements arose in Maharashtra and Tamil Nadu about the same time and for similar reasons.

Why the Movement Started in the South

In trying to explain why the Dravidian movement started in the South and not in the North, Lloyd Rudolph and Susanne Rudolph, in their several studies, could only say that the Brahmans were very conspicuous in the South, as the only true Aryan twice-born, while in the North, there were several Non-Brahman twice-born castes, like Kshatryas and Vaisyas, and a new caste also came into prominence since the Mughal days who competed successfully with the Brahmans in securing a good share of Government jobs and places in the learned professions: the Kayasthas. The Brahmans lost their dominance in the North after the advent of the Muslim conquerors. Even after the arrival of the British, the Brahmans did not rise to any commanding positions. There were not so many temples and places of learning where their services were required. Another factor, however minor it may be, was that the Brahmans—men and women—were generally not distinguishable from the others by dress or manner of speech and behaviour, as is the case in Tamil Nadu. The existence of *agraharams* and numerous temples made their position conspicuous in addition to their overwhelming presence in the services and professions.

The Objectives of the Non-Brahman Elite

The aspiration of the Non-Brahman leadership in the early years of the century was to replace the Brahmans quickly in their dominant position in officialdom and places of political influence and power. But the leadership also realized that without education, economic power, or political influence, the process would not be easy, unless they got outright support from the British bureaucracy. The new Non-Brahman elite which was fast gathering strength expressed their distrust of the new Nationalist movement of the Congress, as in their view, with its Brahman leadership the Congress would stifle the progress of the ordinary people after the British rule was eliminated. The new leadership was openly hostile to the Nationalist movement and stood solidly behind the British.

The Non-Brahman Manifesto and Non-Brahman Leadership

Their apprehensions were expressed in the Non-Brahman Manifesto of 1916. The manifesto, and the South Indian People's Association which issued it, stood firmly against the transfer of power from the British to what they feared would be Brahman overlordship. Soon after, in August 1917, the South Indian Liberal Federation was formed to function as a political organization under the leadership of Dr T. M. Nair, P. Theagaraja Chettiar, and Dr C. Natesa Mudaliar. Though it would have been a sacrilege some years ago to comment on the leadership, I would like to make some observations. But for the fact that the Presidency of Madras included a part of Kerala, Dr Nair would not have been in Tamil Nad politics, and in his native Kerala, the movement never took root at all, though Brahmanical orthodoxy was at its worst there. Chettiar was a Telugu-speaking businessman, and the other was a Mudaliar. Nair was the most prominent spokesman of the Federation and he had his personal reasons. It was a closely-knit elite of rich people from the higher echelons of society, who in no way represented the masses, or knew them, or could speak their idiom. They did not seriously contemplate any social reconstruction or economic uplift to benefit the masses. The fact was that the movement never approached the masses and it was largely urban oriented. There is no evidence of their ever having thought of the depressed classes. As landlords, they could hardly afford to take any note of them. The membership of their organization consisted only of the first generation of educated upper-caste Non-Brahman graduates or educated professionals. They were worried about the growing number of Brahmans in Public Services and in the District Boards which had been set up as a first measure of local self-Government, and about the Brahman influence in the Home Rule movement, which was very vocal in Madras, under the leadership of Dr Annie Besant.

The British Attitude Towards the Non-Brahman Movement: A Review

In this connection it is interesting to see what the British Administration thought in those days of this Brahman dominance in the spheres of learning and Government services.

The British bureaucrats foresaw the trend towards Brahman dominance in the Madras Presidency, though they constituted only 4 per cent of the population, and realized the wisdom of arresting its pace in the interest of social justice. Even in the small legislature that was constituted under the Minto–Morley Reforms, the Brahmans were dominant. Even as early as 1907, the Home Department of the Government of India, in drafting a Scheme for Indian participation, suggested for the legislative council of Madras, 17 non-official seats to be filled by special electorates of Caste and Occupational groups, and this system gave substantial representation to Non-Brahmans, including Christians and Mohammedans. This method of communal representation in the Legislature was strongly criticized all over India. Needless to say, it was badly received by the Press in Madras, as repugnant to national solidarity. In fact, it was condemned as a vicious design to kill the young patriotic movement before it could gather strength. It was another manifestation of 'divide and rule', said a leading Newspaper under Brahman control. The only support the scheme received was from the Muslims and the Non-Brahmans, who were not organized to mobilize any public opinion, and they had no newspapers of their own to give expression to their views. In fact, the lack of unity amongst the Non-Brahman castes prevented any nomination of a leader acceptable to all the castes. Each caste in fact wanted a representation, and any caste left out felt aggrieved. All these were to change substantially, though not radically, in 1917, when the Justice Party emerged as a political factor. The Non-Brahman elite was developing, and largely owing to the apprehension about Brahman dominance flourishing under any system of Home rule, anti-Brahman propaganda was launched on public platforms and in the few papers and journals which were started then for this specific purpose. Matters came to a head in 1916. The election of the members of the Imperial Legislative Council was held under the Minto–Morley Scheme. Dr Nair, the leading light of the Non-Brahman movement, was defeated by the limited electorate, and a Brahman was elected. This was taken as a challenge to the Non-Brahman cause and things began to move fast thereafter. This has already been referred to as a personal factor that determined Dr Nair's interest in the new movement.

The British policy, at least as far as the Madras Presidency was concerned, was to encourage the new development. Here was a group of people who wanted them to stay in India indefinitely, and who preferred British Rule. It was natural for the British to encourage and support this development.

Some 'Might Have Beens' of History

When the Non-Brahman movement was gathering strength, the Brahman leadership could have acted with greater wisdom. Rajaji, though not at the helm of Congress affairs in Madras, had tremendous influence over the party. The other leaders were also men of character and ability. But none of them was able to tear the veil of *Maya* that clouded their thinking and vision. They should have been able to foresee the inevitability of the Non-Brahman claim for some sort of communal representation and social justice. They should have tried to pacify E.V. Ramaswami, their old friend and Congress colleague in the years to follow. The Brahman leadership, always sure of their divine right and intellectual superiority, failed to allay the apprehension in the minds of the Non-Brahman elite, that they were trying to perpetuate their anachronistic dominance. The result of this failure was the resounding call, half a century later, by the leader of the Dravida Munnetra Kazhagam, that theirs was a Government by the fourth caste, i.e., a Sudra Government. The basis for this Sudra Raj was prepared by the Non-Brahman Manifesto, and its cornerstone was laid by the Justice Party.

Tamil Renaissance

Before we begin to evaluate the achievements of the Justice Party, I would like to say a few words about the awakening in the literary and cultural spheres that began during this period. The Nationalist movement itself gave a tremendous fillip to the study of ancient Hindu culture and literature. Any political revolution is accompanied by this kind of renaissance. Under the encouragement given by the Dravidian awakening, Tamil literature blossomed forth in all its splendour. Tamil Music, Art, Poetry, and Drama took distinct shape. Tamil prose expanded and developed in all its manifold variety. Spoken Tamil got special attention, and was developed to a degree that could not have been anticipated in the nineteenth century. The writers and orators of the Dravida Munnetra Kazhagam have contributed a great deal in this direction. I must add, however, that all this revival was not supported solely by the Non-Brahman or Dravidian movement. The Congress, too, had its share of the credit, and Brahman poets and scholars have their honoured place in Tamil revivalism.

Chauvinism

As a side-effect, there developed an excessive chauvinism, to find in ancient Tamil and the Tamil Country everything that the modern world wants. It also led to the Anti-Hindi agitation, with very doubtful benefits either to Tamil or to the Tamil people. The extremists are not convinced yet, that neither Hindi, Sanskrit, nor English, will harm Tamil. The rest of India, which regarded all South Indians as Madrassis and black barbarians, began to know the Southern people better and to appreciate their qualities and historic contribution. In a sense, Dravidianism initially shook them up. The unfortunate tendency that Dravidianism and Tamil chauvinism represented, in the earlier demand for a separate Dravidasthan, was given up by the far-seeing statesman, Anna, and attempts are being made to merge the Tamilian resurgence into the mainstream of Indian nationalism and the cultural renaissance that is taking place all over the country.

In conclusion, I must observe that the renaissance of language and culture is not peculiar to the Tamils, nor a special gift of the Dravidian movement. Such renaissance has taken place in Kerala, Gujarat, Bengal, and Orissa, to mention only a few states. It is only an aspect of the greater revivalism. The Dravidian movement gave it a special twist and linguistic fervour and made it more distinctive and chauvinistic.

LECTURE 2

The Varying Political Phases of the Dravidian Movement

The Non-Brahman movement in the Madras Presidency falls into three clear phases: (1) From the Non-Brahman Manifesto in 1916, to 1926. This is the period of the Justice Party. (2) The movement under Periyar's leadership, from 1926 to 1949, which had a definite Dravidian overtone. This period covers the founding of the Dravida Kazhagam and the Self-Respect movement. (3) From 1949 when Anna broke away from Periyar. This third phase is purely political and cannot properly be treated strictly as a continuation of the Non-Brahman movement. As a social and political agitation, the Non-Brahman or Dravidian movement may be said to have withered away by 1949, though political and social life in Tamil Nadu since then has been permanently influenced by the ideas of the Justice and Dravidian phases of the original movement.

Self-Government under British Guidance

In 1916 the British rulers were inclined to concede some form of self-government, and were willing to share their power with some selected Indian elements. They found the atmosphere in Madras getting more congenial for this purpose. A group of people from the landed aristocracy was organizing a party which 'was not in favour of any movement to undermine the influence and authority of the British Rulers', as the Manifesto clearly defined its political attitude. This view was further defined in the *Non-Brahman*, the official organ of the South Indian Liberal Federation. 'Our goal is the goal of Self-Government, but we want to be led there by the British.' It is worth recording at this stage that the Federation was not called the Dravidian Liberal Federation, but the South Indian Liberal Federation. In a Memorandum submitted to the Government of Madras, this Federation argued that there could be no proper territorial representation, at least in the Madras Presidency. Dr Nair, in a speech quoted in T. Vardarajulu Naidu's book, *The Justice Movement*, asserted that there was no tradition of self-government in India, and that Indians required training by gradual stages towards self-government. It must be emphasized that the Justice Party at no time was against Independence or self-government. Their only point was that it must come gradually, as, in their opinion, Home rule meant Brahman rule. They argued that in elections, Non-Brahmans could not successfully compete against Brahmans, and made a case for communal electorates for Non-Brahmans, on the basis of their numbers, property qualification, and tax-paying capacity. At this present date, with the experience of several elections behind us, one feels aghast that a 96 per cent majority should seek safeguards against a petty minority of 4 per cent. In spite of these representations, and the sneaking sympathy that the British had for the Justice Party, the Montagu–Chelmsford report rejected the idea of special Non-Brahman electorates, as the idea of safeguards for the majority against a minority was inconceivable to them. The question of determining the nature of the electorate was left to be further examined by the Southborough Committee, set up in 1918.

Communal Electorates

A series of Non-Brahman Conferences were held in this connection, to canvass support for communal electorates. There was even a suggestion to boycott the Committee. The Southborough Committee reported against conceding separate electorates for Non-Brahmans, who outnumbered the Brahmans in a ratio of 22 to 1, taking caste Hindus alone, and on the basis of the property and other qualifications recommended for the voters, the ratio was 4 to 1. The Committee felt that the Non-Brahmans should organize themselves and get their fair share of representation by the sheer weight of numbers. The Government of India, which had sympathy for the Non-Brahman movement, did not accept the Southborough Committee's views. The Government was apparently strongly influenced by the views of the Madras Government, that the argument based on numerical strength may be sound in a country accustomed to democratic institutions, but taking the reality of social and political factors into account in the southern Presidency, the numerical superiority of the Non-Brahmans would not prevail, and the Government would be left in the hands of a Brahman-dominated oligarchy. Therefore, the Government of India recommended that at least 30 out of 61 general Non-Muslim seats in the Madras Council should be reserved for Non-Brahmans, leaving the other seats to open contest. But the battle for reservation was not won so easily, and the Non-Brahman leaders were in no mood to give up. They were fast acquiring political and negotiating skill and pursued the matter both in India as well as in England. In spite of the Government of India's recommendation, the Government of India Act of 1919, as passed by the British Parliament, while admitting the principle of reservation, left the number of seats to be so reserved, and the modalities, to be settled by the locally contending parties. Just about this time, something favourable to the Non-Brahman cause had happened, namely, the transfer of Lord Willingdon from Bombay to Madras as Governor. It is believed that the transfer was effected with the purpose of helping the Justice Party, as Willingdon had by then successfully managed similar agitations in Bombay. But the position taken up by the Non-Brahman leadership was that 75 per cent of the seats should be reserved for Non-Brahmans. Even Willingdon could not solve the tangle, though he was prepared to stake his reputation for 50 per cent of the seats. Next came the Meston Award, which dealt a severe blow to the Non-Brahman leadership, as it agreed to only 28 seats and asserted 'that Non-Brahman numerical superiority should be exploited by proper organization.' All this bitter fighting over seats engendered anti-Brahman feelings, and the hatred of the Brahman became almost a creed of the followers of the Non-Brahman movement. Ultimately a compromise solution was provided by the Government, very much on the lines of the views of Lord Willingdon: a 50 per cent reservation with the right to the Non-Brahmans to contest any number of seats in excess. The fear of the Non-Brahman leadership, that their majority would be reduced to a minority in the Council, vanished. A majority was given all the protection normally given to a minority in a plural society—a unique feature in political history anywhere. In the long run, whether future historians will acclaim this as a triumph for the Non-Brahmans remains a question mark.

Electoral Success of the Justice Party

In the three successive elections held under this system, in 1920, 1923 and 1926, in a House of 98, the Non-Brahman majority was 57, 61, and 56. The Brahmans, with their small numerical strength, returned 17, 14 and 18 members, demonstrating that their strength did not depend on numbers alone. The other 24 seats, a constant number, were for special interests, including Muslims. In view of this majority, from 1920 to 1926, the Justice Party was able to take part in the Dyarchic administration in the State. It cannot be said, however, that all the Non-Brahman masses were with the Justice Party and the Non-Brahman movement. As the history of the Congress movement testifies, there were large numbers of Non-Brahmans of all classes, educated and otherwise, landlords and peasants, in the Congress. But the Congress decided on Non-Co-operation and there was no Congress Party in the Council, even as an Opposition. The Justice Party had no organized opposition party to grapple with in the beginning.

The only dissident voice came from the Brahmans of non-Congress persuasion. The others generally voted with the Government. In the 1923 elections, the Non-Brahmans had a bigger majority (61 against the earlier 57), but some of them did not belong to the Justice Party. A dissident group of the Congress, called the Swarajya Party, under the all-India leadership of C.R. Das, entered the legislature, and there were many Non-Brahmans amongst them. By that time, there was a rift in the Justice Party as well, as power always leads to quarrels over its sharing. In the third election, though there were 56 Non-Brahmans, many of them belonged to the Swarajya Party. They had 40 seats, while the Justice Party had only 20. Of the 40 Swarajya partymen, many must have been Non-Brahmans.

Decline of the Justice Party

The decline of the Justice Party began in 1926, though the party continued till 1937 as a political party. Though a purely Justice ministry was not formed after 1927, the Justicites exercised influence over the Independent ministry that was subsequently formed. It met its electoral doom in the first elections held under the Government of India Act of 1935, when it secured only 12 seats out of the 86 it contested. Thereafter, it lingered in the background. During the years the Justice Party was in office, political scientists and observers felt that here in Madras was the beginning of the two-party system, which is regarded as so very essential for the successful working of parliamentary democracy. Several groups functioned as an opposition, and when the Swarajya Party entered the Legislature, there really was a well-organized parliamentary opposition. The subsequent performance of the Justice Party after the elections, under the Government of India Act of 1935, belied all these hopes. The reason for this political failure to function even as a sizeable opposition party, must be found in the absence of a mass base and the lack of a cadre of village-level workers essential for a party organization. It was a party of leaders. There were no village-level, constituency-level, or even District-level party workers functioning effectively. The glamour of the brightly dressed rajas and zamindars who led the party could not hold together the masses for long. More important still was the lack of homogeneity among the numerous Non-Brahman castes. A few castes, which were traditionally dominant in several localities, dominated the party, and the loaves and fishes of office went to the young graduates of these castes. They entered the Revenue Department and the Judiciary in increasing numbers as Deputy Tahsildars, Deputy Collectors, and Munsiffs, and in later days, came to top positions. There were no crumbs, even, thrown to the aspiring and hungry young men of the lower castes, who came to be known even then as Backward Classes, let alone the depressed classes. Absence of a mass base and a region-wide organizational network brought the Justice Party a quicker end than it deserved. It was left to younger leaders who came several years later to build up the mass base and organizational network, and regenerate the Non-Brahman Party under a different name. That credit goes to the scholar, writer, and orator from Conjeevaram, C.N. Annadurai.

It is not the purpose of this lecture to describe the legislative and administrative achievement of the Justice Party, which were by no means negligible. But what is historically remarkable is the legacy left by the party and the movement, which is influencing and will continue to influence South Indian politics and social life for generations. In creating this legacy, the contribution of Periyar is very impressive, and it deserves careful consideration.

Periyar and the Dravidian Phase

Kasinath Kavlekar, in his study of the Non-Brahman movement, describes the entry of Periyar into the movement as the beginning of the Dravidian phase. Till then it was only Non-Brahman, with the limited objective of getting positions of power and influence in Councils and Boards, and a larger number of jobs in Government services, for educated Non-Brahmans. Periyar ran the movement with larger objectives and undertook social reform work simultaneously with political propaganda. He made it a mass movement and he had the requisite training for it.

Periyar's coming over to the Justice Party was neither deliberate nor accidental. Having been nurtured in the Congress for several decades, and having played a prominent role in the Councils of the Tamil Nadu Congress, it would not have been easy for him to join the Justice Party when he walked out of the Congress. Some years of soul searching must have preceded the decision. It was because E.V.R. was a man of the masses, and could develop mass contact, that the Justice Party elected him as its leader in 1938. Though E.V.R. had left the Congress in 1926, after facing repeated defeats and rebuffs from the Tamilnad Congress over several matters, the most important being the adoption of a Resolution supporting communal representation in the Legislature, a subject which was being hotly debated at that time, he was not sitting idle or nursing his grievances in the intervening twelve or thirteen years. He had already started the Self-Respect or *Suya Mariyadai* movement at a Conference in 1929. He had already taken part in leading the opposition against teaching or spreading Hindi in the South. In fact he had already formulated all his ideas, social, religious and political, which he was to propagate during the next four decades. He strode across Tamil Nad like a colossus.

Demand for Dravida Nad

The Dravidian phase of the movement, as contrasted to the Non-Brahman, raised its head for the first time openly in 1939, when Periyar put forth the demand for Dravidanad before Sir Stafford Cripps during his first political visit canvassing Indian support for Britain's war effort. Periyar also had a resolution passed at a Conference demanding that for the well being of the Dravidians, the Madras Presidency, the home of the Dravidians, should be constituted as a separate state directly administered by the Government of India. This synchronized with the commencement of the propaganda regarding the Two Nation theory formulated by Jinnah. A Tamil weekly, called *Dravida Nadu*, was also started, to propagate this idea of a separate state. This espousal of the cause of a Dravida state led to the identification of the Non-Brahmans of the South as Dravidians, and the word stuck to all movements and parties that sprang out of this phase. This gave it an ethnic colour, which the term Non-Brahman did not. This 'Dravidian' appellation gave rise to a tremendous amount of chauvinism and Tamil revivalism, on an unprecedented scale. Surprisingly, the other regions of Dravidasthan did not respond to this cry for a separate state. This development was too much for the older elements of the Justice Party, the knights and Dewan Bahadurs and Zamindars. The matter was further aggravated when in the 1944 Salem Conference, Periyar demanded the resignation of party members from all government jobs, the surrender of titles, etc. He was putting into practice the lessons he had learnt in the Congress.

Emergence of the Dravida Kazhagam and Dravida Munnetra Kazhagam

The conservative elements of the old Justice Party withdrew their association with Periyar's movement, and whatever was left was converted into the Dravida Kazhagam. Periyar and his young apostles, headed by Anna, were already preparing the ground for this new phase and for the first time, a defiantly populist Non-Brahman movement, stubbornly calling itself Dravidian, came into existence under younger and more revolutionary leadership. This was to change the destiny of Tamil Nadu unmistakably in the coming years. The Dravida Munnetra Kazhagam (DMK) was formed in 1949 by what might be called a split in Periyar's Kazhagam. From the very beginning, its objective was political, the capturing of power through the ballot box. Before we come to this phase, the lasting achievements of Periyar must be considered.

Atheistic and Self-Respect Movements

Periyar is known as an uncompromising atheist, who wanted to break Hindu idols. He denigrated Hindu Gods and Goddesses, and vilified the Sanskritic epics and *puranas*. He has a hard core of followers in the atheistic pursuit, but I doubt whether it has made any substantial dent in Hindu ritualism and the temple worship of the masses. I can well understand the logic of Periyar's iconoclastic atheism. He was a rationalist. He wanted to destroy the caste system. But he realized that caste is an integral part of the Hindu religious system, built round the theistic pantheon represented in the Sanskritic epics and *puranas*. Caste is described as God-ordained. Even the *Gita* affirms this. *Chatur varnam maya srishti*, says Bhagawan. The iconoclast's reaction to this relation between caste and religion would be to destroy the faith in gods and the caste system so that the Hindu social structure would automatically wither. But Hinduism is very tenacious and it has withstood many such strong attacks. Periyar's teachings have made people think, and numerous reforms have been slowly effected. Man's attitude towards religion has undergone changes.

Periyar's lasting contribution is the concept of Self-Respect or *Suya Mariyadai*. People at that time ridiculed Periyar because he could not even think of a pure Tamil phrase—*Suya* and *Marjatha* (*Mariyadai*) are of Sanskrit origin. The practical person that Periyar was did not bother about this. The word *Thanmanam* was considered to replace *Suya Mariyadai*. But the word *Suya Mariyadai* held its ground against Tamilian chauvinistic substitution. It is the Self-Respect movement that has transformed the outlook of all Non-Brahmans in Tamil Nadu, including Muslims, Christians, and Scheduled castes. Every Tamilian now thinks he is inferior to none and has developed a sense of his own worth. The feudal concepts that guided human relationships are fast disappearing. The idea of superiority and inferiority by birth or calling is no longer tenable. This is a kind of revolution that has no parallel in Indian history. The caste system is slowly loosening its ritual hierarchical nature, though it is still there, especially in the rural areas. Periyar, apart from his rationalistic attack on God and religion, did not make any strenuous efforts to mitigate the evils of the caste system, or to bring about equality amongst the castes in other respects. But what he accomplished through the Self-Respect movement entitles him to be remembered as one of the greatest figures in the history of social reform in India. Even after his death, his influence is spreading in areas outside Tamil Nadu. Though Periyar's immediate followers did not grow in numbers, his ideas spread steadily amongst all sections of people, even those unconnected with the Justice Party or the Kazhagam. In my opinion, his greatest contribution was that he taught us to set our minds free and hold our heads high.

Anna's Epoch

C.N. Annadurai was a good Tamil scholar, well read in English Literature, Politics, and Economics, and a master of Tamil and English oratory. Along with half-a-dozen frontline lieutenants of E.V. Ramaswami, he formed the Dravida Munnetra Kazhagam, with the definite purpose of making it a modern political party, and not merely a vehicle of E.V.R.'s iconoclasm. His first approach was towards the common man. He had successfully convinced the Tamil masses that wiping away the tears from their eyes was his foremost concern. As he began to gain strength, and as he felt that political power would sooner or later be in his hands, he realized that preaching of hatred would not pay. Brahman-baiting was slowly given up, and appealing to the Tamilian's past glory and the excellence of ancient Tamil Literature succeeded in arousing Tamil chauvinism, which was essential to build up the strength of the party in its early stages. As he grew in political stature, he changed his role from a rabble-rouser and proved himself to be a politician of statesman-like qualities, and a far-sighted administrator.

Propaganda Triumphs

There was no difference between the Dravida Kazhagam of Periyar and the Dravida Munnetra Kazhagam of Anna as far their social goals were concerned. Periyar devoted his energy to social enlightenment, the removal of superstition and the tyranny of the sacerdotal caste, and the elimination of the political and administrative influence of the Brahmans. He spoke and wrote tirelessly and led many whirlwind propaganda tours. The Dravida Munnetra Kazhagam sought to gain the very same ends through capturing political power. The Dravida Munnetra Kazhagam organized demonstrations and protest meetings on a wider scale, and in 1953, the best opportunity for a demonstration of power came its way, when Rajaji, during his brief Chief Ministership, introduced an Educational Reform measure for imparting traditional occupations to students in schools, as part of the vocational educational programme. It also organized a train-stopping movement, to protest against Jawaharlal Nehru's criticism of the Dravida Munnetra Kazhagam. Rajaji's Education Bill was withdrawn, giving the Dravida Munnetra Kazhagam a taste of political success. It led repeated agitations against Hindi and kept up the tempo of agitation, attracting large numbers of the student community into its fold.

Contesting Elections

In 1956, at a conference in Trichy, the Dravida Munnetra Kazhagam decided to contest the 1957 elections and issued a Manifesto. In this Manifesto, all the negative positions for which the Dravida Kazhagam movement was known, found expression, but on the issue of a separate Tamil Nad, it adopted an attitude approving the existing Federal Structure of the Constitution—but it wanted each state to have the right to secede. Some diehard partymen might have thought this was a climbdown. But this was a sure sign of Anna's political foresight. There was some condemnation of what was regarded as the Northern exploitation of the natural resources of the South. There were several socialist overtones in the Manifesto, which proclaimed that the party stood for a classless, casteless society. Kamaraj at that time was the Congress Chief, and being a man of the masses, coming from the lower strata of society, was hailed by Periyar, Anna's Guru, as a true Tamilian, for whom alone all followers of the Dravida Kazhagam should vote. Periyar vigorously campaigned for Kamaraj and against the Dravida Munnetra Kazhagam. The 1957 elections brought an overwhelming victory for Kamaraj, as the Congress captured 133 seats, with 45.3 per cent of the votes cast. The Dravida Munnetra Kazhagam made its debut into the Madras Assembly with 15 seats and 14.6 per cent of the votes cast. This is a glaring example of the manifest evil of the 'First Past the Post' principle of the single member Constituency system. Some political Commentators called this the Congress multiple factor. With a minority vote, an organized party, by contesting in a large number of constituencies against an unorganized opposition, can win an overwhelming majority of seats. The Dravida Munnetra Kazhagam also won two Lok Sabha seats. But being the largest single opposition group in the Madras Legislative Assembly it formed the official opposition. The lesson learnt in this election was that the Dravida Munnetra Kazhagam's strength lay mainly in the large urban areas. It soon captured the Madras City Corporation and in alliance with the Communists, made a strenuous and successful attempt to capture most of the city and town municipalities.

By this time an internal conflict arose which led to the final parting of ways for E.V.K. Sampath, one of the founders of the DMK. Strangely enough, Sampath's outspoken criticism of the leadership was that they had given up their original plan of Dravidasthan. So it is ironic that after a year, he joined the Congress, and became one of its trusted leaders in Tamil Nad.

D.M.K.'s Climb to Power

The next election was due in 1962. In the new election manifesto, a more realistic attitude was taken and the emphasis was on economic problems: rising prices. The D.M.K. also softened in practice and in speech its attitude towards Brahmans, in many ways. Capturing 50 seats in the local Assembly, with 27.10 per cent of voter support, it became the greatest challenge to the Congress in the Southern state in all its history. It also sent 7 members to the Lok Sabha. The success of the D.M.K. movement must not be judged only by its score of 50 seats; in 15 constituencies, it lost by less than a 1000-vote margin. By this time the Dravida Munnetra Kazhagam leaders had learnt their political lessons, and had proved themselves to be expert election managers. They had expanded their geographical base further beyond the big cities and the northern districts of the state, and their flags and slogans were seen and heard all over the southern districts. It was a pity that Anna lost the election, but he was soon elected to the Rajya Sabha. In the next general election of 1967, the party swept the polls with a landslide victory, and the Dravida Munnetra Kazhagam was firmly in power, with Anna as the Chief Minister. As a writer in the *Economist* described it, for the first time, black men with unpronounceable names were in the seats of power. This marks the beginning of a new age in the politics of Tamil Nad. Though Anna did not live long to guide his party and shape it into a well-disciplined political force, he made certain of one thing. The age of Brahman leadership in politics—the politics of any major party in Tamil Nad—was over, so also Brahman dominance in Government service. The rule of the Sudra had begun.

Two-Party System

One can safely say at this stage that some sort of a two-party system, which we hoped for fifty years ago when the Justice Party was founded, might materialize. The Congress may some day regain its strength and may seize power from a Dravida splinter party, but that Congress will be Non-Brahman oriented, and will have to bear all the outward trappings of a Dravidian Party, though it might speak in a different idiom. As one of our respected leaders said, only a party with a Dravidian outlook will get the sympathy of the voters. Just as the Dravida Kazhagam gave place to Dravida Munnetra Kazhagam, the Dravida Munnetra Kazhagam split again into two parties. Perhaps there may be other splits and partial reunions. That seems to be the course in Indian politics. What is happening in the Congress may be repeated in Tamil Nad too, with the inheritors of the Dravida Kazhagam and Dravida Munnetra Kazhagam heritage. But there will always be a powerful Dravidian-oriented party, either in power or in opposition.

Rule of the Sudras

When I mention the Rule of the Sudras, I am reminded of the predictions contained in the *Mahabharata* and the *Srimad Bhagavatam* that in Kaliyuga, Sudras will rule. But the Sudra of that age was one of the *chathur varnas*. The term Sudra of the present day embraces a few thousand castes, each with their own conception of ritual superiority. Which Sudra will rule is the question one should try to answer now. As I indicated in general terms, the succession from Brahman dominance first passed on to the higher castes among Non-Brahmans, who again form only a small percentage of the total population. The Non-Brahman movement, it is needless to say, has not brought about any homogeneity amongst castes. If the adult franchise has succeeded in anything, it has definitely succeeded in arousing caste consciousness and caste rivalry. The succession is already passing from the high-caste Non-Brahmans to the more numerous backward-class Non-Brahmans. In every political party, this inner party struggle based on class or caste grouping goes on, either openly or covertly. When there is a charismatic personality, a large group from different castes tends to rally round that person, as happened with Kamaraj and Anna and one or two others. We have yet to wait and see how fast the succession passes down to the leadership of the lowest classes in the Sudra fold and then to the scheduled castes. The leavening and levelling down of all castes into a well-knit homogeneous democratic society is a process which will take time. Modernization, industrialization, urbanization and faster means of communication and transport, extension of trade unions, Communist ideas—all these are contributing to the equalizing and unifying process. But we still have a long march ahead.

LECTURE 3

Castes as Pressure Groups

In the last two lectures I explained the growth of the Non-Brahman movement and its political and social consequences in general. There is nothing like a Non-Brahman caste or community, as I have repeatedly observed. The term covers everybody other than the Brahman and includes the Harijans, Christians, and Mohammedans. Leaving aside the Christians and Mohammedans and the Scheduled Castes, there must be a few hundred major castes and a few hundred minor castes. Even the last Census Report to record caste names did not enumerate all castes. But for political considerations it is necessary to take careful notice of some of the major castes. For our purpose, the Scheduled Castes can be taken as one unit; though there is a hierarchy of different castes, two of them being the most numerous and important. Towards the end I deal with the problem of the Harijans in general—but not as a pressure group.

The Distribution of Major and Minor Castes

The caste topographical map of Tamil Nadu presents an interesting picture of the interplay of the major agricultural castes. In every district, there is a fair proportion of Harijans, ranging from 15 per cent to 22 per cent, giving an average of 18 per cent. They are largely agricultural labourers, and in the pre-Independence days, no better off than slaves and bonded serfs. Above them come the proper agricultural castes, the Vanniakula Kshatryas in Chingleput, North and

South Arcot Districts, Salem and Dharmapuri, in many areas matching or exceeding the Harijans in number. In Trichy and Tanjore Districts, they are confined to a few taluqs, and in the rest of the State, they are thinly spread. In the southern districts of Madura, Ramnad, and Tirunelveli, the Kallars and Maravars occupy a similar position. The Vanniyars and Maravars include a minority of small land owners and cultivating tenants, but the bulk of the people are agricultural labourers, doing the same work as the top layer of the Harijans. The other major caste is the Kongu Vellalas, who are the important landholding and cultivating classes in Salem, Coimbatore, and part of the Madura district, with the difference that few of them are agricultural labourers as such. There are three other major castes, who are not exclusively agricultural, namely, the Idayars or Yadhavas, the weaver caste of Kai Kolar, and the Shanans, better known as Nadars. The Vellalas, according to the Census Report, are numerically the largest. But all of them are not the Karkarthars or Saivite Vellalas and Mudaliars. The Kongu Vellalas are not separately enumerated, and their present population is estimated at 25 to 30 lakhs. There are nearly a hundred sub-castes, including even a fictional caste called Veerakodi Vellalas, and all of them are grouped together under 'Vellalas'.

Traditional Upper Castes

Traditionally, land had been owned substantially by Brahmans, Vellalas of the higher sub-divisions, Naidus, and Reddiars. Owing to the impact caused by education, government service, and other professions, and the passing of Zamindari and tenancy legislation, Brahman land ownership has declined, but the others still retain their prominent position. Literacy amongst them was always higher than the average, and in the earlier years of the Non-Brahman or Dravidian movement, the beneficiaries displacing the Brahman came largely from these higher Hindu Non-Brahman castes. They are dominant castes, and they exert pressure effortlessly as their interests demand.

Naturally this position would not be meekly accepted by the other Non-Brahman castes, especially the numerically bigger castes. In fact, the resentment against their inferior ritual position in the caste hierarchy began as early as the last years of the nineteenth century and this resentment led to different consequences.

Sanskritization

The first step these major castes took was what is now called Sanskritization by sociologists: the adoption of the Brahman, Kshatrya, or Vaisya appellation in place of the old caste name. A Brahman caste name will only evoke contempt and will never pass muster, as the Nadars discovered very early when they adopted the rituals and signs of the twice-born. The next best are Kshatrya and Vaisya. The other features of Sanskritization are observing Brahman feasts and rituals, and becoming fully or partially vegetarian.

Vanniakula Kshatrya

The Pallis or Padayachis, as they were known, adopted the caste name Vanniakula Kshatrya, even towards the last two decades of the nineteenth century. Their Maha Sangam was founded about the same time as the Indian National Congress itself, and several social reforms were brought about, but nobody appears to have taken their Kshatrya origin seriously, by giving them a status next to Brahmans. Their own leaders accept this. Though they are the biggest single community amongst caste Hindus, nowhere are they in the position of becoming a dominant caste, though they overrule some smaller castes in their localities by weight of their numerical superiority. One reason for this is the low level of educational achievement and the absence of a sizeable upper crust, there being very few big landlords, merchants, or moneyed people. In sheer frustration, the caste politicized itself in the belief that success in elections would bring them the status of a dominant caste and prominence in politics and administration.

Toilers' Party

A young man from Cuddalore, from a good middle-class family, founded the Toilers' Party in the late 1940s, and organized the Vanniya caste, particularly in South Arcot and Chinglepet. Another lawyer, who already had some political experience, did similar work in North Arcot and nearby areas, under the name of Toilers' Commonweal Party. The formation of the two parties, representing the largest single caste, made the caste a major pressure group. It is worth noting that in spite of its size, not many of this caste joined the Justice Party or the Non-Brahman movement earlier, or the Dravida Kazhagam movement later. The caste had maintained its individuality, and developed pride in its role as the leading backward caste. Without much effort or money, the two Toilers' parties together secured, in their electoral debut in 1952, 24 seats in the Madras Assembly and a few in Parliament too. As the leadership was not united, Rajaji, who formed the ministry, won over one of the leaders with a following of six, and saw to it that the Commonweal Party was dissolved. It was perhaps the first instance of mass defection engineered by the Congress leadership. A few years later, Kamaraj did to the main Toilers' Party what Rajaji did to the Commonweal Party. The Toilers' Party ceased to exist as a Legislative Party, till it was revived again in 1963. But it met with no electoral success, as the caste men by that time lost faith in the caste-based party and leadership. In spite of the groups' merger with the Congress, the M.L.A.s of the caste in the Assembly functioned together unofficially as a pressure group for promoting the advancement of their fellow caste men, especially in getting jobs and honorary appointments to places of importance. The functioning of the Vanniyar caste, whether as a party, or as an unofficial pressure group, clearly indicates the slow displacement of the forward castes by the backward castes in all regional political parties. Their efforts bore better results in the matter of Backward Class representation in the services and in seeing that an adequate number of the caste were chosen as candidates for election by every contending political party. In every party in the Tamil Nad Assembly, there are Vanniyars. There are traditional Congressmen, and there are equally committed persons in the other parties. With charismatic leadership, they may try to capture the organizational machinery of one of the existing parties and dominate it.

The Nadars

The caste, 'Shanan', as it was originally known in the earlier decades of the century, apart from being considered very low in the social ritual scale, was regarded as untouchable in some parts of Tirunelveli and Kanyakumari. Hence the tenacity with which its leaders decided to uplift their position. As I observed earlier, Sanskritization by calling themselves some kind of Brahmans, was a failure, as it only exposed them to ridicule. They tried to improve their lot economically, first by becoming transporters and traders in jaggery (the product made out of tapping the palmyrah palm), and then gradually spreading to retail and wholesale trade in spices, grains, firewood, etc. In the course of two or three generations, they became a respected trading and industrial community in Madurai and Ramnad Districts and later in all urban areas in the State. There was an organized attempt to improve the education of the younger generation and their Sangam took steps to establish their own schools and colleges. In this, they had the example and assistance of their people who went over to Christianity, in large numbers, very early. Their social consciousness even led them to ask for the removal of the caste name from the list of backward communities, though subsequently they realized their mistake, and petitioned for restoring reservation. A fairly substantial crust of a well-to-do trading class has developed—not in any way comparable to the professional trading community of Chettiars—and the community was lucky to produce a leader of Kamaraj's eminence. The caste, however, is not politically as conscious as the Vanniakula Kshatryas, but it is nevertheless a force to be reckoned with. Every political party would like to have their support in the southern districts, and in every election, Nadars have been elected to the local Assembly and to Parliament. They pull their weight, and their politicians join together in the caste interest, in whatever party they may be. They have not shown preference for any political party, though their first choice would be Congress. Every party leader tries to accommodate Nadars in positions of power. The caste has no political ambition to form a party or to dominate one, but furnishes an example of successful group effort, unparalleled by any other Tamil Nadu caste. The only comparison would be with the Ezhavars of Kerala.

The Nadar leadership, being largely from the trading classes, believes in maintaining good relations with the Government of the day, whatever be its political complexion. Their general attitude is non-partisan. They have made no effort to ally themselves with any other major caste to form a larger block. Their rivalry and suspicion of the powerful Maravar caste in the southern districts, stands in the way of any alliance between them. The Vanniyars, a numerically larger caste, with greater political consciousness and reasonable success in elections, cannot match its success as a pressure group with that of the Kallar, Maravar, or the non-partisan Nadar caste. Politics has strengthened caste consciousness among the Vanniyars but has had no such impact on the Nadars, whose caste consciousness is kept well under control.

Kallars and Maravars

This is another large group whose impact on the politics of Tamil Nadu deserves some study. The Maravars of Tirunelveli and Madurai, and the sister community of Kallars, who spread out from Ramnad District, together constitute perhaps the second largest single community. There is an allied caste called Agamudiars, and taking this along with the other two castes, the larger group is sometimes called Mukkulathor: the three clans. The impression of the Tamil Nadu Backward Classes Commission was that, while the Kallars and Maravars would like to unite with the Agamudiars, the latter, especially from Thanjavur District, do not show any such affinity. Their literacy rate has always been higher, and traditionally, they have been a service caste. The percentage of agricultural labourers amongst them is smaller. They would like to associate with the Tuluva Vellalars, who sometimes call themselves a branch of the Agamudiars. The Kallars and Maravars have the advantage that many Zamindars and Princelings flourished in their castes, and held powerful positions, till recently, in the southern districts. The Raja of Ramnad is a Maravar and the Raja of Pudukottai is a Kallar. Apart from this aristocratic heritage, in recent times they produced leaders like Muthuramalinga Thevar and Mookiah Thevar, and there was a tendency for Maravars to favour the Forward Bloc. But Kallars and Maravars are to be found now in all political parties. The Maravars constitute 13 per cent of the population of Tirunelveli, and about 9.5 per cent of the Ramanathapuram District. The Kallars form 9 per cent of the population in Madurai, and 10 per cent in Thanjavur. Taking the Kallars and Maravars together, they constitute a power in the three southern districts. They have been able to return to the State Assembly a number of M.L.A.s far in excess of the percentage of their population. The reasons apparently are the strength of their martial tradition, caste cohesion, and competent political leadership. Though the bulk of the people are poor agricultural labourers and cultivating tenants, they are making good progress. They are becoming highly politicized and have an eye on the winning post. If allied with the Vanniyars of the northern districts, they would form a powerful caste combination; but chances of such collaboration are remote. But they are a force to reckon with politically, and they will manage to have the last word on any matter concerning the southern districts, despite the Nadars' achievements in many fields.

Number Alone is Not a Determining Factor: Yadhavars and Kammalars

I have dealt with the ascriptive tendencies of three of the major castes. Their strength largely depends on the population being concentrated in sizeable numbers in some areas. This gives them considerable political weightage. There is at least one major caste with a bigger population than the Nadars or Maravars or Kallars—I refer to the Idayars or Yadhava caste—but as the population is scattered fairly evenly in all the districts, they do not command a decisive voice even in one Assembly constituency. Political parties do not find it necessary to put up a Yadhava candidate, unless it be on consideration other than caste. In no Assembly have they been able to send more than 4 or 5 members, and they cannot aspire to become a pressure group in politics as the other major castes have managed to become. The position of other castes without concentration in at least some areas is worse still. The Kammalar group, or that of the oil-monger (Vaniyan), which has its population thinly spread over all the districts, has no chance of returning an M.L.A. Similar is the lot of the weaver caste. The numerically big castes manage to send a good number of M.L.A.s, though not in adequate proportion to their population. The thinly spread castes have no chances at all, under the present system of election. But the dominant castes, by their social, economic and political influence at the local and State level, manage somehow to get themselves more than adequately represented. The exception is the Brahmans, who form 3 per cent of the population and should expect 7 or 8 members at least to be elected, but they have none.

To function effectively as a political pressure group is easier for the dominant castes and they do so in practice, whatever be the complexion of the Government in power. Mere number alone does not count, except when it enables a larger number of M.L.A.s to be returned. The economic and other achievements of the caste are equally important. If, from a caste, there are one or two powerful ministers with discreet caste loyalty, and a strong coterie of M.L.A.s around each, one can say that there is a nucleus of a pressure group. It will be more effective, if outside of politics, the caste is well represented among the superior Government servants, amongst High Court Judges, and other professions.

Communal Representation

Any examination of the position of castes will not be complete unless a reference is made to communal representation in public services. The growth in power, and the ability to arouse public opinion and government support in favour of the major Backward Communities, are largely due to the communal concession policy pursued in the Presidency since the beginning of the century, and in turn, the agitational strength of particular castes has from time to time changed and shaped the communal representation policy.

It must be mentioned at the outset that the communal representation policy in the Madras Presidency is anterior to the Non-Brahman or Dravidian movement. The list of Backward or Depressed Classes, as it was known then, owes its origin to the Grants-in-Aid code framed in 1885. This code provides for aid to poor students from the untouchable or depressed castes. This list was reviewed and amplified in 1906 and 1913. Till 1913, no attempt was made to distinguish the backward castes from the depressed castes. A list of castes other than depressed castes was prepared in 1925. The two lists were further revised on the basis of the 1931 Census. The purpose of maintaining these two lists was only to regulate the grant of half school-fee concession. After Independence, the half-fee concession was converted to full-fee concession to the Scheduled Castes and Tribes alone. The list of Scheduled Castes is a statutory list under the constitution. The list of Backward Classes was revised from time to time, on the basis of the educational and social backwardness of the castes agitating for inclusion in the list compiled by the State Government. The facilities originally contemplated were confined to fee concessions in schools. This however greatly helped the progress of education of these people.

Because of the social awakening and political consciousness of the masses, a number of castes in the Backward Class list agitated for facilities on a par with Scheduled Castes. Some of them even petitioned for inclusion in the list of Scheduled Castes. In 1957, the Government of Madras approved of a list, for the first time, of Most Backward Classes, with the purpose only of granting more educational concession, and not for reservation in appointments.

The Communal G.O., 1921

The story of communal representation in the services, however, as distinct from educational concessions, begins only with the Non-Brahman manifesto of 1916. The Tamil Nadu Backward Classes Commission Report gives the following statistics of employment in Government Services: 'It is on record that between 1894 and 1904, in the provincial Civil services, out of 16 officers 15 were Brahmans, among 21 Assistant Engineers, 17 were Brahmans, out of 140 Deputy Collectors 77 were Brahmans, and out of 128 District Munsiffs 98 were Brahmans.' This was inevitable, as, according to E.F. Irschick, who had made a deep study of this subject, during these years, between 67 per cent and 71 per cent of the graduates of the Madras University came from a single community: Brahman. As a result of the Non-Brahman agitation from 1915, Government introduced the principle of communal representation in services from 1921, by introducing a system of rotation of recruitment among five different groups. This is hailed as one of the greatest achievements of the Justice Party. This system of appointments based on rotation under 5 categories continued for 25 years—till Independence. I do not intend to pursue the course of communal representation, and the modification made to the list from time to time. My purpose in giving this brief resume, of communal concession in education and communal representation in the services, is only to underscore the relation between the political and social awakening of the Non-Brahman castes (including the Scheduled castes) and their desire for a greater share in the service and educational opportunities provided by the State. The Justice Party gave the lead, and any amount of preaching of the theory of equality before the law could not check the movement, and the

Congress Government after Independence continued the same policy, and even amplified it. Needless to say, the Dravida Munnetra Kazhagam and the Anna Dravida Munnetra Kazhagam will do nothing to weaken or discourage the policy of representation based on caste or class. The term 'class' is but a euphemism. In fact, the Madras or Tamil Nadu example is now copied and even elaborated in other states. This progress of the backward class or caste representation has now provoked counter-attack from the forward castes even in Tamil Nadu. Things have come to a stage now that backwardness is becoming a vested interest. Once a caste is included in the list, it is impossible to remove it. Political parties will regard such an action as nothing short of political suicide, as they view everything from the 'voting strength' point of view. More and more castes are included in the list. Against the views of the Backward Classes commission, several castes with large population have been included in the list after 1971, so much so that nearly 80 per cent of the population is backward (including Scheduled Castes and Tribes). In fact, there are so many loopholes in the wording of caste names and in the administrative orders, that every caste, other than the Brahman, can find its way into the backward class list. This in fact is going on continuously, and the disparities are widening, instead of reducing. Social justice will be abused and rendered ineffective if the State does not review the policy from time to time, at least once in ten years.

Unequal Beneficiaries

What is happening is an unfortunate trend. The list of backward classes is being expanded and the proportion of reservation has also increased, now covering almost 70 per cent of the appointments and seats in educational institutions. The forward classes have always opposed reservation, as discouraging talent and depriving the state and society of the services of the meritorious. This agitation is spreading in all the states. Apart from this, the really backward classes have always complained that a few forward or progressive castes, included in the list, manage to secure for themselves a share of the reserved quota far in excess of their number. In Tamil Nadu, according to the Backward Classes Commission, a few castes with a total population of 20 or 25 lakhs, had managed to secure more than 60 per cent of the reserved posts in Government services and seats in educational institutions. In view of this, the less progressive among the backward castes claim proportional representation, an almost impracticable proposition.

Reservation to be Revised

Modern society and modern thinking will not admit that environmental and social handicaps cannot be eradicated by conscious effort in a generation or two. There is plenty of talent amongst the backward castes, as we have seen from their progress in the professions, examinations, and service achievements. The Nadar community has demonstrated this remarkably. This talent will flourish better with some competition. The leaders of the backward classes must realize that they cannot depend on State support forever. Now youngsters are beginning to depend too much on the reservation support. The Non-Brahmans, and particularly what are known as the backward classes, have had advantages secured for them by reservation in admission to educational institutions, and by liberal reservation in government service. It is true that at present this reservation is confined to State services, and not to the Central services, public sector, and business organizations. This, however, is under examination by the Backward Classes Commission appointed three years ago by the Janata Government. It is only fair that reservation is conceded for the Backward Castes in Central Services, as it has been done for Scheduled Castes and Tribes. As far as Tamil Nadu is concerned, some backward castes have made good progress. Some are lagging behind. On the whole, the progress is not adequate enough to bring them on a par with the forward classes. Inevitably, the progress is uneven. The young men and women require to put in more effort and not to depend too much on reservation.

Removal of the Upper Crust

There are two tendencies which have become noticeable. Reservation has helped the backward classes for nearly six decades from the 1920s to the 1980s—practically three generations. The benefit of reservation has gone mostly to the few top castes amongst the backward, and to an increasing layer of upper crust in each caste. The filtration process has not been thorough or uniform. This is not surprising, and is to some extent unavoidable. It would be a step in the larger interests of society and of the backward classes themselves, if a check is applied to both these tendencies. There has been thinking on these lines among administrators; but the opposition of vested interests has been too strong to carry out the necessary pruning. But sooner or later, the removal of the two kinds of upper crust will become unavoidable; otherwise we will be encouraging the castes to form a class system within the caste system—not an altogether desirable trend in a democratic and socialistic society.

I have not included the Harijans in my discussion on the Non-Brahman movement, as this movement affected mainly the ranks of the Non-Brahmans other than the Scheduled Castes. Reservation for the Scheduled Castes in educational institutions and services, and representation in the legislature, are guaranteed under the Constitution itself, and both Central and State Government have been adopting various measures to enable these people to avail themselves of their opportunities. But here again, the beneficiaries have been a small upper crust, drawn from one or two of the more progressive castes amongst them. The general economic improvement among them is perhaps a little more noticeable than is the case with the lower strata of the backward classes. This has inevitably led to clashes between them in various places. The land-owning classes who employ agricultural labourers, and their fellow cultivating tenants, are very reluctant to accord equality of treatment to the Scheduled Castes. The people of the Scheduled Castes, on their part, are now very conscious of the special constitutional protection that they enjoy. Having imbibed

Self-Respect ideas from the Non-Brahman movement, and egalitarian ideas from the labour movement they no longer tolerate the indignities inflicted on them by the caste Hindus. If the social and political fabric is to be preserved, both the State and Central Governments, and Hindu society at large, should secure for the Scheduled Castes, their place in the sun.

Explanatory Notes

I. An Exercise in Biography (1958)

CHAPTER 1

p. 13. **I am 54 (completed 53)**: This is standard South Indian usage. Sattanathan declares that he has completed fifty-three years of his life, and is, at the time of writing, in his fifty-fourth year.

p. 13. **Shencottah**: a town in the south of present-day Tamil Nadu. The name is an Anglicized form of the Tamil name Sengottai (*sen-kottai*), literally, 'Red Fort'. Some local inhabitants attribute the name to the reddish soil of the area; others believe that in a bygone era, a fort, the seat of a local chieftain, did exist. At the time of which Sattanathan is writing, Shencottah belonged to the **Princely State of Travancore** (p. 32n.) and was located on its boundary with **Thirunelveli** (p. 17n.) district in British India.

p. 15. **First World War**: 1914–18.

p. 15. **Humayun's legendary story**: The *Humayun-Nama* (1552), written by Gulbadan, daughter of Babar, the first Mughal emperor of India, tells how when Humayun, Babar's heir, fell seriously ill, Babar prayed for his recovery, pledging his own life for that of his son. Babar died as Humayun recovered. See Gul-Badan Begam, *The History of Humâyûn (Humâyûn-Nâma)*, transl. Annette S. Beveridge (London: Royal Asiatic Society, 1902), 105–9.

p. 15. **Sanskritized middle classes**: The term 'Sanskritization' (see also Lecture 3, p. 178n.), now standard usage in sociology, was coined by M.N. Srinivas, in his *Religion and Society among the Coorgs of South India*, to describe the process of upward mobility of the lower castes: 'A low caste was able, in a generation or two, to rise to a higher position in the hierarchy by adopting vegetarianism and teetotalism, and by Sanskritizing its ritual and pantheon. In short, it took over, as far as possible, the customs, rites, and beliefs of the Brahmins.' See M.N. Srinivas, *Religion and Society among the Coorgs of South India* (1952), new edn, introduced by André Béteille (New Delhi: Oxford University Press, 2003), 29. As Sattanathan implies, this kind of upward mobility is also linked to a rise in social class: the effect of Sanskritization is especially manifest among those sections of the lower castes who have attained, or aspire to, middle-class status. Here Sattanathan describes Sanskritization as extending to language, in the use, by the aspirant classes, of words of Sanskritic origin (such as *amma* for 'mother') in preference to the purely Tamil (non-Sanskritic) equivalent, in this case, *aathal*.

p. 16. K: Narayanan Kasamuthu Sattanatha Karayalar (*c.* 1851–1917). His descendants still live in the ancestral home in Shencottah.

p. 17. **they belonged to two different communities**: Karayalar belonged to the **Idayar** or **Yadhava** caste, a pastoral or shepherd caste, higher up in the social hierarchy of the low castes ('**Sudra**', p. 134n.) than the **Padayachi** or **Vanniyar** caste of agricultural workers (see Lecture 3, p. 178) to which Sattanathan's family belonged.

p. 17. **Thirunelveli**, known in English as 'Tinnevelly' during the colonial period, was the chief town of an eponymous district located in south-eastern India, in the southern part of present-day Tamil Nadu, and belonging to **the British Indian province of Madras** (p. 49n.).

Chapter 2

p. 22. **the family deity**: See chapter 6, pp. 66–8 and n.

p. 23. **the piper, the drummer, the *taalam* or time-keeper, and the background piper**: The 'piper' plays the instrument that Sattanathan later (p. 120) refers to by its Tamil name, ***naadaswaram***, a wind-instrument similar to a clarinet, but longer. The 'drum' is the two-sided *thavil*, slung horizontally around the percussionist's neck and beaten with the hand on one side and a stick on the other. The *taalam* is a small cymbal used to keep time (the word *taalam* also signifies the beat of a piece of music). The second *naadaswaram* backs up the first.

p. 24. ***pandal***: canopy or awning.

p. 25. **to elaborate their musical theme**: In South Indian classical (Carnatic) music, the musician, performing a set piece or composition, displays his virtuosity in long passages of improvisation, based on the scale (*raagam*), or certain of the musical phrases of the piece.

p. 25. ***Balai! Sabaash!***: expressions of approbation, equivalent to 'Bravo!' 'Well done!'

p. 25. **Pillay** or Pillai, also **Saivite Vellala**: the highest of the Tamil Non-Brahmin castes, often stricter than the Brahmins in their religious observances and adherence to ritual.

p. 26. ***kaavadi***: This form of penance, which consists in carrying an elaborate and heavy structure on the shoulders over long distances, is especially associated with the worship of **Subramania** or **Muruga** (see below).

p. 26. **Subramania**: See **Muruga**, below.

p. 26. **Muruga**: Also bearing the Sanskritic names, **Subramania**, Skanda, or Kartikeya, and probably representing a synthesis of the Aryan and Dravidian pantheons (see Lecture 1, p. 153), the Tamil god Muruga or Murugan, a son of Shiva, is an important deity in Tamil religion from a very early period. There is evidence to indicate that the worship of Murugan (the youthful god) or Velan (the god with the spear) among the Tamil people dates to prehistory—see K.A. Nilakanta Sastri, *A History of South India: From Prehistoric Times to the Fall of Vijayanagar* (1955), 4th edn, introduced by R. Champakalakshmi (New Delhi: Oxford University Press, 2003), 51–2. Muruga is the god of youth and beauty. Shrines dedicated to him are typically located on hill-tops.

p. 27. **objectionable food**: any food considered to stimulate the appetites, including many of the foods that grow in the earth, such as garlic and onions.

p. 28. **during Id . . . the custom of 'playing the Tiger'**: The 'Pulikali' or Tiger Dance is performed by Muslims in the Kerala region, not during Id, but Muharram, the festival of the martyrdom of the Prophet's grandson, Hussain. Muslim men in tiger costume, with masks and body paint, dance and parade through the streets. The tiger symbolizes Hussain's valour.

Chapter 3

p. 29. **the old *gurukulam* system:** The ancient Indian system of education, dating back to the Vedic period (first millennium BCE), in which pupils resided with their *guru* (teacher), as part of his *kulam* (family), for the period of their education. The initiation ceremony belongs to the rituals associated with this system. In modern times, the system lingers in the performing arts.

p. 29. **Saraswati *pooja*, *Vijaya Dasami*:** The day of the worship of Saraswati (a *pooja* is a ceremony or ritual of worship), the Victorious Tenth day. These are consecutive days that fall within of the festival of Navarathri ('nine nights') in Tamil Nadu, which celebrates the slaying of the buffalo demon, Mahishaasura, by the goddess Durga. The ninth day of the festival is sacred to Saraswati, the goddess of learning and the arts. The following day, the day of Durga's victory, is considered auspicious for the start of any new venture or pursuit, especially in education.

p. 29. **the sacred symbols:** the Tamil letters that spell the word 'Om'.

p. 30. **the pupils sat on the floor with sand spread before them:** This method of instruction in village schools had been practised for centuries; it is remarked, for instance, by the Italian traveller Pietro Della Valle in 1623. See *The Travels of Pietro Della Valle in India*, transl. G. Havers (1664), new ed., with a life of the author, introduction and notes by E. Grey (New Delhi: Asian Educational Services, 1991), 227–8.

p. 32. **the Princely State of Travancore:** Colonial India was comprised of two kinds of administrative units: 'provinces', directly under British control, and 'princely states', administered internally by their Indian rulers, under British protection. The state of Travancore, ruled by the Maharaja of Travancore, was located in the south-west of present-day Kerala, between the **Western Ghats** (p. 43n.) and the Arabian Sea, running about 174 miles from its northern boundary to its southernmost tip at **Cape Comorin** (p. 111n.).

p. 35. **Certain cousinly relations alone have that right:** In many South Indian castes, cousins, when they are children of siblings of different sex, are entitled to marry, this marital right being known as *murai*. Thus a boy is entitled to marry his father's sister's daughter; a girl is entitled to marry her mother's brother's son (or indeed, by *murai*, her mother's brother himself). The children of same-sex siblings, however, are themselves considered siblings, and not permitted to marry.

p. 35. **the usual professions of the caste**: in this case, probably the cultivation of the land. Other occupations of the **Padayachi** or **Vanniyar** caste (see Lecture 3, p. 178) caste in that area included musicianship and freshwater fishing, in both of which, as well as in agriculture, Sattanathan's father was involved.

p. 36. **a particular caste—toddy-tapping being their hereditary profession:** In Tamil Nadu, toddy, here, palm-liquor, was traditionally drawn from the palm by the **Nadar** caste, also known as **Shanan**. For a fuller account of the Nadar community, see Lecture 3, pp. 180–1.

p. 36. **Tinnevelly**: See **Thirunelveli** (p. 17n.).

Chapter 4

p. 41. **Tenkasi**, whose name means 'southern Kasi (Varanasi)', is located in Thirunelveli district, about 53 km to the north-west of Thirunelveli, and is known for its temple of Vishwanatha (Shiva), *c.* fourteenth century.

p. 43. **Quilon**, called Kollam in Malayalam, a port located on the Arabian Sea, on the west coast of India in present-day Kerala. Historically of some strategic importance, Quilon was a large commercial town and railway terminus of the state of Travancore.

p. 43. **the Western Ghats**: mountain range running along the western coast of the Indian peninsula to its southern tip.

p. 44. **I was a Tamilian, and not a Malayalee, from my tuft of hair**: The practice of shaving the front portion of the head, and wearing the hair long at the back, in a tuft, was common among Tamil Non-Brahmin men, but not among Malayalis.

p. 45. **Kuttalam**, at the time 'Courtallum' in English, is located about 170 m above sea level in the Western Ghats in Thirunelveli district, about 59 km to the north-west of Thirunelveli. Popular, during the colonial era, with Indians and Europeans alike, it is a spa town, famous for its waterfalls, which are believed to have medicinal properties. According to Bishop Caldwell in 1881, 'It may be asserted without risk of exaggeration that Courtallum is the finest fresh-water bathing place in the world.' See R. Caldwell, *A Political and General History of the District of Tinnevelly, in the Presidency of Madras, from the Earliest Period to its Cession to the English Government in A.D. 1801* (Madras: Government Press, 1881), 8.

p. 46. ***namaskaaram***: respectful salutation or bow, with palms joined together.

Chapter 5

p. 49. **the British Indian province of Madras**: The southern Indian province of Madras consisted, under the British, of present-day Tamil Nadu, much of Andhra Pradesh, and parts of Kerala. For the distinction between 'province' and 'princely state', see **the Princely State of Travancore** (p. 32n.).

p. 50. **Vijayanagar Feudatories**: nobles who ruled lands held by feudal tenure under the kings of the Vijayanagar empire, the last great Hindu empire of South India, founded in the 1340s and continuing, despite its decline, till the mid-seventeenth century. In its heyday, the empire spanned the Telegu-, Kannada-, and Tamil-speaking regions. Originally viceroys or representatives, appointed by the Vijayanagara kings to administer provinces such as Madurai and Tanjavur, these feudatories, known as **Nayaks** (p. 155n.), became, with the decline of the Vijayanagar empire, the *de facto* rulers of their provinces.

p. 50. **Naidu**: nomenclature borne by a group of prosperous and socially-advantaged Telugu Non-Brahmin castes.

p. 52. **very low caste**: an 'untouchable' caste by the Vedic system, now, 'Dalit', or officially, '**Scheduled Caste**' (p. 184n.), but at the time, 'depressed class', lower down on the caste hierarchy than the **Sudra** (p. 134n.) or '**backward class**' (p. 149n.) to which Sattanathan belonged.

p. 55. **fast and feast**: 'fast' here implies that no rice was eaten at that meal. Among many South Indians, 'meal' signifies that rice is eaten; any other repast, no matter how substantial, is 'tiffin'.

p. 55. ***idli* or *dosai***: Made from the same batter, about four parts rice to one part black lentils, *idli*, a steamed savoury cake, and *dosai*, a savoury pancake, are standard breakfast or tiffin fare in South India.

p. 55. ***saambaar***: a traditionally South Indian, liquid, lentil-based dish, with vegetables.

p. 55. **Such was the even tenor of my childhood life**: Just audible, here, is the echo of Thomas Gray's frequently-anthologized *Elegy Written in a Country Churchyard* (1751), ll. 75–6: 'Along the cool sequester'd vale of life/They kept the noiseless tenor of their way.' Gray is also describing the rural poor.

p. 57. **the harvests of both seasons**, one taking place in January, at the time of Pongal (see p. 59 and n.), the other in July–August.

p. 58. **Chit Fund**: This kind of co-operative organization of a group of subscribers is among the oldest of existing financial systems in India, and, on the auction principle outlined by Sattanathan, continues to flourish all over the country.

p. 59. **the most sacred holiday of the Tamils . . . Pongal Day, which falls on the first day of the Tamil month *Thai***: Pongal, the most important of the Tamil festivals, is primarily a rural festival of thanksgiving for the harvest, taking its name from the ceremony of the boiling over (*pongal*) of the brass pot in which newly-harvested rice is cooked. Usually performed at sunrise, the ceremony marks the beginning of *Thai*, the auspicious tenth month of the Tamil calendar.

p. 60. **flat rice offered in worship**: rice dry roasted in the husk, then pounded. Called *aval* in Tamil, it is commonly used as a ritual offering.

p. 63. **burial ghat**: cemetery; the word 'ghat' in this context is probably an Anglicization of the Tamil word *kaadu*, as in *sudu-kaadu* (cremation ground). At the time of which Sattanathan is writing, the norm among low-caste Non-Brahmins was to bury their dead. Nowadays they prefer cremation.

Chapter 6

p. 66. **pearls were traditionally associated with the southern districts**: The districts of Madurai and Thirunelveli in southern Tamil Nadu belonged to the ancient Tamil kingdom of the **Pandyas** (p. 154n.), which controlled the pearl fisheries along the South Indian coast. Pearl fishing still continues at Tuticorin, the seaport of the ancient kingdom.

p. 66. **not a god known to the Hindu pantheon, nor . . . one of the popular deities of Dravidian folklore or legend . . . the local patron deity of the tribe:** Here 'Hindu' signifies the established Sanskritic or Aryan pantheon, as distinct from the gods that are Dravidian in origin. The deity Sattanathan is describing belongs to neither tradition, but is peculiar to a single family. The word 'tribe' is used casually, to refer to the extended family.

p. 68. **ordained priest of his generation,** i.e., designated by family mores. In this instance, the deity is purely familial, but in the larger social community also, especially in rural areas, Non-Brahmins, usually members of a numerically dominant caste in the area, officiate as priests in shrines and temples and at religious ceremonies, although, with the progress of sanskritization, Brahmin priests are increasingly the norm.

p. 68. ***chombu*:** corruption of *chembu*, metal vessel.

p. 69. **S.K.:** Subramania Karayalar (d. 1928).

p. 70. **'S':** Sattanathan, the given name of the founder of the family, see K (p. 16 and n.).

p. 70. **Trivandrum,** in the south-west of the state of Travancore, was the state capital, as it is of present-day Kerala, and takes its name from the presiding **deity of the state** (p. 114n.).

p. 75. **the most successful person among those practising music as a profession in the district:** Chitrai Nayakar (d. 1925) rose, in his day, to considerable fame as a ***naadaswaram*** (p. 121n.) virtuoso. Family recollection has it that he had performed by invitation as far afield as the durbar of the Maharaja of Mysore (probably Krishnaraja Wodeyar IV, r. 1894–1940) and the Murugan temple at Kathirgamam in Sri Lanka.

p. 75. **the beautiful name Sundarapandyapuram:** *Sundara* means 'beautiful'; the suffix *puram* indicates a place name. The beautiful god, Sundara Pandya, is a Tamil avatar of Shiva, who takes earthly form in the ancient line of the **Pandya** (p. 154n.) **kings of Tamil Nad.** Celebrated in the Tamil verse-narrative, *Thiruvilaiyaadal Puranam* ('Story of the Sacred Games', *c.* seventeenth century), by the poet-saint Paranjothi Munivar, Sundara Pandya is an alluring and playful god, only occasionally reminding us of his better-known, more fearsome manifestation. Sattanathan was especially fond of the *Thiruvilaiyadal* stories.

p. 75. **More about him I will have to say later:** The eminent musician was to become intimately connected with Sattanathan, not only by the marriage of Sattanathan's sister to the musician's nephew (see chapter 10), but by Sattanathan's own marriage in 1929—outside the span of the present fragment—to Meenakshi, a daughter of the musician's second wife. In the more complete account of his life that Sattanathan originally intended, the musician would no doubt have figured again, as Sattanathan's father-in-law.

p. 76. ***cheedai***: small hard balls of deep-fried rice flour, a savoury South Indian snack.

p. 76. **the old Maharaja of Travancore (Sri Moolam Thirunal)**: Moolam Thirunal Rama Varma (1857–1924) ruled as Maharaja of Travancore from 1885 to 1924.

p. 78. **S.S.L.C.**: Secondary School Leaving Certificate, the qualification awarded to a student on the completion of his schooling, requisite for enrolment in a pre-University (Intermediate, p. 94n.) course.

CHAPTER 7

p. 79. ***Ramayana* and *Mahabharata***: The two great Indian (Sanskrit) epics. The origins of the *Mahabharata*, which describes itself as the composition of the mythical sage, Vyasa, can be dated to *c.* 400 BCE, although the final compilation, some 100,000 verses in all, took shape over centuries. The *Ramayana*, shorter by far, and ascribing itself to another legendary sage, Valmiki, is of the same date or slightly later.

p. 79. **Swami Vivekananda**: Born Narendranath Dutta, the Bengali religious and social reformer later known as Swami Vivekananda (1863–1902), extolled India's cultural and spiritual heritage, and became a source of inspiration for the nationalist movement. Beginning with his address at the

1893 World Parliament of Religions in Chicago, Vivekananda achieved great success as a publicist of Hinduism in North America and Europe, gaining for it a philosophical and intellectual stature that it had previously lacked in the West.

p. 79. **a boy who eventually rose to be a distinguished Mathematician:** S. Sivasankaranarayana Pillai (1901–50) or S.S. Pillai, as he was known, a brilliant number theorist and one of the most outstanding of Indian mathematicians in the twentieth century, was, till his tragic death in an air crash in 1950, Sattanathan's dearest and most long-standing friend.

p. 79. **the legend of Vikramaditya:** Tales of the valour and wisdom of the legendary ruler, Vikramaditya, of the ancient city of Ujjayini in central India, are told in a Sanskrit text of unknown authorship, *Simhasana Dvatrimsika* (*c.* thirteenth century), which probably draws from an older oral tradition. The legendary Vikramaditya is said to be the founder of the Vikrama or Samvat era (beginning 58 BCE), the basis of a system of dating still in use in North India. Chronologically incompatible with this is another popular identification, of Vikramaditya with the historical Chandragupta II (*c.* 376–415), ruler of the vast Gupta empire that stretched across most of North India at the height of what is sentimentally regarded as India's 'golden age'.

p. 79. ***Kamba Ramayana*:** Tamil version (*c.* twelfth century) of the *Ramayana*, by the poet Kamban.

p. 79. ***Mahabharata* by Villiputhur Alwar:** The *Bharatham* (*c.* 1400), by the poet Villiputhuraar, is a Tamil version of the *Mahabharata* in 4350 verses. The term **Alwar** (p. 154n.) denotes a Tamil Vaishnavite saint.

p. 80. **Rama:** the seventh avatar of the god Vishnu, and the model king and hero of the *Ramayana.*

p. 81. **A year previously, when the German submarine 'Emden' cruised round the Indian seas:** Sattanathan is misremembering both the date and the type of naval craft to which he refers. The German light cruiser (not submarine), *SMS Emden*, perhaps the most romanticized ship of World War I, under her commanding officer, Kurt von Müller, inflicted heavy damage on Allied shipping in the Pacific and Indian oceans in the second half of 1914, not 1917, as in Sattanathan's narrative.

p. 81. ***Kaliyuga***: 'Black era': the present age of chaos and evil which, according to Hindu belief, immediately precedes apocalypse.

p. 81. **Pandavas**: Collective name for the five brothers, heroes of the *Mahabharata*; the epic recounts their victory in the great battle against their cousins, the Kauravas.

p. 81. **Ravana's *Raakshasas***: Ravana, the adversary of Rama and the great anti-hero of the *Ramayana* is, in the epic, the *raakshasa* (demon) ruler of the kingdom of *raakshasas*, Lanka.

p. 81. ***vimanas***: celestial vehicles.

p. 81. **Krishna**: The ninth avatar of the god Vishnu, and the guiding spirit of the *Mahabharata*.

p. 81. **Congress . . . the nationalist movement . . . Gandhi**: Nationalisms of various kinds began to be manifest in India in the last decades of the nineteenth century; the Indian National Congress came into being in 1885. Its early agenda, to increase the participation of Indians in governance and administration, was modest, but gradually, the demand for *swaraj* (self-rule) gained momentum. In 1907, at its annual meeting, at Surat on the west coast of India, Congress declared *swaraj* to be its goal. In 1919, Mohandas Karamchand Gandhi (1869–1948) entered nationalist politics, and, without formally holding office, soon took control of Congress. Gandhi's charisma and vast mass following made him the icon of the nationalist movement thereafter.

p. 81. **. . . self-government . . . Independence**: Self-government was at first envisaged as a government of India by Indians under the Crown, but scepticism grew about the implementation of such devolution, and at its Lahore Session in 1929, Congress demanded full independence by the following year.

p. 82. **Swamiji**: The title *Swami* denotes a Hindu religious or spiritual guru; the Hindi suffix *ji* indicates reverence or respect.

p. 82. **Ramakrishna**: Born Gadadhar Chatterjee in rural Bengal, Ramakrishna Paramahansa (1836–86), a mystic and advocate of religious tolerance, was Vivekananda's guru.

p. 82. **the Brahmo Samaj**: In 1828, the Bengali intellectual Raja Ram Mohun Roy (1772–1833), a pioneer of religious and social reform, founded the Brahmo Samaj, a religious organization based on monotheistic and ecumenical principles, and seeking to amalgamate Hinduism with the liberal humanism of the West.

p. 83. **Vallam**, near Kuttalam.

p. 85. **clarionet and horn**: The clarionet, in this instance, is the same as the Western instrument; the horn, called *kombu* in Tamil, is a wind-instrument in the shape of a cow's horn.

Chapter 8

p. 88. **the Jesuit College of St Joseph's**: The Jesuits date their presence in India to the arrival of St Francis Xavier in Goa in 1542. St Joseph's College was founded by the Jesuits in 1844 in Nagapatnam, a port town on the coast of present-day Tamil Nadu, to the south of Madras. The college was affiliated to the University of Madras in 1866, and in 1883, was transferred to Trichy (Tiruchirapalli).

p. 88. **Lane-Poole's book on Muslim India**: Stanley Lane-Poole, *Mediaeval India under Mohammedan Rule (AD 1712–1764)* (London: Fisher Unwin and New York: Putnam, 1903).

p. 88. **Lyall's on British India**: Alfred Lyall, *The Rise of British Dominion in India* (London: John Murray, 1893).

p. 88. **Tout's and Green's books on English History**: Thomas Frederick Tout, *A Short Analysis of English History* (London: Macmillan, 1891) and John Richard Green, *A Short History of the English People* (London: Macmillan, 1898).

p. 90. **Donor's**: Not Subramania Karayalar, who actually donated the money, but his father, Sattanatha Karayalar, in whose memory the money was donated.

p. 90. **a day in January–February**: The date is reckoned on the basis of the Tamil lunar calendar, and thus varies from year to year.

p. 91. **P.W.D.**: The Public Works Department, a governmental body in charge of the upkeep and maintenance of public lands and holdings.

p. 92. **Malabar**: The region adjoining the south-west (Malabar) coast of India. The name 'Malabar' signifies a mountainous or hilly region.

Chapter 9

p. 94. **Intermediate Examination**: pre-University examination, taken at the end of a two-year course which follows the completion of the student's school education.

p. 97. **mercy as described by Shakespeare**: in Portia's famous speech to Shylock in *The Merchant of Venice*, IV. i. ll. 183ff.

p. 98. **our College**: the Maharaja's College, Trivandrum, established in 1866 as a college affiliated to the Madras University, the maharaja at the time being Ayilam Thirunal (r. 1860–80). In 1924, the College split, its Arts and Sciences departments becoming two separate colleges (see p. 109). They were re-amalgamated in 1942, when the institution was given its present name, University College.

p. 100. **C.R. Das . . . the Swarajya Party**: The Swarajya Party, a splinter group of Congress, led by Chittaranjan Das (1870–1925, popularly called 'Deshbandhu', the nation's friend) and Motilal Nehru (1861–1931), was established during Gandhi's temporary withdrawal from political activity in the 1920s. Gandhi called off his campaign of non-cooperation in 1922; he was arrested on 10 March 1922, and jailed for two years. The Swarajya Party was formed as a constitutionalist party, to contest elections to the provincial and central legislative councils under the provisions of the **Government of India Act of 1919** (p. 164n.) for increasing Indian participation in government. The party's avowed intention, in ending Gandhi's boycott of elections to the legislatures, was to fight the British on their own ground, and it won a large number of seats in both the Central and Provincial legislatures in the elections of 1923. The decision to lift the boycott of the councils caused a rupture in Congress, between the 'pro-changers'—Das and Nehru and their followers—and the 'no-changers', those in favour of continuing the boycott.

p. 100. **Phookan of Assam**: Tarun Ram Phookan (1877–1939), a lawyer, was among the key leaders of the Indian Nationalist movement in Assam. He became President of the Assam Provincial Congress Committee (APCC) in July 1921, soon after it was constituted, and was at the same time elected by the APCC to the All-India Congress Committee.

p. 101. **C.R., as Chakravarthy Rajagopalachari was then known**: Chakravarthy Rajagopalachari (1879–1972), lawyer and intellectual from Salem in Tamil Nadu, at this time known as 'C.R.', but later more popularly referred to as **'Rajaji'**, was among the top rank of the Congress leadership in the period before Independence and, after Independence, became India's only Indian Governor-General in 1948. (The post was later replaced by that of President when the Republic was declared on 26 January 1950.) Subsequent to the events described here by Sattanathan, Rajagopalachari, as leader of the 'no-changers', took the opposite side to Das on the issue of the boycott of the legislative councils.

p. 101. **A. Rangaswamy Iyengar of the *Swadesamitran***: A. Rangaswami Iyengar (1877–1934), lawyer, constitutional expert, and political scientist from Tanjore in Tamil Nadu, joined the English daily, *The Hindu*, in 1910, as Assistant Editor and Manager, leaving it in 1915 to edit the *Swadesamitran* ('Friend of Independence'), the first major Tamil newspaper, started as a weekly in 1882, and becoming a daily in 1899. (Rangaswami left the *Swadesamitran* to rejoin *The Hindu* as editor in 1928.) Twice Congress Secretary, Rangaswami became nationally known as editor of the *Swadesamitran*.

p. 101. **Vaikam Satyagraha**: A landmark in the history of the caste struggle. In Kerala, where caste discrimination was especially extreme, a small group of demonstrators started a *satyagraha* (roughly, 'truth force', a term coined by Gandhi to signify non-violent protest) on 30 March 1924, at the temple of Shiva at Vaikam, demanding entry for untouchables to the temple and the public roads adjoining it. The protest quickly gained national attention and was joined by major national figures. It ended twenty months after it began, with access opened to some temple roads. In 1936, the Temple Entry Proclamation of the last Maharaja of Travancore, Chitra Thirunal Balarama Varma (see **the young prince**, p. 117n.) finally opened all temples and temple roads in Travancore to worshippers, regardless of caste.

p. 101. **E.V. Ramaswami Naicker** (1879–1973), social reformer and iconoclast, and later, as founder of the Dravidian or Non-Brahmin movement, known in Tamil Nadu as **Periyar** ('the great one'; p. 149n.), was at this time in the top rank of the Tamil Nadu Congress, and had been elected President of the Tamil Nadu Congress Committee in 1920 and 1924. He took a leading part in the Vaikam Satyagraha, thereby earning another of his sobriquets, Vaikam Veerar ('Vaikam Hero'). For a detailed account of E.V. Ramaswami's impact on Tamil politics and cultural identity, see Lecture 2, pp. 167–71.

p. 101. **P. Varadarajulu Naidu** (1887–1957), physician and journalist, E.V. Ramaswami's close associate and sympathizer, and like him a great orator, was, with Ramaswami, among the leaders of the Tamil Nadu Congress.

p. 101. **Satyamurthi**: S. Satyamurthy (1887–1943), parliamentarian and C.R. Rajagopalachari's main rival among the leaders of the Tamil Nadu Congress was, like Rajagopalachari, a Brahmin. Sattanathan is making the point that it was the Non-Brahmin, rather than the Brahmin leaders, who had the more prominent standing.

p. 101. ***satyagrahis***: those engaged in *satyagraha* (see under **Vaikam Satyagraha**, above).

p. 101. **Akalis**: The term *Akali* is roughly translatable as 'follower of the Eternal One'. In the early 1920s, the term was adopted by Sikh volunteers who undertook to wrest control of the *gurdwaras* (Sikh temples), from hereditary, often non-Sikh priests. Their method was non-violent resistance (they are to be distinguished by the Babbar Akalis, a militant group with similar political objectives) and they were strongly supported by Gandhi and the Indian National Congress.

p. 102. **Rabindranath Tagore** (1816–1941) of Bengal, the most renowned of Indian poets in the twentieth century. His reputation in the West was established with the publication, in 1912, of his English translation of *Gitanjali* ('Song Offerings', a collection of poems published in Bengali in 1910), with a preface by William Butler Yeats. He was awarded the Nobel Prize for literature in 1913, the first Asian to be awarded the prize. Subsequently, he was knighted in 1915, but returned the knighthood in 1919, in protest against the British atrocities at Jallianwala Bagh in Amritsar (where British troops, under Brigadier General Reginald Dyer, massacred hundreds of peaceful demonstrators on 13 April 1919). Tagore, whom Gandhi, among others, called 'Gurudev' ('Respected Teacher'), was sympathetic to, if not actively involved in, the nationalist movement. The national anthem of independent India is a Hindi version of a Bengali composition by Tagore.

p. 102. **Sarojini Naidu** (1879–1949), poet and activist, was very much in the public eye in the period leading up to Independence. Called the 'Nightingale of India' on account both of her poetry and her celebrated voice, she toured the country widely from about 1915, lecturing on topics such as nationalism and the emancipation of women. She was elected President of the Indian National Congress in 1925.

p. 102. **his daughter-in-law**: Protima Devi (1893–1969), the wife of Tagore's son Rathindranath, was closely involved in his various projects, and usually accompanied him on his travels.

p. 102. **C.F. Andrews**: Charles Freer Andrews (1871–1940), came to India as a Christian missionary in 1904, and by 1906, became openly and actively involved with the nationalist movement. In 1913 he went to South Africa (**see the South African agitation**, p. 103n.), at the request of the then President of the Indian National Congress, Gopal Krishna Gokhale (1866–1915), where he met Gandhi, with whom he worked closely thereafter. Andrews met Tagore in England in 1912, and was from then on his devoted friend. When Gandhi and Tagore met for the first time at Santiniketan in 1914, it was with Andrews as their link.

p. 102. *Gitanjali*: see under **Rabindranath Tagore**, above.

p. 102. **Viswa Bharathi University**: In 1901, Tagore founded a school at Santiniketan (literally, 'abode of peace'), which was expanded, in 1921, to a residential university, the Viswabharati University. Today, the university is a nationally recognized institution.

p. 102. **the Forest Gurukulas of ancient India**: A topic dear to Tagore. The ancient model of *gurukulas* (places of learning; see chapter 3, p. 29 and n.) located in forests was the ideal on which Tagore founded his own school at Santiniketan, later the Viswabharati University. At a fund-raising event for the Viswabharati University, therefore, the topic was entirely apropos.

p. 103. **the South African agitation**: In 1894, Gandhi founded the Natal Indian Congress, and from 1896, began to practise and propagate his method of *satyagraha* or passive non-violent resistance, for the rights of the Indians in South Africa. By 1914, when Gandhi left South Africa, significant gains had been made, not the least of these being the organization of South African Indians into a unified community with a common cause.

p. 103. **a German poet . . . the people cried for light, light, and then it came:** This was probably a misunderstood or misremembered reference to the popular, if apocryphal, version of Goethe's last words: 'Light, more light!'

p. 104. **a young lecturer**: R. Sivaramakrishnan (1899–1945), who was lecturer in English Literature at the Maharaja's College and, following his distinguished performance in the examination mentioned by Sattanathan, was sent to Jesus College, Cambridge, as part of his training.

p. 104. **I.C.S.**: Indian Civil Service. See also **Superior Civil Service** (p. 127n.)

p. 104. **N.R. Pillai** (1898–1992) who graduated from Trinity Hall, Cambridge, in 1922, rose to great eminence in the Indian Civil Service, and, after Independence, was Secretary-General of India's Ministry of External Affairs from 1952 to 1960.

p. 105. ***vaidyam***: traditional, i.e. indigenous and non-Western, medical practices.

CHAPTER 10

p. 107. **Honours courses . . . Pass course**: At the time there were two types of undergraduate course leading to a Bachelor's degree: the three-year, academically demanding, Honours course, and the ordinary two-year Pass course, of a lower academic level than the Honours course.

p. 109. **Arts College in Thaicaud**: see under **our College** (p. 98n.).

p. 109. **K.V. Rangaswamy Aiyangar** (1880–?), a well-known historian, who wrote and published extensively on ancient Indian history, was Principal of the Arts College in Thaicaud from its inception in 1924 till 1928, and again from 1930 to 1933.

p. 109. **Pericles or the Magna Carta or Julius Caesar**: Sattanathan's choice of examples is telling: the topics all pertain to the history of democracy.

Pericles (495?–429 BC), under whose leadership ancient Greece is said to have reached the peak of its glory, is credited with the fostering of democracy by his promotion of the rights of the ordinary citizen. The *Magna Carta* ('Great Charter'), signed by King John of England in 1215, a document that placed checks and curbs on the absolute power of English kings, is considered the landmark first step towards constitutional government and the guarantee of individual rights. Julius Caesar (100–44 BCE), the legendary military and political commander of ancient Rome, was pivotal in the transition from the Roman Republic to the Roman Empire.

p. 110. **Chandrasekhar**: The Oxford-educated C.V. Chandrasekharan (1889–?) later became Principal of the Arts College in Thaicaud, at the end of K.V. Rangaswamy Aiyangar's tenure as Principal, from 1928 to 1930, and again from 1933 to 1935.

p. 110. **textbook on Constitutional History, written by Miss Chambers**: Annie Muriel Chambers, *A Constitutional History of England* (London: Methuen, 1909).

p. 110. **The whole class burst into laughter**: In Tamil, as in some other Indian languages, punning is a main mode of humour, and a special delight is taken in puns on foreign words.

p. 111. **Scott Christian College, Nagercoil**: The Mission School founded in 1809 in Nagercoil (headquarters of Kanyakumari district in present-day Tamil Nadu) by missionaries of the London Missionary Society in Travancore, attained the status of a College affiliated to the University of Madras in 1893. The College was named after Septimus R. Scott, Chairman of the Board of Directors of the London Missionary Society, in recognition of a generous benefaction.

p. 111. **K.B. Sundarambal** (1908–80), the best-known actress on the Tamil stage in the early twentieth century, was later the first major star of the Tamil screen, her success owing largely to her singing voice. She was paid a record Rs 1 lakh for the title role—a male part—in the film *Nandanar* (1935), and went on to attain her greatest celebrity in the title role of *Avvaiyar* (1953). An ardent nationalist, Sundarambal, who sang patriotic songs at public meetings, was an asset to the Tamil Nadu Congress. Her nomination to the Madras Legislative Council in 1951 began the intertwining of politics and film that characterizes Tamil Nadu politics to the present day.

p. 111. **Suchindram temple**: Suchindram is about 13 km from Cape Comorin (see below); its temple, whose origin dates back into legend, contains thirty shrines dedicated to various deities and is a rare instance of a temple where the Trinity of the Hindu Pantheon (Brahma, Vishnu, and Shiva), represented in a single idol, is worshipped. Another famous idol is a 22-foot statue of Hanuman, the monkey god.

p. 111. **Cape Comorin . . . the temple**: Cape Comorin is the British name for Kanyakumari ('the virgin'), at the southernmost tip of the Indian subcontinent, and at the time, the southernmost point of Travancore state. The town takes its name from the Virgin Goddess, the deity to whom its temple is dedicated: the young maiden Parvati, who, by asceticism and penance, won Shiva's love.

p. 111. **The *devadasi* system**: The word *devadasi* translates roughly as 'bondmaid of god'. The system of consecrating girls to a temple deity can be dated to about the ninth or tenth century in South India; such girls remained unmarried, and, highly trained in music and dance, became key proponents of the performing arts traditions. The association of the system with prostitution made the status of the *devadasi* increasingly lowly; in the course of the twentieth century, as a result of legislation as well as social disfavour, the system disappeared.

p. 111. **the procession idol**: the idol in the temple, usually of the main deity, kept especially for peripatetic use.

pp. 111–12. **the salt industry—with which . . . I came to be officially connected**: In 1942, Sattanathan was posted to the Madras Collectorate of Salt Revenue and Central Excise.

p. 112. **Saivite Vellala, see Pillay (p. 25n.).**

p. 112. ***Khaddar* had come into vogue**: The boycott of foreign cloth by wearing *khaddar* or *khadi* (Indian hand-spun cloth) was an integral part of Gandhi's programme of non-cooperation; from 1921 onwards, hand-spun cloth became the badge of nationalists across the country.

p. 113. **the first woman High Court judge**: Anna Chandy, née Jacob (1905–96), was appointed a judge of the Kerala High Court in 1959, the first woman judge of an Indian High Court, and possibly only the second in the world to obtain a judgeship at that level.

p. 113. **a politician**: Sattanathan later (p. 124) identifies this person as Mary Mascarenhas, of whom I can find no trace. On the other hand, Annie Mascarene (1902–63), a prominent woman leader of the Travancore Christians, was a student at the Maharaja's College at the time, and is probably the person referred to here. Mascarene was an active participant in the political agitations in Travancore State in the period leading up to Indian Independence, and was imprisoned several times during 1939–47; after Independence, she became Minister for Health and Electricity in the newly-formed Travancore–Cochin State, but resigned from Congress in 1950, in protest against corruption. In 1951, she was re-elected to the **Lok Sabha** (p. 173n.) as an Independent, but was defeated in the following general elections, when she retired from public life. If Mascarene is indeed the person referred to by Sattanathan, his changing of her name might perhaps be attributed to a lapse of memory, or an attempt to disguise identity, although this is inconsistent with his identification of other figures in his narrative.

p. 113. **a third renounced the world**: Identified further on in the narrative (p. 124) as 'Saradamma'. Later in life, she retreated to an ashram in Kulathur, near Trivandrum. Sattanathan did not forget his old college friend; in the early 1950s, when he visited Trivandrum with his family, he sought her out in her retreat.

p. 113. **Monkumpu, near Aleppey**: The island village of Monkompu is in the central part of present-day Kerala, the nearest sizeable commercial town being Alleppy (Alappula in Malayalam), formerly a port of some importance.

p. 114. **the famous shrine of Padmanabha, the patron deity of the state**: The temple of Padmanabha—Vishnu in his reclining form on the serpent Ananta (eternity)—in Trivandrum dates to antiquity. In 1750, Martanda Varma (r. 1729–58), the most famous of the Travancore rulers, dedicated his kingdom to Padmanabha; thenceforward, he and his successors ruled Travancore as *Padmanabha dasa*, the servant of Padmanabha. Trivandrum, the state capital, takes its name from the temple deity: Tiruananantapuram, the place of the sacred Ananta.

p. 114. **we removed our shirts, and tied our upper cloths around our waists**: The tradition that male worshippers remain bare-bodied within a temple's precincts, probably as a sign of humility, is still practised in many Kerala temples today.

p. 114. ***Makkathaayam*** **or** ***Marumakkathaayam***: Inheritance by the son (*makkan* in Malayalam) or inheritance by the sister's son (*marumakkan*). The system of matrilineal inheritance, by which a man's heir is not his son, but the son of his sister or of his sister's daughter, or the descendant of a common ancestress, was, until the middle decades of the twentieth century, the norm among the Kerala royal families and other high-caste Kerala Non-Brahmins, such as the Nairs.

p. 114. **a Yadhava**: see under **they belonged to two different communities** (p. 17n.).

p. 114. **if his God did not incarnate as a Yadhava cowherd**: According to Hindu mythology, Krishna, the avatar of Vishnu, was born in a Yadhava clan, a clan of cowherds and cattle-rearers and, till he gained his royal inheritance, was himself a cowherd.

p. 115. ***voothu purai***: '*Ootu pura*' in Malayalam. The entitlement to be fed gratis at these feeding places was an ancient privilege of the Brahmins of Travancore. In his *Native Life in Travancore* (1883), the missionary Samuel Mateer writes, 'it seems evident that the Ótooperahs for feeding Brahmans should by degrees be abolished; . . . Nowhere is there a parallel in civilized countries to the waste on Brahmans, the undue preference of this class of subjects, and the abuses hitherto prevalent in the administration of this so-called charity.' See Samuel Mateer, *Native Life in Travancore* (London: W.H. Allen, 1883), 369.

p. 115. **Gopala Menon**: A. Gopala Menon (1889–?) who graduated with a B.Com. degree from the London School of Economics in 1924, and later served as Principal of the Arts College, from 1935 to 1937.

p. 115. **Tampi**: Arumanai Narayanan Tampi (1892–?), of the Travancore royal family, studied law in Madras, not England, and in 1922 graduated with a degree in history from Christ Church, Oxford. He was appointed Assistant Professor in History at the Maharaja's College in 1924, as Sattanathan records.

p. 116. **the Dewan of Travancore**: In this case, T. Raghaviah, Dewan of Travancore from 1920 to 1925.

p. 117. **there were two Maharanees**: Moolam Thirunal had no sisters; his two adopted nieces, Setu Lakshmi Bayi and Setu Parvati Bayi, were the

Senior and the Junior Maharanis respectively. Setu Lakshmi Bayi had no sons; thus, the eldest son of the Junior Maharani was the old Maharaja's heir. By right of seniority, the Regency belonged to the Senior Maharani, but the Junior Maharani, as the mother of the heir, also had a claim.

p. 117. **The poor old man died:** Moolam Thirunal died on 7 August 1924.

p. 117. **the young prince:** Subsequently, the last Maharaja of Travancore, Chitra Thirunal Balarama Varma (1912–91; r. 1931–49), a good friend of Sattanathan's in later years.

p. 117. **the impeachment of Aurangzeb:** The Mughal emperor Aurangzeb, (1618–1707; r. 1658–1707), under whom the Muslim empire in India attained its greatest power and breadth, is also known to history for his ruthless and inhumane treatment of opponents and enemies, and for his religious bigotry, evinced in his persecution of Hindus and his destruction of Hindu temples.

p. 119. **my younger sister . . . became a big girl, and was staying indoors:** In rural Tamil Nadu, girls, once they attain puberty, do not leave the household quarters till they are married.

p. 120. ***naadaswaram*:** See under **the piper, the drummer, the *taalam* or time-keeper, and the background piper** (p. 23n.).

p. 120. ***Vidwan*:** maestro.

p. 121. **quack *vaidyar*:** A *vaidyar* is one who practises *vaidyam*; the word 'quack' in this context does not signify a fraudulent person, but a practitioner of alternative, i.e., non-Western, medicine.

p. 122. **R. Srinivasan** later became Principal of the Science College in 1937–8, and 1941–2.

Chapter 11

p. 127. **Superior Civil Service:** At the time of which Sattanathan is writing, the civil services were divided into three classes or categories, 'Superior', 'Provincial', and 'Subordinate'. The most prestigious of these, the Superior services, were divided into the all-India services (which included, for instance, the Indian Civil Service, the Indian Police Service, and the Indian

Educational Service) and the Central Services, which dealt with the Indian states, including, for instance, posts and telegraphs, customs, and railways.

p. 128. **the Principal of a college in Madura**: The college is subsequently (p. 140) identified as Madura College, established in 1889, one of the earliest institutions of higher education to be founded by Indians. The principal at the time was V.R. Venkataraman, who served as principal from 1924 to 1928.

p. 128. **Pachaiyappa's College, Madras**: The Pachaiyappa's Central Institution, a school founded in 1842 under the provisions of the will of the philanthropist Pachaiyappa Mudaliar (1754–94), became a first-grade college in 1889. Till 1947, the college admitted only Hindus.

p. 129. **My salary was nominally Rs 100, but I would be paid only Rs 80**: This kind of shortfall, between the salary specified in an employee's contract, and the actual amount that the employee is paid, still obtains in many private institutions in India.

p. 129. **another College—Alwaye in Travancore**: the Union Christian College, founded in 1921 in Alwaye (Aluva in Malayalam, to the north of Cochin, in the central part of present-day Kerala), as an inter-denominational co-operative effort of the non-Roman Catholic churches of the state.

p. 129. **British Resident in Travancore**: A representative of the British Raj, who acted as advisor to the Indian ruler of a princely state. In 1926, the Resident was Charles William Egerton Cotton (*c.* 1875–1931).

p. 131. **the heaven-born tribe**: The name 'Brahman' signifies 'of Brahma'. So identified with the Creator himself, Brahmins claim to be 'heaven-born', this claim being underlined by the **sacred thread** (p. 152n.) ceremony, which signifies a second, spiritual birth in addition to the ordinary mortal birth.

p. 131. **Ayangar**, also Iyengar: see **an Iyer or an Iyengar?** (p. 146n.).

p. 134. **'sudra fellow'**: The Sudra is the low or menial caste, fourth in the four-tier hierarchy defined by the traditional Hindu (Vedic) system.

p. 135. **the Holy City**: Madurai, known generally as the city of temples, is, for Tamilians, especially marked as the Holy City by its temple of Meenakshi, thought to have been built by the **Pandyas** (p. 154n.) *c.* seventh century, and rebuilt in its modern shape by the Nayaks (p. 155n.) by the end of the fourteenth century. According to legend, Meenakshi's consort, Shiva, was incarnated here as the legendary ruler Sundara Pandya, the city and its people being under his particular care ever since.

p. 135. **Ramesvaram**: Located in the south-east of present-day Tamil Nadu, Rameswaram is famous as the site of a temple, *c.* seventeenth century, said to be built on the spot where Rama set his feet on his journey to Lanka to wage war against the demon, Ravana. The architectural glory of the temple is its 700-foot-long pillared halls, opening into decorated galleries crosswise.

p. 136. **In spite of my suffering from the prejudices of Brahmans, I continued to be a robust nationalist**: See Lecture 1, pp. 157–8, for an explanation of the Non-Brahmin antipathy to the nationalist movement.

p. 136. **Raja of Panagal**: P. Ramarayaningar (1866–1928), who assumed the title 'Raja of Panagal' in 1922, was Chief Minister of Madras State from 1921 to 1926.

p. 136. **E.V.R.**: See **E.V. Ramaswami Naicker** (p. 101n.).

p. 136. **Annie Besant**: See **The Home Rule movement . . . Dr Annie Besant** (p. 158n.).

Chapter 12

p. 137. **Ramnad**: The chief town and headquarters of an eponymous district in southern Tamil Nadu.

p. 138. **University Training Corps**: The University Corps, established under the Indian Defence Act of 1917 to address the shortage of recruits to the Indian armed services, was replaced, under the Indian Territorial Act of 1920, by the University Training Corps, the precursor of today's National Cadet Corps. The U.T.C., whose members were students in Indian universities, represented an important milestone in the Indianizing of the armed services.

p. 139. **This gentleman became a politician, and later became a minister**: M.A. Manickavelu Naicker (1896–1964), a lawyer, was a member of the

Madras Legislative Council from 1926 to 1937, later founding the **Toilers' Commonweal Party** (p. 179n.). When C. Rajagopalachari became Chief Minister of Madras state in 1952, he took Naicker into his cabinet, and Naicker was retained, as Revenue Minister, in **Kamaraj**'s (p. 172n.) cabinet.

p. 139. **Dr Subbarayan**: Dr P. Subbarayan (1889–1962), was Chief Minister of the Madras Government from 1926 to 1930.

p. 139. **the Justice Party**: See **the South Indian Liberal federation** (p. 157n.).

p. 139. **Dyarchy**: 'Dual rule': a system of dual government instituted in the Indian provinces by **the Government of India Act of 1919** (p. 164n.). The Provincial Legislatures were enlarged, with a majority of their members consisting of elected representatives. The provincial administration was by two parallel executives: one, the Governor's Executive Council, independent of the Provincial Legislature and in control of certain departments such as finance, the other, a ministry appointed by the Governor from the elected members of the Legislature and answerable both to the Governor and to the Legislature, the ministry being in charge of departments such as education and public health.

p. 140. **Fort St George**, the first British fort in India, was built in 1640, although its present shape owes largely to remodelling carried out after it was recovered from the French in 1748 (it was captured in 1746). Named after England's patron saint, the fort, formerly the headquarters of the British South Indian administration, now houses the Legislative Assembly and Council and the administrative offices of the Government of Tamil Nadu.

p. 141. **National College, Trichy**: The National High School, Trichy, was founded in 1886 by three Brahmins, G. Sesha Iyengar (1856–1937), B.S. Venkataramana Sarma (1866–1931), and P.G. Sundaresa Sastri (1851–1954), whose object was to establish a high-quality educational institution where the Hindu faith would be safeguarded. In 1919, it became the second-grade National College when it opened Intermediate classes, and in 1924, a fully-fledged first-grade college.

p. 141. **Sri Meenakshi College, Chidambaram**, founded in memory of his mother by M. Annamalai Chettiar (see **The leading Chettiar of the time,**

p. 142n.) in 1920, and affiliated to the University of Madras. The college was the forerunner of the present-day Annamalai University (see **The necessary legislation for establishing a university was before the Legislature**, p. 142n.).

p. 141. **Theosophical College, Madanapalle**: The Theosophical College was founded by Annie Besant in 1915 in Madanapalle in present-day Andhra Pradesh. In 1917, during the **Home Rule movement** (p. 158n.), it dissociated itself from Madras University, but was re-affiliated to the university in 1923.

p. 141. **a Health resort for consumptives**: The Union Mission Tuberculosis Sanatorium in Madanapalle, under the charge of a young Danish missionary, Dr C. Frimcdt-Müller (d. 1943), was established in 1915 by the evangelical missions in South India, and had a far-reaching impact on the research and treatment of tuberculosis in the country.

p. 141. **Theosophy**: philosophy or religion of the Theosophical Society, founded in New York city in 1875 by Helena Petrovna Blavatsky (1831–91) and Henry Steele Olcott (1832–1907). The movement took root in India with the arrival of the founders there in 1879. Aside from its mystical and esoteric aspects, the main message of Theosophy is universal brotherhood and a non-denominational code of ethics.

p. 142. **Chidambaram . . . Nataraja**: Nataraja is Shiva as the Lord (*raja*) of Dance (*nata*); in this form, he is a distinctively Tamil god, belonging to the Shaivism of the Tamil country. The temple of Nataraja at Chidambaram, believed to date to the seventh century, rose to fame in the period of the Imperial **Cholas** (p. 154n.) from the tenth century onwards. The bronze images of Nataraja of this period are regarded as landmark achievements in bronze sculpture.

p. 142. **Chettiars**: the major merchant or trading caste of Tamil Nadu.

p. 142. **The leading Chettiar of the time**: M. Annamalai Chettiar (1881–1948), who, as a public benefactor, was knighted in 1923 and in 1929 was granted the title, thereafter hereditary, of 'Rajah of Chettinad'.

p. 142. **The necessary legislation for establishing a university was before the Legislature**: In 1928, a bill to convert the Sri Minakshi College to a university was introduced in the Madras Legislature, and being passed unanimously, became law on 1 January 1929. Consequently the college was enlarged and absorbed into the Annamalai University, which opened on 1 July 1929.

p. 142. **Neelakanta Sastri:** K. A. Nilakanta Sastri (1892–1975), first Principal of the Sri Minakshi College, Chidambaram, and later Professor of History at the University of Madras. Sastri's *A History of South India from Prehistoric Times to the Fall of Vijayanagar* (1955) and other studies of South Indian history are considered landmarks in the field.

p. 143. **'There are fresh fields and pastures outside Chidambaram, and I will seek my fortune in the wide open world.'**: This is a glorious mishmash of the closing lines of Milton's two greatest poems, *Lycidas* and *Paradise Lost*: 'To morrow to fresh Woods, and Pastures new' (*Lycidas*, l. 193; Sattanathan's substitution of 'fields' for 'woods' is a common mistake), and 'The World was all before them, where to choose/Thir place of rest, and Providence thir guide:' (*Paradise Lost*, book xii, ll. 646–7).

p. 143. **St Joseph's College:** see **the Jesuit College of St Joseph's** (p. 88n).

p. 144. **a Protestant Mission college:** The S.P.G. College (the initials standing for the missionary Society for the Propagation of the Gospel) began as a second-grade college in 1873, and in 1882 became a first-grade college. In the late 1920s, it was renamed the Bishop Heber College, after Reginald Heber (1783–1826), a Bishop of Calcutta and a well-known hymn-writer, who died on a visit there.

p. 144. **a pre-eminent lawyer:** Probably A. Rangaswami Aiyar (1869–1964), who joined the Theosophical Society in 1897, and was thereafter closely associated with Annie Besant in a number of her activities.

p. 145. **Saranathan:** V. Saranathan (1892–1948) was Principal of the National College, Trichy from 1921 to 1947, a period that is regarded as the College's 'Golden Age', Saranathan himself being much lauded as a benefactor of the underprivileged and socially deprived.

p. 145. **an Iyer or an Iyengar?** An Iyer, sometimes spelled Aiyer or Aiyar, is a Tamil Saivite Brahmin; an Iyengar or Ayengar is a Tamil Vaishnavite Brahmin.

II. The Dravidian Movement in Tamil Nadu and Its Legacy (1981): Three Lectures Delivered at the University of Madras

Preface

p. 149. **Tamil Nadu Backward Classes Commission:** The term 'Backward Classes' refers to those castes that fall collectively under the broad category of 'Sudra' in the Vedic classification, such castes being socially and educationally backward in modern India. The first Tamil Nadu Backward Classes Commission was constituted in 1969, under the Chairmanship of A.N. Sattanathan, to investigate the disadvantaged position of the Backward Classes in the state. Based on the findings and recommendations of the Commission's report (1971), the state government implemented a policy of quotas or reservations, in education and public sector jobs, for the Backward Classes.

p. 149. **Backward Classes agitation and counter-agitation in recent times:** In 1979, in Tamil Nadu, the ministry of the All-India **Anna Dravida Munnetra Kazhagam** (p. 174n.), under M.G. Ramachandran, issued a Government Order recommending the implementation of the economic criterion prescribed by the Sattanathan Commission, that is, that reservation be confined to members of backward-class families with an annual income of Rs 9000 or less. The protests and agitations that ensued forced the withdrawal of this GO in 1980. At the same time, Ramachandran's government issued a GO announcing the raising of the reservation quota for Backward Classes from 31 per cent to 50 per cent. Both GOs gave rise to extensive litigation questioning their validity, leading to the appointment of the second Tamil Nadu Backward Classes Commission in 1982.

p. 149. **Periyar:** popular sobriquet of E.V. Ramaswami Naicker. The honorific was given him for the first time at an **anti-Hindi** meeting (p. 161n.) on 13 November 1938.

p. 149. ***sishya:*** disciple or student.

p. 150. ***darshan:*** audience.

LECTURE 1

p. 151. **Bombay Presidency:** One of the three administrative zones into which British India was divided (the other two being the Madras and Bengal presidencies). The Bombay Presidency, with its headquarters at Bombay, included present-day Gujarat, the western two-thirds of Maharashtra, and north-western Karnataka.

p. 151. **the Vindhya**: Mountain range in Central India that forms a natural boundary between the north and the south of the country.

p. 151. **Madras Presidency**: The administrative zone, comprising, with its dependencies, the south of the Indian peninsula, with its headquarters at Madras.

p. 151. **the Aryan settlement**: As outlined by the hypothesis, now widely debated, that between 1500 and 600 BCE, groups of Aryans (those speaking an Indo-European dialect), migrated from West Asia to North India through Iran, these migrants being distinguished from the indigenous (Dravidian) inhabitants of the subcontinent.

p. 151. **Buddhism and Jainism may even be called anti-Brahman movements**: Buddhism and Jainism, both religions that originated in northern India *c.* 500 BCE, can be seen to be reactions against the rigidity of a caste-based Hindu society. Neither religion subscribes to the caste system nor asserts the superiority of any one caste.

p. 152. ***Varna***: Literally, 'colour', the Sanskrit term used in the Vedas to signify caste.

p. 152. **exclusively of Dravidian origin . . . no Kshatrya or Vaisya caste of Aryan descent**: The assumption here is that the lowest castes (Sudras and Dalits), and only they, are purely Dravidian, with no Aryan admixture. Kshatrya is the ruler or warrior caste, second in the four-tier Vedic hierarchy; Vaisya is the 'middle-class' caste, consisting of farmers, merchants, and skilled workers, third in the Vedic hierarchy.

p. 152. **Muslim invasion and rule in the ninth and tenth centuries**: The introduction of Islam in India is generally dated to the Arab conquest, *c.* 712 CE, of Sind in north-west India (now in Pakistan). Muslim rule in India began to be established *c.* 1000 CE, with the invasions of the Turkish leader, Mohammed of Ghazni (in present-day Afghanistan).

p. 152. **the Parasurama story**: In Hindu mythology, Parasurama, the sixth avatar of Vishnu, was a Brahmin skilled in martial combat and deadly in his use of the axe (*parasu* in Sanskrit; hence 'Parasurama', the Rama of the axe). To avenge the killing of his father by a king, Parasurama carried out a slaughter of Kshatryas, and in so doing rid the land of many who were immoral or undeserving.

p. 152. **the epics**: The *Mahabharata* and the *Ramayana*.

p. 152. ***Puranas***: Literally (ancient stories), a set of Hindu religious texts compiled *c.* 400–1000 CE, and aimed at inculcating morality and religious feeling in the masses. There are eighteen *Puranas* (six for each of the Hindu Trinity, Brahma, Vishnu, and Shiva). By traditional belief, their author is the sage Vyasa, to whom the *Mahabharata* is also ascribed.

p. 152. ***Karma***: deed or action. By the Hindu concept of *karma*, a person's lot in this life is the consequence of his or her actions in past lives; thus, the notion of *karma* entails upon the low castes the acceptance of oppression and social bondage.

p. 152. ***Punarjanma***: rebirth. Endurance and suffering in this life will bear its fruit in the next.

p. 152–3. **As modern historians like N. Subrahmanian . . . caste culture**: See N. Subrahmanian, *History of Tamilnad (To AD 1336)* (Madurai: Koodal Publishers, 1972), 33–8.

p. 153. **Sangam literature**: ancient classical Tamil literature, *c.* 100 BCE to 250 CE, extant being the Eight Anthologies (*Ettuthogai*) of short poems, the Ten Long Poems (*Pattupaatu*), and a grammar, the *Tolkaapiyam*. The poets and scholars of the period are believed to have gathered at formal assemblies at Madurai, the capital of the **Pandya** (p. 154n.) kingdom of South India, hence the name Sangam ('assembly' or 'gathering' in Tamil). The literature of the Sangam period, being largely secular, and dealing with a range of topics—love, loss, war, trade, governance—is the source of much of our knowledge of the ancient Tamil world.

p. 153. **early post-Sangam literature** (*c.* 200–300 CE), notably, the great Tamil epics, including *Silappadikaaram* by Ilango Adigal and *Manimekalai* by Sittalai Sattanar. The post-Sangam period is marked by the growth of Buddhism and Jainism whose impact is manifest in these works.

p. 153. **the *Thirumandiram* of Thirumoolar**, *c.* 600 CE, is a composition of 3047 verses in nine sections, called 'tantras'. The work, which extols the worship of Shiva and the practice of *siddha* yoga (the rigorous yoga of the adepts), thus belongs to the Saiva Siddhantha tradition of South India. Tradition has it that the author was a cowherd, and so of low-caste origin.

p. 153. **holy thread:** Called *yagnopavitam* in Sanskrit and *poonol* (soft thread) in Tamil, this is a caste marker: a thin white thread worn especially by Brahmin and other upper-caste Hindu boys from their coming of age onwards.

p. 153. ***Sikha*:** The wearing of the hair in a long tuft (*sikha*), traditionally practised by all Hindu males, was particularly important for Brahmins.

p. 153. **some stanza in the second tantra:** The references to the Brahmins' holy thread and tuft are in the first, not second tantra of the *Tirumandiram*, especially stanza 230; also 241 and 242.

p. 153. **In an earlier stanza:** *Tirumandiram*, tantra one, stanza 226.

p. 153. ***Gayathri*;** A Vedic prayer, taught during the ceremony in which upper-caste boys are invested with the sacred thread, and to be recited by them regularly thereafter.

p. 153. ***Maya*:** illusion or unreality. The term signifies the emptiness of the material world in Indian religious thought.

p. 153. **Siddhas:** Ascetics who are believed to have attained superhuman powers by means of prayer and penance.

p. 154. **Saivite Mutts:** A mutt is a Hindu religious establishment where ascetics live together; some mutts own temples or educational institutions. Saivite mutts propagate the worship of Shiva.

p. 154. **the period of the Nayanmars:** The Nayanmars were a group of sixty-three saints, devotees of Shiva. Like the **Alwars** (see below), they led the great Hindu religious revival—a reaction against the spread of Jainism and Buddhism—during the early medieval period (*c.* 400–800 CE) in South India.

p. 154. **Dr Ghurye . . . in his latest edition of *Caste and Race in India*:** See the chapter 'Caste and Politics in Tamilnadu' in G.S. Ghurye, *Caste and Race in India* (1932; Bombay: Popular Prakashan, 1969), 355–403, especially 360–4.

p. 154. **Vellalas:** a major farming caste of Tamil Nadu. The subdivisions of the caste vary widely in social and economic status, the upper subdivisions being considered the highest of the Tamil Non-Brahmin castes.

p. 154. **Parayas:** a formerly 'untouchable' caste of Tamil Nadu.

p. 154. **Alwars:** collective name given to a group of twelve saints, devotees of Vishnu, and, like the Nayanmars, leaders of the Hindu religious revival in early medieval South India.

p. 154. **Sekkilar . . . the *Periya Puranam*:** The *Periya Puranam* (Great Purana), by the poet Sekkilar, is a twelfth-century Tamil work in 4253 verses, proselytizing Shiva by recounting the lives and achievements of the Nayanmars.

p. 154. **the Dravida Kazhagam and Dravida Munnetra Kazhagam:** Periyar was elected leader of the Justice Party in 1940. In 1944, at a conference in Salem, a resolution was passed in the name of the party's secretary, C.N. Annadurai ('**Anna**', p. 161n.), changing the name of the party to Dravida Kazhagam (the party of Dravidians). In 1949, the Dravida Kazhagam split, the breakaway party—under the leadership of Annadurai—calling itself the Dravida Munnetra Kazhagam (the party for the advancement of Dravidians). For a fuller account, see Lecture 2.

p. 154. **Pallavas:** a major ruling dynasty of the Tamil country in the early medieval period, from *c.* 500 to *c.* 800 CE. At its peak, the Pallava kingdom, with its capital at **Kanchipuram**, just south of present-day Chennai, spanned the region in modern Tamil Nadu that consists of the districts of North Arcot, Chinglepet, Chennai, Trichy, and Tanjore.

p. 154. **Cholas:** one of the three major dynasties of ancient Tamil Nadu (the other two being the Cheras and the **Pandyas**, see below), ruling from a period of undetermined antiquity to *c.* 300 CE and, regaining power after the decline of the Pallavas, from the ninth to the twelfth centuries. The Cholas of the early and later periods are usually distinguished as the 'Sangam' and 'Imperial' Cholas respectively. Their territory comprised roughly the districts of Trichy and Tanjore in present-day Tamil Nadu.

p. 154. **Pandyas:** another of the three major dynasties of ancient Tamil Nadu, ruling, with fluctuating power, from a period of undetermined antiquity to arguably as late as the eighteenth century. The Pandyas are especially associated with the southern districts of Madurai and Tirunelveli in present-day Tamil Nadu.

p. 155. **Valentine Chirol . . . (in *Indian Unrest*)**: What Sattanathan offers here as a direct quotation is in fact a very loose paraphrase of Chirol's comments on Brahmins towards the close of chapter 1 of *Indian Unrest*: 'it is amongst high-caste Hindus that for the last three-quarters of a century English education has chiefly spread, and, indeed, been most eagerly welcomed; it is amongst them that British administration has recruited the great majority of its native servants in every branch of the public service'—see Valentine Chirol, *Indian Unrest* (London: Macmillan, 1910), 7. Chirol does not mention 'filtration' here but he does do so later on, in chapter 17: 'Government has concentrated its efforts mainly upon higher education, and has thus begun from the top in the over-sanguine belief that education would ultimately filter down from the higher to the lower strata of Indian society' (ibid., 208). The idea of 'filtration' originates with Macaulay's influential and now infamous *Minute on Indian Education* of 2 February 1835, which advises that English education be imparted to an elite upper class which might then be expected to convey, by slow degrees, the knowledge thus gained to the masses.

This sentence contains my only substantial emendation of Sattanathan's text. The original University of Madras publication reads 'Valentine Chirol, writing in 1910 (in Indian Unrest) compared their position as Government Servants as illustrative of Lord Erskine's Filtration theory'—see A.N. Sattanathan, *The Dravidian Movement in Tamil Nadu and Its Legacy* (Madras: University of Madras, 1982), 4. The mention of Lord Erskine I assume to be a mistake on Sattanathan's part; Chirol nowhere mentions Erskine in *Indian Unrest*; on the other hand, he does specifically refer to Macaulay, on the same page that he disputes the filtration premise.

p. 155. **in Maharashtra**: The Non-Brahmin movement in Maharashtra can be said to have begun with the activism of Jotirao Phule (1827–90), but gained its greatest momentum and success in the 1920s, and should be seen, as Sattanathan rightly suggests, as parallel rather than causal to the movement in Tamil Nadu.

p. 155. **Nayaks**: See under **Vijayanagar Feudatories**, p. 151n.)

p. 156. **Mudaliars**: Vellalas of the northern Tamil regions, of a high social status.

p. 156. **Velirs:** Chieftains of the Sangam era, some of whom were loyal to the Chola kings.

p. 156. **Dalavoys:** 'Dalavoy' was the title of the principal officer of certain Hindu kingdoms of medieval South India, in whom was combined the leadership of both the civil and the military administrations of the kingdom.

p. 156. **Telugu Cholas,** also called Telegu Chodas, a minor Chola dynasty claiming descent from the legendary king Karikala of the Sangam Cholas, and ruling over the southern parts of present-day Andhra Pradesh in the twelfth century.

p. 156. **Reddiars:** Like the Naidus, a socially-advantaged Telegu-speaking caste from present-day Andhra Pradesh, many of whom have settled in Tamil Nadu, especially the northern region of the state.

p. 156. **Lloyd Rudolph and Susanne Rudolph, in their several studies:** See, for instance, *The Modernity of Tradition: Political Development in India* (Chicago and London: University of Chicago Press, 1967), 46–7.

p. 156. **true Aryan twice-born:** The sacred thread ceremony and the learning of the *Gayathri* are considered to mark the spiritual birth of upper-caste Hindu boys, who are thenceforward considered twice-born.

p. 156. **Kayasthas:** an administrative and scholastic caste of northern India, outside of the Vedic system, but considering themselves on par with the Brahmins in terms of caste status. According to tradition, they are an offshoot of the Kshatryas.

p. 157. ***agraharams*:** localities of traditional houses occupied exclusively by Brahmins in order to preserve caste purity uncontaminated by contact with other castes.

p. 157. **Non-Brahman Manifesto of 1916 . . . the South Indian People's Association:** The South Indian People's Association began with a meeting of about thirty Non-Brahmins in Madras in November 1916, when it was resolved to found an association with the primary purpose of publishing newspapers to counter the nationalist position of the dominant Brahmin-owned newspapers in the Madras Presidency (and thus to safeguard the interests of Non-Brahmins). In December 1916, the association issued the

Non-Brahmin Manifesto, whose key political commitment was to continuing British rule. The association published three newspapers: the English daily *Justice*, the Tamil daily *Tiravitan* ('Dravidian'), and the Telegu weekly, *Andhraprakasika*.

p. 157. **South Indian Liberal Federation . . . under the leadership of Dr T.M. Nair, P. Theagaraja Chettiar, and Dr C. Natesa Mudaliar**: The South Indian Liberal Federation, founded by T. M. Nair (1868–1919), P. Theagaraja Chettiar (1852–1925), and C. Natesa Mudaliar (1869–1937), was the political wing of the South Indian People's Association, and was soon known as the **Justice Party**, *Justice* being the name of the English newspaper published by the Association.

p. 158. **Public Services**, comprising the Civil Service, the Audit and Accounts Service, the Police Service, and the Provincial (particularly the Revenue and Judicial) services, all instituted by the British, and constituting the vast administrative infrastructure of the Indian empire. Only a fraction of the Public Services was European, the remainder being recruited from among upper-caste Indians. See also **Superior Civil Service**, p. 127n.

p. 158. **District Boards . . . first measure of local self-Government**: The first measures for local self-government in India were introduced by Lord Ripon (1827–1909), Viceroy of India (1880–4), whose resolution of 18 May 1882 set out the general principles of decentralization. Subsequently, the Ripon resolution became the Bengal Local Self-Government Act III of 1885, providing for a Board in each district, and beneath the District Board, two further tiers of localization.

p. 158. **the Home Rule movement . . . Dr Annie Besant**: Annie Besant (1847–1933), English activist and social reformer, and later a leader of the Theosophical movement, came to India in 1893 following her conversion to Theosophy, and from 1914 became actively involved in nationalist politics. In 1915–16, with Bal Gangadhar Tilak (1856–1920, a leading figure on the extremist rather than the moderate side of nationalist politics), she began the Home Rule Movement, founding a Home Rule League in Madras in December 1816, Tilak having formed another such league, headquartered in Poona, six months earlier. The League's demand was for Dominion Status for India within the British empire. Besant was closely involved with the Indian National Congress and presided over its Calcutta Session in 1917, during which the Home Rule League merged with Congress. However, mainly due to differences with Gandhi, she withdrew from nationalist politics in the 1920s.

p. 158. **the Minto–Morley Reforms**, also known as the Government of India Act of 1909, its architects being John Morley (1838–1923) and Gilbert John Elliot-Murray-Kynynmound, 4th earl of Minto (1845–1914), respectively, Secretary of State for India and Viceroy of India from 1905 to 1910. The act allowed Indians limited representation in the central and provincial legislatures. Where, previously, Indians in the legislatures had been government appointees, the reforms provided for some elected representatives, although the electorate was still mainly from the upper classes and castes. Importantly, the act granted separate electorates for Muslims, and in so doing endorsed a principle of communal representation that was later extended to other communities.

p. 158. **legislative council of Madras**: the provincial legislature based in Madras.

p. 158. **Caste and Occupational groups**: Caste being traditionally defined by occupation, a caste group frequently had an occupational basis and *vice versa*.

p. 159. **leading Newspaper under Brahman control**: *The Hindu*, founded in 1878 as a weekly by a group of six Brahmin nationalists, and becoming a daily in 1878. In 1905 it was acquired by its legal adviser, Kasturi Ranga Iyengar (1859–1923), also a Brahmin and a staunch nationalist, who became its editor.

p. 159. **Imperial Legislative Council**: the central legislature of British India.

p. 159. **a Brahman was elected**: This was the statesman V.S. Srinivasa Sastri (1869–1946), who later left Congress, along with other moderates who rejected Congress's policy of non-cooperation, to found the Indian Liberal Federation in 1922, of which he was the President.

p. 160. **Rajaji, see C.R., as Chakravarthy Rajagopalachari was then known** (p. 101n.).

p. 161. **the Anti-Hindi agitation**: the periodic agitation, 1938–1965, against the institutionalizing of Hindi as the official language of India, for instance, by the imposition of Hindi in educational curricula and as a requirement for the Civil Service, supposedly as an assertion of a unified national identity, but experienced by non-Hindi-speakers as detrimental to their own language and culture, and as disadvantaging them professionally and socially. The first attempt at such imposition was by C. Rajagopalachari, when he was leader of the Congress Ministry elected to the provincial government in 1937; two people were killed in the ensuing agitation, and a number imprisoned. The resistance to subsequent efforts did not wane, the most widespread and violent outbreak of the agitation taking place in 1965. With the accession to power of the Dravida Munnetra Kazhagam under Annadurai ('Anna', below), the imposition of Hindi in Tamil Nadu has been altogether given up.

p. 161. **Madrassis:** The term 'Madrassi' is a dismissive and derogatory term used by North Indians to refer indiscriminately to a native of one of the four South Indian states: Karnataka, Andhra Pradesh, Tamil Nadu, and Kerala.

p. 161. **Dravidastan,** literally, 'land of the Dravidians', comprising the four southern states of India, although, as an autonomous political entity seceded from the Indian Union, it was envisaged as principally encompassing the Tamil Nadu region (there being little support for the notion outside of Tamil Nadu).

p. 161. **Anna:** C.N. Annadurai (1909–69) popularly known as 'Arignar Anna' (wise older brother) or simply 'Anna' (older brother), was the founder of the Dravida Munnetra Kazhagam, which came into power for the first time in Madras state in 1967, since which time no non-regional party, such as Congress, has been able to regain a mass following in the state. A key player in the anti-Hindi agitation, as Chief Minister, Anna changed the name of Madras state to 'Tamil Nadu', and also implemented the two-language formula, Tamil and English, which continues to be the policy of the state.

Lecture 2

p. 162. **Self-Respect movement:** a movement begun by Periyar to raise consciousness in the Non-Brahmin castes, so as to effect their social, economic, and political advancement. A further reference to the movement is made on p. 168, and a fuller account given on pp. 169–71.

p. 163. ***the Non-Brahmin***: the newsletter or magazine of the South Indian Liberal Federation.

p. 163. **Dr Nair . . . quoted in T. Vardarajulu Naidu's book, *The Justice Movement***: See T. Varadarajulu Naidu, *The Justice Movement* (1932; Madras: Dravidar Kazhagam, 1991), 13–14.

p. 163. **Montagu–Chelmsford report**: a report of 1918 signed jointly by Edwin Samuel Montagu (1879–1924), Secretary of State for India from 1917 to 1922, and Fredric John Napier Thesiger, 1st Viscount Chelmsford (1868–1933), Viceroy and Govenor General of India from 1916 to 1921, recommending measures to achieve a limited degree of representative government in the Indian Provinces and outlining the system of dyarchy for the provincial governments. The recommendations of the report became law in the **Government of India Act of 1919**.

p. 163. **Southborough Committee**: a committee headed by Francis John Stephens Hopwood, first Baron Southborough (1860–1947), sent by the Home Government to India to determine the franchise and constituencies to be established under the Government of India Act of 1919 and the procedures for election to the self-governing bodies constituted by the act.

p. 164. **Government of India Act of 1919**: See under **Montagu–Chelmsford report** (p. 163n.).

p. 164. **Lord Willingdon**: Freeman Freeman-Thomas, first Marquess of Willingdon (1866–1941) was Governor of Bombay from 1913 to 1918, and Governor of Madras from 1919 to 1924. In 1931 he became Viceroy and Governor General of India, a position that he held till 1936. A liberal in politics, and sympathetic to the Moderate wing of the Indian Nationalist movement, Willingdon's support for the Non-Brahmin Justiceites, with their support of continuing British rule, rather than the more radically nationalist Congress Brahmins, could justifiably be anticipated. Willingdon's standing with the Non-Brahmins of the Bombay Presidency is attested to by the fact that Chhatrapati Shahu, the Maharaja of Kolhapur (1874–1922; r 1894–1922), a primary agent of the Non-Brahmin movement in Maharashtra, in 1918 petitioned His Majesty's Government for an extension of Willingdon's tenure as Governor—see G.W. Bergstrom, 'Lord Willingdon and India, 1931–6: A Study of an Imperial Administrator' (University of Oxford D.Phil. thesis, 1978), 36.

p. 164. **Willingdon had by then successfully managed similar agitations in Bombay:** See, for instance, Edwin S. Montagu, *An Indian Diary*, ed. V. Montagu (London: Heinemann, 1930), 135. In his diary entry of 2 January 1918, Montagu remarks that Bombay, under Willingdon, 'is far the happiest and most progressive part of India, in which we ought to be able to go much farther than anywhere else', i.e., with the reforms in which Montagu was then engaged, which became the Government of India Act of 1919. Montagu was instrumental in Willingdon's transfer from Bombay to Madras as governor.

p. 165. **the Meston award:** James Scorgie Meston, first Baron Meston (1865–1943), was appointed by the Government of India to arbitrate between the Brahmins and Non-Brahmins on the matter of the number of reserved seats to be allocated to Non-Brahmins in the provincial legislature of Madras. His decision, issued in 1920, came to be known as the Meston Award.

p. 167. **the loaves and fishes of office:** The allusion is to Christ's feeding of the multitude in the miracle of the loaves and fishes (Matthew 15: 36; Mark 8: 6) The point of Sattanathan's metaphor, of course, is that not a multitude, but only a select few are the recipients of the bounty here.

p. 167. **Conjeevaram:** British Indian spelling of **Kanchipuram** (see under **Pallavas**, p. 154n.).

p. 167. **C.N. Annadurai:** See **Anna** (p. 161n.).

p. 167. **Kasinath Kavlekar . . . study of the Non-Brahmin movement:** Kasinath K. Kavlekar, *Non-Brahmin Movement in Southern India, 1873–1949* (Kolhapur: Shivaji University Press, 1979).

p. 168. **a Conference in 1929:** the first Self-Respect Conference, held at Chinglepet, near Madras, on 18 February 1929.

p. 168. **Dravidanad:** synonym of **Dravidastan** (p. 161n.), the Tamil 'nad' ('nadu'), like the Sanskritic 'stan', signifying 'country' or 'region'.

p. 168. **Sir Stafford Cripps . . . canvassing Indian support for Britain's war effort:** In 1939, at the outbreak of the Second World War, India was dragged into hostilities without consultation; the Congress ministries of eight provinces resigned in protest. In December 1941, Japan entered the war; Singapore and Rangoon fell to the Japanese in early 1942, and, as the Japanese rapidly advanced upon India, in March 1942 Sir Stafford Cripps (1889–1952), then Leader of the House of Commons, was sent to India to woo the support of Indian political leaders with proposals for a new Constitution and Dominion Status for India after the war. The Cripps mission failed, and, on 8 August 1942, Congress passed its landmark 'Quit India' resolution, urging the immediate ending of British rule.

p. 168. **a separate state directly administered by the Government of India**, i.e., to be granted Dominion Status separately from the Indian Union.

p. 168. **Two Nation theory formulated by Jinnah**: the basis on which Pakistan was created. Mahomed Ali Jinnah (1876–1948) left the Indian National Congress in 1920, and in 1934 became the leader of the Muslim League, an organization founded in 1906 to safeguard the interests of Indian Muslims, and which Jinnah had joined in 1913, although at the time remaining a loyal member of the Congress. Initially an emissary for Hindu–Muslim unity, by 1940 Jinnah was referring to Hindus and Muslims as 'two nations'. In the Lahore Session of the Muslim League in March 1940, the historic 'Pakistan Resolution' was passed, demanding that the regions where Muslims were numerically the majority be constituted sovereign and autonomous.

p. 168. **A Tamil weekly, called *Dravida Nadu***: This weekly, which achieved great popularity, was started in 1942 by Anna, who was at the time Periyar's chief lieutenant.

p. 169. **Dewan Bahadurs**: 'Dewan Bahadur' was a title accorded by the British Raj to an Indian who had excelled in a profession or an endeavour.

p. 169. **1944 Salem Conference**, i.e., the same conference at which the Justice Party became the Dravida Kazhagam.

p. 170. ***Gita***: The *Bhagavad Gita* ('Song of God'), a long poem in eighteen cantos in the sixth book of the *Mahabharata*. The poem, often considered the essence of Hinduism, is the revelation of the eternal truth by Krishna to Arjuna, one of the five Pandavas, as he stands on the brink of the great war.

p. 170. ***Chatur varnam maya srishti***: 'The four castes are my creation', *Bhagavad Gita*, canto 4, verse 13.

p. 170. **Bhagawan**: God; here Krishna, the speaker and Supreme Being of the *Bhagavad Gita*.

p. 170. **pure Tamil phrase . . . *Thanmanam***: The ideology by which the Non-Brahmin castes identify as 'Dravidian' entails the rejection of what is perceived as 'Aryan' (synonymous, in this context, with 'Brahmin') influences, including the Sanskritization of the Tamil language. Tamil vocabulary that is free of Sanskritic derivation is upheld as the 'pure' language; the phrase *Thanmanam* for self-respect is 'pure' in this respect, unlike *Suya Mariyadai*, as Sattanathan explains.

p. 171. **to set our minds free and hold our heads high**: This paraphrases the famous nationalistic lines from Tagore's *Gitanjali*: 'Where the mind is without fear and the head is held high;/Where knowledge is free.'

p. 172. **an Educational Reform measure**: The idea of vocational training in their hereditary occupations for school students was first introduced by C. Rajagopalachari in 1937, when he became leader of the provincial ministry under dyarchy. The idea had to be set aside even at the time because it was considered to endorse caste distinctions by promoting caste-based labour. In 1952, when Rajagopalachari became Chief Minister of Madras State, he again introduced the vocational educational scheme. Widespread opposition forced its withdrawal, and Rajagopalachari resigned as Chief Minister in 1954.

p. 172. **train-stopping movement, to protest against Jawaharlal Nehru's criticism of the Dravida Munnetra Kazhagam**: In 1953, the DMK launched a major agitation, including the stopping of trains by party activists, whose target was threefold: first, Rajagopalachari's educational reforms; second, the renaming of the town of Kallakudi in Trichy district, 'Dalmiapuram', after a North Indian cement company which owned a factory near the town; and third, the criticism allegedly expressed by Nehru about the party's Dravidianist demands. (Confronted by the DMK's demand for greater representation of Tamil history and culture in school curricula, on the occasion of his visit to Madras to inaugurate a science exhibition in 1953, Nehru is alleged to have uttered the word 'nonsense'.)

p. 172. **existing Federal Structure of the Constitution**: As established by the Constitution, India is a union of states, with a (closely rather than loosely) federal structure of government. The legislative and executive functions of government are divided between the centre and the states, there being a parliament at the centre and individual legislatures (called legislative assemblies) in each state.

p. 172. **Northern exploitation of the natural resources of the South**: A popular slogan of the DMK was *Vadakku vaazhkirathu; Therkku theykirathu* ('The North prospers; the South decays').

p. 172. **Kamaraj**: K. Kamaraj (1903–75), freedom fighter, popular leader and Congress stalwart, joined the Congress Party in 1921, later heading a Congress ministry as Chief Minister of Madras State, a position he held from 1954 to 1963.

p. 173. **The Madras Assembly**: The legislature of Madras State, now Tamil Nadu.

p. 173. **'First Past the Post' principle of the single member Constituency system**: On the British model, an Indian state is divided into constituencies, each party fielding a single member to stand for election in a constituency, and each constituency being represented by the single person who secures a majority in that election. The party which secures the greatest number of constituencies, that is, is 'first past the post', becomes the majority party, even if it has secured only a minority of the actual number of votes cast. This is especially likely when the opposition is unorganized, that is, when there are several opposition parties: in such a case, the opposition parties together might secure a majority of the total votes, although no single opposition party secures a greater number of votes than the victorious party.

p. 173. **Lok Sabha**: House of the People, the lower house of the Indian Parliament.

p. 173. **Madras City Corporation**: The Madras Corporation is a city council, politically more or less independent of the state government in power, and responsible for areas such as housing, environment, public spaces, health and hygiene in Madras city.

p. 173. **Communists:** Before the DMK began to contest elections, the Communist Party of India (CPI) was, after Congress, the second most important electoral party in Madras State.

p. 173. **E.V.K. Sampath** (1926–77), a nephew of Periyar, left the Dravida Kazhagam with Anna to found the Dravida Munnetra Kazhagam, and, in the 1957 elections, became a member of the Lok Sabha. Growing differences with Anna led to Sampath leaving the DMK in 1961 to form the Tamil Desiya Katchi, or Tamil Nationalist Party (TNP); the TNP merged with Congress in 1964.

p. 174. **Rajya Sabha:** Council of States, the upper house of the Indian Parliament.

p. 174. **As a writer in the *Economist* described it:** Sattanathan's recollection has rather exaggerated the words of *The Economist*'s correspondent. The International Report on the 1967 elections in Madras State, in the issue of *The Economist* dated 8 July 1967, states merely: 'For the first time in centuries, the dark-skinned, low-caste people of Madras are in the seats of power' (*The Economist* ccxxv, no. 6463, 107). There is no mention of the unpronounceable names.

p. 174. **the Dravida Munnetra Kazhagam split:** In 1972, M.G. Ramachandran (1917–87), film-star and popular icon, and main rival to M. Karunanidhi (1924–), the leader then, as now, of the DMK, broke away to form his own political party, the Anna Dravida Munnetra Kazhagam.

p. 175. **predictions contained in the *Mahabharata* and the *Srimad Bhagavatam* that in Kaliyuga, Sudras will rule :** The predictions about the ascension of Sudras in Kaliyuga are in Book 3 (*Vanaparva*, the Book of the Forest), section 188, of the *Mahabharata*. The *Srimad Bhagavatam*, a Sanskrit work celebrating Krishna, of epic proportions, but belonging to the category of *Puranas*, takes equal place in Hinduism with the *Ramayana* and the *Mahabharata*. Traditionally ascribed to Vyasa, the legendary author of the *Mahabharata*, it is now believed to have been composed much later, *c.* 1000 CE, in South India. Book 12, chapter 1, predicts the rule of Sudras in Kaliyuga.

p. 175. **the adult franchise**, established by the Constitution of independent India, twenty-one being the qualifying age.

LECTURE 3

p. 176. **Harijans:** 'God's people', Gandhi's name for the formerly 'untouchable' castes. Once acceptable usage, it is no longer so, having been rejected by the people it designates as euphemistic and patronizing, their preferred designation being 'Dalit' (oppressed).

p. 176. **Scheduled Castes:** See **Scheduled Castes and Tribes** (p. 184n.).

p. 176. **in the pre-Independence days:** India became independent on 15 August 1947.

p. 176. **Vanniakula Kshatryas:** The title 'Kshatrya' and other aspects of the caste are explained on pp. 178–80 .

p. 177. **Kallars:** As the name indicates, the traditional occupation of the caste was theft, but it has long been primarily a caste of cultivators.

p. 177. **Maravars,** formerly a warrior caste, but now, like the Kallars, a caste of cultivators.

p. 177. **Kongu Vellalas,** also known as Kounder or Gounder, in the past, of low social status, but now one of the most influential castes in the Coimbatore, Salem, and Trichy districts of Tamil Nadu state. The epithet 'Kongu' refers to their native land, Kongunadu, which principally comprises the Coimbatore region, in the west of Tamil Nadu.

p. 177. **Idayars:** see **they belonged to two different communities** (p. 17n.).

p. 177. **Shanans, better known as Nadars:** see **a particular caste—toddy-tapping being their hereditary profession** (p. 36n).

p. 177. **Karkarthars:** a branch of the Saivite Vellalas.

p. 177. **fictional caste called Veerakodi Vellalas:** This is a caste found in the old Princely State of **Pudukottai** (p. 182n.). A 'fictional' caste is one which, rather than having an established basis, is self-invented, to promote the interests of the group or to secure benefits.

p. 177. **Zamindari and tenancy legislation:** legislation in Tamil Nadu state directed towards curbing the rights of landlords and protecting those of the tenant-cultivator; this includes the Tamil Nadu Cultivating Tenants Protection Act and Rules of 1955, the Tamil Nadu Cultivating Tenants (Payment of Fair Rent) Ordinance of 1956, and the Tamil Nadu Agricultural

Lands (Record of Tenancy Rights) Act of 1969, as well as the Tamil Nadu Land Reforms (Fixation of Ceiling on Land) Acts of 1961 and 1970.

p. 178. **as the Nadars discovered very early**: In the 1860s, the Nadars began to press their claim to twice-born status, but abandoned the claim by the 1920s.

p. 178. **Pallis or Padayachis**: see **they belonged to two different communities**, p. 17n.

p. 178. **Maha Sangam**, known as the Vanniya Kula Kshatrya Sangam, the association or organization (*sangam*) of the Vanniyars. Sattanathan's epithet 'maha', literally 'big' or 'great', in this context emphasizes inclusiveness and breadth.

p. 179. **A young man from Cuddalore . . . the Toilers' Party**: In 1951, at a state-wide conference of the Vanniya Kula Kshatrya Sangam, it was decided that a political party, representing the caste, should be formed under the name, Tamilnad Toilers' Party, with the object of contesting the 1952 elections. The party was headed by S.S. Ramaswami Padayachi (1918–92), then only thirty-three.

p. 179. **Another lawyer . . . Toilers' Commonweal Party**: Subsequent to the formation of the Toilers' Party in 1951, rivalries between local Vanniyar organizations led to the formation of a second caste party of Vanniyars, the Toilers' Commonweal Party, under the leadership of M.A. Manickavelu Naicker (see **This gentleman became a politician, and later became a minister**, p. 139n.). The Toilers' Party was dominant among the Vanniyars of South Arcot and Salem districts, while the Commonweal Party held sway in the North Arcot and Chinglepet districts.

p. 179. **M.L.A.**: Member of the Legislative Assembly, i.e., the State Legislature.

p. 180. **Sangam**: Here, 'association' or 'organization'. The main Sangam of the Nadars, known as the Nadar Mahajana Sangam, was formed in 1910.

p. 181. **Ezhavars of Kerala**: A caste whose traditional occupations included toddy-tapping, like the Nadars, as well as coconut-palm cultivation and coir-making. Like the Nadars too, they were formerly considered a polluting caste, but have since gained considerably in social and caste status. The great social reformer, Narayana Guru (1854–1928), has been instrumental in their uplift.

p. 181. **Agamudiars**: Broadly classed as an agricultural caste, although Sattanthan describes them as having more traditionally been a service caste, i.e., employed in 'white collar' occupations.

p. 182. **Tuluva Vellalars**: Tamil Vellalas who trace their origins to the Tulu region of southern Karnataka.

p. 182. **Raja of Ramnad**: The hereditary ruler, surnamed 'Setupathi', of Ramnad district in southern Tamil Nadu. The Rajas of Ramnad were known as patrons of the arts, and were prominent in public life.

p. 182. **Raja of Pudukottai**: The hereditary ruler, surnamed 'Tondaiman', of the erstwhile Princely State of **Pudukottai**, in the central region of present-day Tamil Nadu.

p. 182. **Muthuramalinga Thevar**: See **Forward Bloc** (below).

p. 182. **Mookiah Thevar**: P.K. Mookiah Thevar (1926–79), a **Forward Bloc** (see below) politician and associate of Muthuramalinga Thevar.

p. 182. **Forward Bloc**: a political party started by the radical nationalist Subhas Chandra Bose (1897–1945) in 1939. The Tamil Nadu faction of the Forward Bloc, under the leadership of the charismatic U. Muthuramalinga Thevar (1908–63), was more or less a caste party of the Mukkulathor (see **p.** 181).

p. 182. **Kammalars**: a caste of smiths, craftsmen, and artisans.

p. 184. **Grants-in-Aid code framed in 1885**: The first step towards affirmative action to promote the welfare of the under-privileged sections of society, now so ingrained a characteristic of the Indian social and political agenda, was the framing of Grants-in-Aid Code by the Madras Government in 1885, which provided for financial assistance in education to students of what were then the 'untouchable' castes.

p. 184. **Scheduled Castes and Tribes**: The official designation of the formerly 'untouchable' castes and tribes. The term 'Scheduled Castes' came into use with the Government of India Act of 1935, which contained provisions for the welfare of the 'depressed classes', the actual 'Schedule' of castes and tribes falling within that category being made by the Government of India (Scheduled Castes) Order of 1936. The usage was perpetuated in the Constitution of independent India, a detailed listing being made by the Constitution (Scheduled Castes) Order and the Constitution (Scheduled Tribes) Order, of 1950.

p. 185. **Most Backward Classes:** A category within a category, introduced in order to allow for differing levels of social disadvantage. The 'most backward' are those castes that are considered the most disadvantaged of the Backward Classes, and who benefit therefore, by a reserved quota within the reserved quota for the Backward Classes. In Tamil Nadu, the Vanniyars are numerically the largest of the Most Backward Classes.

p. 185. **G.O.:** Government Order.

p. 185. **E.F. Irschick:** See Eugene F. Irschick, *Politics and Social Conflict in South India: the Non-Brahmin Movement and Tamil Separatism, 1916–29* (Berkeley and Los Angeles: University of California Press, 1969), 18–19.

p. 186. **Anna Dravida Munnetra Kazhagam:** see the **Dravida Munnetra Kazhagam split** (p. 174n.)

p. 187. **reservation is confined to State services, and not to the Central services, public sector, and business organizations:** This is no longer the case. The Mandal Commission's (see **the Backward Classes Commission . . . Janata Government**, below) recommendation that 27 per cent of vacancies in civil posts and services under the Central Government be reserved for backward classes was implemented with effect from 7 August 1990.

p. 187. **the Backward Classes Commission . . . Janata Government:** On 20 December 1978, the party in power being the Janata Party (constituted in 1977), Morarji Desai (1896–1995), then Prime Minister of India, announced the Government of India's decision to appoint a Backward Classes Commission, the second such commission to be appointed by the Central Government. The Commission was appointed on 1 January 1979, with B.P. Mandal (1918–82) as Chair, and it had in fact submitted its report in December 1980, before the date of Sattanathan's lectures. However, the report had little impact till August 1990, when V.P. Singh (1931–), then Prime Minister of India, heading a National Front government (a coalition of the Janata Dal, constituted in 1988, and various regional parties), announced the government's intention to implement the Mandal report. The announcement provoked the notorious riots of the early 1990s in North India, when several upper-caste youths immolated themselves, and several more were killed in clashes with police.

p. 188. **clashes between them in various places**: Typically, these have between the Vanniyars and the Parayars in northern Tamil Nadu, and between the Thevars (Maravars) and the Pallars (like the Parayars, a 'scheduled' caste), in southern Tamil Nadu.